Divided Korea

Divided Korea

Toward a Culture of Reconciliation

ROLAND BLEIKER

BORDERLINES, VOLUME 25

 University of Minnesota Press

Minneapolis

London

Earlier versions of the Introduction were published as "Identity and Security in Korea," *Pacific Review* 14, no. 1 (2001): 121–48, and "Towards a Culture of Reconciliation in Korea," *Peace Review: A Transnational Quarterly* 14, no. 3 (September 2002): 297–302. Parts of chapter 3 appeared as "A Rogue Is a Rogue Is a Rogue: U.S. Foreign Policy and the Korean Nuclear Crisis," *International Affairs* 79, no. 4 (Summer 2003): 719–37. Parts of chapter 5 were published as "Alternatives to Peacekeeping in Korea: The Role of Non-State Actors and Face-to-Face Encounters," *International Peacekeeping* 11, no. 1 (2004): 143–59.

Published by the University of Minnesota Press
111 Third Avenue South, Suite 290
Minneapolis, MN 55401-2520
http://www.upress.umn.edu

Library of Congress Cataloging-in-Publication Data

Bleiker, Roland.
    Divided Korea : toward a culture of reconciliation / Roland Bleiker.
        p.   cm. — (Borderlines ; v. 25)
    Includes bibliographical references and index.
    ISBN 0-8166-4556-6 (acid-free paper)
    1. National security—Korea (South)—History.   2. National security—Korea (North)—History.   3. Korea (South)—Foreign relations—Korea (North).   4. Korea (North)—Foreign relations—Korea (South).
    5. Security, International—Moral and ethical aspects.   I. Title.
    II. Borderlines (Minneapolis, Minn.) ; v. 25
    UA853.K6B55   2005
    355'.0330519—dc22
                                                                    2004025263

Printed in the United States of America on acid-free paper

The University of Minnesota is an equal-opportunity educator and employer.

12 11 10 09 08 07 06 05   10 9 8 7 6 5 4 3 2 1

To Kim Yong Joo

Contents

Preface
A Rogue Is a Rogue Is a Rogue

There is something about this peninsula which has repelled investigation.
—ISABELLA L. BIRD, *KOREA AND HER NEIGHBOURS:*
A NARRATIVE OF TRAVEL, WITH AN ACCOUNT
OF THE RECENT VICISSITUDES AND PRESENT
POSITION OF THE COUNTRY, 1897

Old times must be sent away.
—KO UN, "SONG OF PEACE FROM JEJU ISLAND"

Few conflicts are as protracted as the one in Korea, where deeply
hostile and anachronistic Cold War attitudes have posed major security problems for half a century. To be more precise, two specters
haunt the peninsula: a military escalation, even outright war, and a
North Korean collapse, which could easily destabilize the northeast
Asian region.[1]

Dealing with North Korea is perhaps one of the most difficult security challenges in global politics today. Totalitarian and reclusive,
ideologically isolated and economically ruined, it is the inherent
"other" in a globalized and neoliberal world order. Yet North Korea
survives, not least because its leaders periodically rely on threats, such
as nuclear brinkmanship, to gain concessions from the international
community. The latest such attempt occurred in the autumn of 2002,
when Pyongyang admitted to a secret nuclear weapons program and
subsequently withdrew from the Nuclear Nonproliferation Treaty.

From then on, the situation rapidly deteriorated. By early 2003 both the United States and North Korea were threatening each other with outright war. Even Japan, in its most militaristic posture in decades, publicly contemplated the possibility of a preemptive strike against North Korea.[2]

The dangers of North Korea's nuclear brinkmanship are evident and much discussed. Miscalculations or a sudden escalation could precipitate a human disaster at any moment. Equally dangerous, although much less evident, are the confrontational and militaristic attitudes with which some of the key regional and global players seek to contain the volatile situation. Particularly problematic is the approach of the most influential external actor on the peninsula, the United States. Washington's inability to see North Korea as anything but a threatening "rogue state" seriously hinders both an adequate understanding and potential resolution of the conflict. Few policy makers, security analysts, and journalists ever try to imagine how North Korean decision makers perceive these threats and how these perceptions are part of an interactive security dilemma in which the West is implicated as much as is the vilified regime in Pyongyang. Particularly significant is the current policy of preemptive strikes against rogue states, for it reinforces half a century of American nuclear threats toward North Korea. The problematic role of these threats has been largely obscured, not least because the highly technical discourse of security analysis has managed to present the strategic situation on the peninsula in a manner that attributes responsibility for the crisis solely to North Korea's actions, even if the situation is in reality far more complex and interactive.

A fundamental rethinking of security is required if the current culture of insecurity is to give way to a more stable and peaceful environment. Contributing to this task is my main objective of this book. I do so by exploring insights and options broader than those articulated by most security studies specialists. While pursuing this objective I offer neither a comprehensive take on the Korean security situation nor a detailed update on the latest events. Various excellent books have already done so.[3] I seek not new facts and data but new perspectives. I identify broad patterns of conflict and embark on a conceptual engagement with some of the ensuing dilemmas. I aspire to what Gertrude Stein sought to capture through a poetic metaphor:[4] the political and moral obligation to question the immutability of the status quo; the need to replace old and highly problematic Cold War thinking patterns with new and more sensitive attempts to address the dilemmas of Korean security.

BETWEEN SEOUL, PANMUNJOM, AND PYONGYANG

Before I outline exactly what rethinking Korean security entails, I must be honest and present my own reasons for seeking to understand these dilemmas. I am doing so not to aggrandize myself or to suggest that my person was or is of any relevance to the events in question. I am doing so because a story, subjectively experienced as it inevitably is, can at times capture a political dilemma more precisely than (or at least differently from) the type of scholarly work that will follow. Also, I feel that this is the only intellectually honest approach, particularly when it comes to engaging a topic like Korean security, which is emotionally and politically charged to the point that a detached and objective analysis is simply impossible.

I urge readers who prefer to do without this personal contextualization to jump to the Introduction right away. But I would be disingenuous if I presented the result of my research as if there had been no other possibility from the beginning. As if the "I" did not have anything to do with it. As if the facts lay out there, ready to be discovered and unveiled in their authentic meaning—the author a mere messenger, picturing and enframing events at their time and place of occurrence and carrying them to a far-off destination, where they unwrap and shine in their original brightness. The voyage cannot be erased and neither can the framing, the fading, the restoration work, indeed, the author's interference with the events themselves. Writing is a story whose traces should be left intact, laid open for the reader to outline and verify, to correct and redraw. Hence the need to present the context of my perspectives. Hence the confession, with Milan Kundera, that "the only thing we can do is to give an account of our own selves. Anything else is an abuse of power. Anything else is a lie."[5]

I first arrived in South Korea on a late September night in 1986. In the early hours of the next day I was driven up from Seoul to Panmunjom, where I was to take up the position of chief of office of the Swiss delegation to the Neutral Nations Supervisory Commission

(NNSC). "In front of them all," bellowed a young U.S. soldier as we crossed a bridge over the Imjin River and approached the most militarized landscape I had ever seen: the so-called Demilitarized Zone, or DMZ. My new home turned out to be even more surreal: located right at the barbed-wire fence that divided the peninsula, our barracks were surrounded by military observation posts and loud-speakers on both sides. The latter were competing with each other every night, blaring propaganda speeches and music into an other-wise pristine and stunningly beautiful landscape.

My experiences during the next two years form the origin of this book. The NNSC is an odd institution that symbolizes Korea's strug-gle to turn half a century of hot- and cold-war confrontations into a political arrangement that can bring stability, perhaps even peace. Established with the Armistice Agreement in July 1953, the purpose of the NNSC was to supervise two clauses in the agreement that prohibited the introduction of new military personnel and weapons. Five ports of entry were designated on each side, and the NNSC was given the task of controlling them. The commission's neutrality consisted of each side's choosing two nations that did not actively participate in the war. North Korea opted for Czechoslovakia and Poland. Switzerland and Sweden were selected by the southern side, which was formally represented by the United Nations Command. With the intensification of the Cold War the idea of retaining cur-rent levels of military personnel and equipment became a farce. An arms race soon took hold of the peninsula, and by June 1956 all NNSC inspection teams had been completely withdrawn. With its official purpose gone, the NNSC radically shrunk. By the time I arrived in 1986, the Swiss delegation consisted of a mere six people, compared to the more than one hundred who initially controlled the ports of entry. We still dutifully filed reports about incoming military personnel and weapons, but the actual purpose of the NNSC was informal. It consisted of establishing links across the DMZ at a time when there were few meaningful interactions between North and South Korea. NNSC members regularly met in Panmunjom's Joint Security Area (JSA) and embarked on frequent visits to both sides.

Being able to cross the otherwise hermetically sealed DMZ and travel between North and South Korea was a rare privilege, an op-portunity to see two countries that were clearly of the same nation but seemed to be located on different continents, if not planets. At least they were diametrically opposed in their central political passions: virulent anticapitalist and anti-imperialist sentiments permeated the North, while an equally strong anti-Communist discourse dominated the South.

Each time I returned from the North I had difficulties describing or even comprehending what I had seen and experienced. At a visual level a beautiful but poor countryside stood in contrast to the capital, Pyongyang, which boasted gigantic architectural ambition, featuring anything from gargantuan statues and towers to modern multilane boulevards. Uniformed traffic regulators were systematically positioned on the latter, except that they had no traffic to regulate, at least no more than the occasional lost-looking truck limping along. Then there was the personality cult, perhaps unmatched in history, that surrounded the country's first leader, Kim Il Sung and his son and successor as head of state, Kim Jong Il. Once accustomed to the hagiographic routine that permeates all aspects of life, I was particularly taken aback by the omnipresence of the authoritarian state and the general militarization of society. Countless features make up this central theme, from a tightly controlled and highly propagandistic media to the organization of so-called mass games, involving tens of thousands of children delivering a stunning but frighteningly flawless performance. It is not my purpose here to discuss these and other features. They are, in any case, part of a well-rehearsed image of North Korea that is experienced by the increasing number of journalists, tourists, and businesspeople who visit the country.

The visual contrast with the South was at its most extreme when one traveled in one evening from the nearly dark and seemingly deserted northern city of Kaesong southward through the fortified and rather eerie DMZ and then directly on, into the bustling metropolis of Seoul, where millions of flashing neon signs appear to keep an even greater number of people hyperactive for twenty-four hours a day. But beside these stunning differences were just as many similarities, and they went beyond a shared cultural tradition. The South also had an authoritarian regime, led by Major General Chun Doo-hwan. It dominated the country, perhaps not quite as tightly as in the North, but the control and militarization of South Korean society were nevertheless remarkable, all the more because these aspects were reinforced through the significant and very visible presence of U.S.

military forces. Similar as well was the role of an omnipresent state, basing its legitimacy on a process of demonizing the archenemy across the DMZ. Indeed, hatred for the political system on the other side of the border was as pronounced and widespread in the South as in the North. It permeated all aspects of society, from the state-censored media to the realm of the everyday, as, for instance, in the form of popular game machines that asked a player to use a hammer and hit as many randomly surfacing targets as possible—each signifying a North Korean spy trying to infiltrate the South through tunnels dug beneath the DMZ.

The constructed nature of these antagonistic perceptions became particularly evident if one had the opportunity to visit and talk to people on both sides of the barbed-wire fence. It was clear that the prevalent images of the "evil other" were based far more on stereotypical and manipulated images than on what the vilified people on the other side of the DMZ actually were, did, and believed. But in the context of a hermetically divided peninsula, where virtually no communication and information passed from one side to the other, each state could easily promote propagandistic regime-legitimization processes without running the risk of having its claims questioned by the population. Look at what happened in mid-November 1986, when rumors spread in South Korea that North Korea's leader, Kim Il Sung, had died. The origin of these rumors was South Korean government reports of North Korean broadcasts intercepted along the DMZ, as well as photographs of a North Korean flag flying at half-mast in Panmunjom. Over the next few days my NNSC colleagues and I observed the flag in question, but at no point was it located at half-mast. Except, of course, for a few seconds twice a day, when it was hoisted in the morning and lowered again in the evening. It was thus easy to take photographs of the flag flying at half-mast, but only the power and legitimacy of the state could imbue these highly partial visual interpretations with a power strong enough to generate a sustained political crisis that fixated politics in the South for days—most likely to detract attention from problematic domestic issues.

We saw occasional breakthroughs in our daily work, but they were always followed by an eventual setback. On one occasion, for instance, we NNSC members sought to organize an informal get-together during which all stake-holding parties (mostly South Koreans, North

Koreans, Americans, and Chinese) could talk to each other in a relaxed and constructive atmosphere. Doing so was no easy task, and it was certainly unusual, for the official meetings of the Military Armistice Commission were formal and tense. They consisted of no more than an exchange of brief prepared statements in which each side accused the other of violating the Armistice Agreement. We did succeed in creating an informal forum. The political atmosphere in Panmunjom improved, but a few months later tensions reemerged to the point that the parties could not even agree when to meet. The South introduced daylight savings time but the North did not. Neither side was willing to adjust to the other's clock. This very pattern of constant progress-regress was evident not only in mundane daily affairs. Even at the highest level a step forward was always followed by two steps backward.

After I left Panmunjom in 1988 I stayed for a semester at Seoul's Yonsei University, trying to improve my language skills and cultural understanding. But even after I moved on, settling in Canada, the United States, and eventually Australia, the memory of Korea never left me. Part of my heart seemed to have stayed behind, alongside my appendix and wisdom teeth, which were removed in a makeshift clinic just south of the DMZ. I observed Korea from a distance, not as a specialist but as an international relations scholar and, above all, as a person fascinated with a country and its people.

The idea of embarking on systematic research about Korean security came only a decade later, in 1998, when I had the opportunity to return for a year, as visiting professor at Pusan National University. I was immediately struck by how much the old one-step-forward-two-steps-backward pattern still dominated security politics. The very day I returned marked the presidential inauguration of Kim Dae-jung, who was a dissident under house arrest when I first arrived in Korea in the mid-1980s. By 2000 his so-called Sunshine Policy, which promoted a more tolerant approach toward the North, would yield a spectacular success: an unprecedented summit meeting with the North Korean leader Kim Jong Il. But the ensuing sense of euphoria was soon replaced by an equally dramatic reemergence of tension over North Korea's nuclear ambition. It became clear that no diplomatic agreement or security arrangement could bring lasting peace and stability to the peninsula, at least not as long as the underlying sources of conflict—the tensions over antagonistic identities—remain unresolved. I was equally stunned by the persistence of intellectual patterns. Over the years I sought to keep track of the latest books and journal articles on Korean security. But year after year the various publications looked more and more alike. They seemed to discuss just about everything, from details on weapons capabilities and conflict scenarios to the latest diplomatic wrestling match—everything except, I thought, what really mattered: the antagonistic identity patterns that were driving the conflict in the first place.

Gathering the courage to start a large research project on Korean security was not easy, for few topics have produced as much literature. Taking on this massive body of knowledge as a mere "hobby Koreanist" was a rather daunting idea, no matter how passionately I felt about it all. This was all the more the case because increasing attention was now given to work by more critically inclined authors, such as Moon Chung-in, Paik Nak-chung, Bruce Cumings, Leon Sigal, Katherine Moon, Scott Snyder, and Hazel Smith, to name just a few. Add to this the insufficiency of my Korean-language competence, despite sustained and rather laborious attempts to acquire and then update my rudimentary linguistic skills. In the end I simply decided to take the plunge, dilettantish as my dive (and subsequent landing) may well be. I jumped into the void mostly because I had a long and strong passion for Korea and because I had an equally strong and passionate conviction that the puzzles of Korean security need to be scrutinized in a novel and radically different manner. Perhaps there is even an advantage in not being a specialist, for one's mind is not yet molded by well-rehearsed disciplinary conventions, nor does one have a professional reputation and career at stake, at least not in that particular discipline. An outsider may thus pronounce what an insider cannot, which is why some commentators argue that a rethinking process actually requires a "stranger's account."[6]

The disciplinary boundaries of scholarship on security and inter-Korean relations became visible as soon as I started to conceptualize my project. I worked out a grant proposal that described rethinking Korean security through an interdisciplinary approach that presents the conflict not in conventional geopolitical and ideological terms but as a struggle over competing forms of identity. Reactions to this idea were mixed. Many people were wonderfully supportive, even

though I had not yet sufficiently worked out the details of my project. But I found quite a few discouraging reactions too, particularly
from security experts. One anonymous referee who evaluated the
proposal stressed that a project that examines linkages between
identity and security would be an exercise in "academic anthropology" and thus of little relevance to "policy-making circles." This
person identified a number of "questionable assumptions" in my proposal, such as the suggestion that "security dilemmas are socially
constructed." What does this mean? the author wanted to know.
"Can they be thought away?" As a result of this skepticism the critic
was particularly concerned that my project sought to embark on
a *genealogy* of Korean security, which I introduced, as accessibly
and as free of jargon as I could, as an effort to analyze how hostile
identities are not naturally given but have emerged in the context of
specific political struggles. A genealogical inquiry, which is meanwhile
a fairly well recognized research tool in the humanities and social sci-
ences, seemed nevertheless inappropriate to this reviewer: "Studying
family lineages? Surely some other meaning must be intended."

The controlling mechanisms of security discourses surfaced again
when I actually embarked on systematic research for this book, involving archival work and interviews, most notably in Korea and the
United States. A lot of people, from academics to defense analysts
and policy makers, were extremely generous in giving me their time
and perspectives on issues of Korean security. I also attended various
workshops and conferences, trying as much as I could to get a grasp
of the respective debates. But despite my enthusiasm, I had great difficulties understanding the language of security experts, which was
full of acronyms, technical details, and obscure metaphors. Clarity
failed to emerge even as I acquired more fluency in the academic jargon. Quite to the contrary. I became more frustrated because I was
unable to communicate what I felt so passionate about: the need to
take into account identity issues and rethink Korean security along
interdisciplinary lines. The prevalent linguistic and academic conventions seem to make it impossible to address security issues in
ways other than the prescribed technical, realist, and militaristic
manner. This is, of course, not a new experience. Carol Cohn wrote
in detail about the practices of inclusion and exclusion that are established throughout the language of defense analysis.[7] I am thus
fully aware that my attempt at providing a different conceptual base

for understanding and dealing with Korean security will not be uniformly applauded or even understood. All I can do is give my best and hope that I can act, with Nietzsche, "against time, and thus on time, for the sake of a time one hopes will come."[8]

Grassroots practitioners often seemed more open to multiple perspectives than the detached specialist of high politics. I learned a great deal from the development community, which has been active in North Korea since a famine devastated the country in 1995. In this context I had the opportunity to evaluate the political dimensions of the Swiss Development Agency's humanitarian assistance program in North Korea. Should one provide humanitarian aid in an attempt to alleviate the disastrous effects of famine? Or would such assistance merely obstruct badly needed change, helping to sustain an authoritarian regime and thus further perpetuating human rights abuses? The answers are not easy, of course, and I certainly do not pretend to have found them. But having to come up with a position that had immediate and very real consequences for people forced me to contemplate ethical dilemmas in a way that I could not have done had I simply judged the issues from the safe distance of an ivory tower, where relatively little is at stake.

Most of this book was written during the winter of 2002–2003, while I was a Humboldt Fellow in Berlin. I had first intended to conduct a systematic comparison of Korea and Germany, profiting from structural similarities between the two countries and from Germany's dozen years of experience with unification. In the end I had to concede that security dilemmas in Korea are, above all, linked to very specific political, historical, and cultural constellations. But studying the German precedent nevertheless turned out to be extremely useful, far more than is evident from the occasional references that appear in this book. Living in the eastern part of Berlin (in Prenzlauer Berg), literally right next to where the Wall used to slice the world into Communist and capitalist parts, made me especially aware of the arbitrary but highly consequential nature of political boundaries. Writing in Berlin also gave me the necessary distance from Korea while being constantly reminded, in a daily and practical manner, that even in politically unified Germany people from the east and west still retain a very different sense of identity, which causes significant social and political tension.

Engaging the practical dilemmas of Korean security also brought me back for a couple of days to the Swiss camp in Panmunjom, where issues of continuity and change were particularly evident. As I was strolling through the camp in the spring of 2002, much looked like fifteen years before, at least at first sight. The barracks had not changed, nor had the atmosphere, which was as surreal as ever. But the rusty barbed wire on the fence had been replaced with brand new material. Other things had changed too. The collapse of the Berlin Wall made the DMZ look like a Cold War theme park, albeit a frighteningly real one. Tensions were all too evident and conflict all too likely to escalate, perhaps even more so than at any time in the past. I wondered what the world looked like for those North Koreans I had met and worked with in the mid-1980s. Many may no longer be alive. Half a decade of recurring famines had devastated the country and its people. Those who were still there belonged to an extremely isolated state that had lost all its traditional allies and trading partners. Even our NNSC colleagues, the Czechs and Poles, had long since switched sides. "In front of them all" echoed through my head as we rolled out of Panmunjom on our way south. I took one more look back, but all I could see was a large red flag rapidly fading in the distance.

Acknowledgments

Given that this book emerged over a period of almost two decades, I am grateful to a correspondingly large number of people who were kind enough to help me in my effort to understand Korea and its security challenges. During my initial stay in Panmunjom I came to appreciate my Swiss, Swedish, Polish, and Czech colleagues at the Neutral Nations Supervisory Commission. I spent many an hour in debate with them, particularly Herbert Amrein, Theodor Brönnimann, Jean-Paul Dietrich, Urs Fischer, Christoph Glauser, Pierre Jordan, Pierre Monod, and Michel Obrecht, as well as Olof Kitti, Goran Tornerhjelm, Jan Langer, and Andrzey Pokrzewnicki. I also would like to thank the people of Tae Sung Dong for their hospitality, and I am grateful as well for the opportunity to learn from our North Korean, South Korean, Chinese, and American interlocutors, most notably Lee Jong Dae, Lee Chang Bok, Kim Byung-Ick, Park Sung Il, Son Chang Sun, Lee In Sub, Lee Gunsik, Zhang Huaping, William Pendley, Mike Graziano, and Jim Ball. An Chi Hong, Lee Hyung Sook, Doug and Joe Bond, Marc Flegenheimer, and Kim Verwarst facilitated my reintegration into "civilian life" during my first stay at Yonsei University.

During the subsequent decade in Toronto, Vancouver, Boston, and Canberra, I was lucky that people supported me in my effort to keep my passion for Korea alive. My thanks to Richard Stubbs, Julia Schtivelman, Adam and Sonhi Deutsch, Kal Holsti, Don Baker,

Sheena Trimble, John Ravenhill, and Ron Duncan. During my year at Harvard University's Program on Nonviolent Sanctions, a joint research project with Doug Bond and Lee Myoung-soo gave me the chance to look at Korea in an interdisciplinary way. At the same time Kim Yong Joo, to whom this book is dedicated, taught me more about cross-cultural crisscrossing than I could ever absorb. The turning point in the gestation of this book came in 1998, during two semesters that I spent at Pusan National University. There I gathered the courage to pursue a systematic research project on Korean security, mostly thanks to my wonderful students and the kind support of my colleagues and good friends, Chun Hongchan, Hoang Young-ju, Kim Changsoo, Kim Sangyong, Lee Kab-soo, Moon Kyoung-hee, and Tsche Kwang-jun.

I am particularly grateful to two extraordinarily generous foundations that supported the research for this book: the United States Institute of Peace (USIP) and the Alexander von Humboldt Stiftung. At USIP I would like to thank Deepa Olapally, Taylor Seybolt, Bill Drennan, and April Hall; at the Humboldt Foundation, Manfred and Ute Osten, as well as Brigitte Eßer-Trojan. My gratitude also goes to James Cotton, Jim George, and Andrew Mack for endorsing my grant proposals and to several anonymous referees who subsequently assessed them.

Moon Chung-in not only kindly hosted my second stay at Yonsei University (in 2002) but also provided insightful comments on large parts of the manuscript. In Jeju-do I enjoyed the hospitality of Kang Kun-Hyung and his colleagues from Jeju National University, most notably Ko Choong-Suk and Chang Won-Seok. Thanks also to Kelly Wong and Tina Blumel for being such generous hosts in Washington, D.C., and to Jane Bennett and Bill Connolly for providing a theoretical break in Baltimore from my more policy-oriented research. In New York I would like to thank Lili Cole at the Carnegie Council for inviting me and my colleague Hoang Young-ju to take part in her project on history and reconciliation. And in cyberspace I am very grateful to Stephen Chan for encouraging me to venture into domains of Asian and international politics that my more reserved Swiss instincts would otherwise have left untouched.

In the course of my research I conducted a fair number of interviews—far more than those that are visible in the final text.

A wide range of people shared their insights with me, from policy makers, aid workers, military personnel, and security specialists to politicians, academics, students, and, not least, average Koreans concerned by the political situation on the peninsula. For reasons of confidentiality and research methodology I have not drawn directly on these interviews, but traces of them undoubtedly appear here and there, testifying to how much I have learned from them. The mere thought of trying to remember all the interlocutors makes me realize that I will undoubtedly fail to mention many of them, for which I apologize in advance: Bill Callahan, Chun Chae-sung, Bruce Cumings, Nick Eberstadt, Hong Guang-yob, Hwang Byong-Moo, Peter Gey, Gerrit Gong, Donald Gregg, Hyun In-taek, Kang Kun-Hyung, Kim Dong Sung, Kim Hyuk-Rae, Kim Sae-Jung, Kim Soonam, Don Kirk, Kwon Youngmin, Jeon Woo Taek, Lee Seok-Soo, Lim Sung Hack, Min Sung Kil, Katherine Moon, Don Oberdorfer, Park Hahnkju, Park Myung-Lim, Harold Piper, Ryoo Kihl-Jae, Hazel Smith, Scott Snyder, Boudewijn Walraven, and Käti Zellweger.

During my return visit to Panmunjom in 2002 I was gracefully received by Adrien Evéquoz, Christof Gertsch, Hansjürg Reber, and Mattias Waeber. Equally generous with their time and willingness to share insights were the people from the Swiss Development Agency, most notably Werner Wirz, Paul Egger, Hubert Eisele, and the Pyongyang resident coordinator, Ueli Müller. During my research year in Berlin, Claus Offe offered me an intellectual home at Humboldt University's Institut für Sozialwissenschaften. Thanks as well to other colleagues in Berlin and elsewhere in Germany: Ralf Bönt, Ulla Gläßer, Sieglinde Gstöhl and Heiko Prange, Helga and Elmar Kilz (plus Doro and Lorentz), Michael Kreile, Ekkehart Krippendorf, Hans-Joachim Maaz, Hans Maretzki, Heiner Meulemann, Ruth Owen, Werner Pfennig, Choe Hyondok, Jörg Potthast, and Dieter Senghaas.

The University of Minnesota Press was very supportive, not least because it took on a somewhat unusual project even at a stage where it had not yet been entirely worked out. I want to thank Carrie Mullen and Jason Weidemann, as well as the editors of the Borderlines series, David Campbell and Mike Shapiro. Thanks also to Polly Kummel for her excellent copyediting. Two referees provided insightful comments on the manuscript; I can only hope that my revisions have done justice to them. At my home institution, the University of Queensland, I would like to acknowledge my dean and head of school, Linda Rosenman and Paul Boreham, respectively, for providing me with the leave necessary to complete this book. I also want to thank Nadja Alexander, Mark Beeson, Stephen Bell, Alex Bellamy, Chris Diamond, Marianne Hanson, Martin Leet, Cindy O'Hagen, and Barbara Sullivan—to name just a few of my unusually supportive colleagues. Bill Tow, who knows far more about East Asian security affairs than I ever will, kindly read and commented on the entire manuscript. During many years of the preparation phase of this book, Christine Sylvester was an intellectually stimulating partner who helped me re-view Korea: a special thanks to her. Last but most certainly not least, I am grateful to David Hundt for helping me access and understand some of the Korean-language sources, which would otherwise have remained out of my limited linguistic reach. Unless indicated otherwise, all translations from Korean sources into English were done in collaboration with David Hundt, and all translations from French and German into English are my own.

Finally, I want to thank several anonymous referees who evaluated earlier published essays and people who commented on presentations of various drafts, most notably at Yonsei University, Korea National Defense University, Pusan National University, Humboldt University, and Free University Berlin, as well as at the annual convention of the International Studies Association in Los Angeles (March 2000) and the annual conference of the British International Studies Association in London (December 2002).

Note on Transliteration

Transliterating Korean, which is based on the hangul alphabet, into romanized English has never been straightforward. For decades the McCune-Reischauer system had been widely used in Western publications. In July 2002 the South Korean government introduced a new transliteration system; see http://www.korea.net/learnaboutkorea/ hangeul/revised4.html and http://www.mct.go.kr. The new system is now largely standard practice in the South, but not all Western scholars working on Korea have adopted it. I long hesitated between the two options but in the end decided on the new system, in part because it simplifies the transliteration process, in part because it moves closer to North Korea's method of transliteration (see http:// en.wikipedia.org/wiki/Revised_Romanization_of_Korea), thus symbolizing a linguistic attempt to overcome some of the many schisms that divide the peninsula. As is standard practice, I retain the romanized spelling of Korean names as they appear in standard English-language publications, even if these are not consistent with the new system. I also retain the Korean practice of placing surnames before the given names, except when the latter are of a Western nature or the author seemingly wanted his or her name to appear in anglicized form.

Introduction
Rethinking Korean Security

Let us see who will win and who will be defeated in the fire-to-fire standoff.
— [NORTH] KOREAN CENTRAL NEWS AGENCY

We are all one people.
— KIM DAE-JUNG, PRESIDENT OF SOUTH KOREA,
PYONGYANG, JUNE 2000

Hey, man, cry your eyes out.
— KO UN, "BLUE SKIES"

One of the key features of politics in Korea is a persistently recurring state of military tension. The roots of this conflict are historical: as a result of the emerging Soviet-American rivalry at the end of World War II, the Korean peninsula was tentatively divided along the thirty-eighth parallel. With the creation of two politically and ideologically separate Korean states in 1948, and their subsequent confrontation during the Korean War, the patterns for conflict in northeast Asia were set. In 1953 the Armistice Agreement ended three years of intense fighting that killed more than a million people. But the memory of violence and death continues to dominate politics on the peninsula. More than half a century later, and more than a decade after the collapse of the Berlin Wall, Korea remains hermetically divided between a Communist North and a capitalist South, caught in a tense and highly anachronistic Cold War stalemate. The presence of weapons of mass destruction, combined with a hostile rhetoric and the intersection of great power interests, has created an ever-present danger of military confrontation. Nearly two million troops face each other across the dividing line at the thirty-eighth parallel. Conventional security approaches, based on deterrence and realist ideology, have failed to bring lasting security to the region.

In addressing the present impasse, I advance a fundamental rethinking of Korean security. Two components are essential in this endeavor: presenting new conceptual perspectives on existing security dilemmas and deriving from them recommendations about how to promote a more stable and peaceful political environment.

I begin by drawing attention to the recurring patterns of conflict on the peninsula and the resulting need to rethink security policy. The next two sections spell out what such a rethinking entails, with regard to both the domestic and the international context. Key here is an examination of the statecentric nature of security policy and an effort to present the respective dilemmas not only as geopolitical and ideological issues, as they are conventionally regarded, but also as questions of identity. The role of identities must be scrutinized at various levels, from the individual to the national to the international. The linkages between them are essential for understanding how threats emerge and generate security dilemmas. I then present the two key normative suggestions that I advance in this book. They revolve around the need to combine an ethics of dialogue with an ethics of difference. Expressed in other words, dialogue beyond the control of the state is essential for the promotion of peace but not enough. Needed as well is a broader notion of tolerance and forgiveness: a recognition that the other's sense of identity and politics may be inherently incompatible with one's own. I end the introduction by drawing attention to the policy relevance of my suggestions. They deal not only with the culture of insecurity that has caused tensions for decades but also with a second major source of destabilization in northeast Asia: the potential collapse of North Korea.

RECURRING PATTERNS OF CONFLICT

Diplomatic breakthroughs in Korea are usually followed by the reemergence of conflict. The latest rounds exemplify this deeply entrenched pattern. Tensions rose in 1993 when North Korea threatened to withdraw from the Nuclear Nonproliferation Treaty. William Perry, then U.S. secretary of defense, considered the subsequent crisis the only time during his tenure when he "believed that the U.S. was in serious danger of a major war."[1] An agreement, signed in October 1994, managed to avert an open conflict. Pyongyang consented to freeze its nuclear program in return for a number of U.S., South Korean, and Japanese promises, including aid, heating oil, and the eventual construction of two light-water nuclear reactors that would provide North Korea with energy sources. A relatively tolerant U.S. attitude significantly defused tensions and provided momentum for South Korea's then president, Kim Dae-jung, and his so-called Sunshine Policy, an approach that called for a conciliatory political atmosphere and more interaction between North and South. The result was a historic summit meeting between the two heads of state, held in Pyongyang in June 2000. An atmosphere of hope soon engulfed the peninsula. There were family reunions. There was talk of reconciliation. There were plans for a return visit to Seoul by North Korea's leader, Kim Jong Il.

Less than two years after the historic Pyongyang summit, the usual Cold War tensions returned to the peninsula. North Korea retracted several planned confidence-building measures and embarked on actions that were interpreted as military provocations. The new U.S. president, George W. Bush, adopted a more confrontational policy, which intensified in the wake of the terrorist attacks of September 11, 2001. Bush used his State of the Union address in early 2002 to single out North Korea as one of three nations belonging to an "axis of evil." Soon afterward, the Defense Department, in a report to Congress, included North Korea in a group of seven nations that were potential targets of preemptive nuclear strikes. Pyongyang reacted in an angry manner, warning that it would abandon the agreed-to freeze of its nuclear weapons program, which it subsequently did. While South Korea persisted with a conciliatory position, the overall situation rapidly deteriorated. By early 2003 Pyongyang spoke of the possibility of "total war," while Washington countered that "no military option's been taken off the table."[2]

One can argue about who is to blame for the renewed tensions in Korea. To engage these debates is not the purpose of this book, at least not in the conventional sense. Instead I seek to understand and deal with the more fundamental question of why such standoffs keep emerging and reemerging in the first place. The persistently recurring pattern of conflict suggests a more deeply entrenched structural problem, one that goes far beyond short-term tactical maneuverings of policy makers. The key actors, issues, and policy perspectives change constantly, but the nature of the problem remains the same. This is why fundamentally new forms of thinking and acting are required, for it is hardly possible to find a way out of the current security dilemmas through the political mind-sets that have created them in the first place.

Without dealing with questions of reconciliation and forgiveness, the present culture of insecurity is unlikely to give way to a more peaceful order. But the task of constructing a nonviolent future out of a violent past is, of course, not easy. How is one to facilitate nonviolent coexistence among people divided by the memory of pain and death? What are they to remember? And how? What are they to forget? And why? These difficult but fundamental questions are hardly ever posed in Korea, where antagonistic Cold War rhetoric and a general climate of fear and distrust continue to drive interactions between the key actors.

A sustained diplomatic breakthrough cannot occur without first promoting a *culture of reconciliation*. To argue this is, of course, not necessarily new or radical. Many security experts would readily agree. Jang Si Young and Ahn Pyong-Seong, for instance, stress that genuine peace is unlikely in the immediate future because "it will require considerable time for the two Koreas to promote exchanges and confidence building" before any progress can be made.[3] But in the logic of prevailing realist security thinking, the absence of a culture of reconciliation calls for a reinforcement of conventional defense postures. This is why Jang and Ahn argue that a "sustained build-up of its military strength is essential [to South Korea's] security." A similar logic underlies the U.S. position toward North Korea. It is based on the assumption that the only "genuine alternative to war with North Korea is now, and always has been, credible deterrence."[4] But militaristic and statecentric approaches to security (which continue to guide policy making, media coverage, and many influential academic analyses) reproduce the very dangers that they wish to ward off. A detailed study by Moon Chung-in, for instance, has shown how various attempts to manage the Korean conflict through the conventional logic of military deterrence have turned out disastrously. They have "driven North and South Korea into the trapping structure of a vicious cycle of actions and reactions."[5]

THE DOMESTIC CONTEXT

A fundamental rethinking of security is required if Korea is to find a way out of the present stalemate. Chapters 1 and 2 begin this task by analyzing the historical emergence of antagonistic identities and the manner in which they have become intertwined with contemporary security dilemmas. Much as Gregory Henderson described the essence of Korean politics as revolving around a "physics of centralization,"[6] one could view identity as the key to understanding security on the peninsula. To be more precise, the present security dilemmas can be seen as emerging from a fundamental but largely ignored tension between the idea of Korean identity and its rather different practical application. A strong, almost mythical, vision of homogeneity permeates both parts of Korea. It portrays the division of the peninsula as a temporary disruption of Korean identity and assumes that unification will eventually recover the lost national unity.[7] Enforcing such trends is a strong cultural fear of the notion of outsideness, of absolute otherness. This is why the other side of the divided peninsula must be seen as part of a whole. Anything else would be too terrible to contemplate.[8]

In contrast to this mythical homogeneity we find the reality of half a century of political division, during which the two Koreas have developed identities that are not only distinct but also articulated in direct and stark opposition to each other. The memory of war continues to dominate Korean politics. Antagonistic identity constructs, born out of death, fear, and longing for revenge, are continuously used to fuel and legitimize aggressive foreign and repressive domestic policies. Indeed, much of the conflict in Korea is based on identity constructs that portray the opposite side of the divided peninsula not only as an ideological archrival but also, and perhaps more important, as a threatening "other," as something that is inherently evil and thus incompatible with one's own sense of identity. Over the years these antagonistic forms of identity have become so deeply entrenched in societal consciousness that the current politics of insecurity appears virtually inevitable.

The tension between these two contradictory aspects of Korean politics, the strong myth of homogeneity and the actual reality of oppositional identity practices, contains the key to understanding both the sources of the existing conflict and the potential for a more peaceful peninsula. To highlight identity is not to deny that security policies in divided Korea have been dominated by strategic and ideological motives. The point, rather, is to acknowledge that the ensuing dilemmas were, and still are, also part of a much more deeply seated practice of defining security through a stark opposition between self and other. This mind-set, which defines security as a protection of the inside from the threat of a hostile outside, turns into a collective mind-set that greatly increases the risk of instability and violent encounters.

Antagonistic identity constructs are crystallized in the state, which is seen as the only meaningful security actor. This statecentrism not only entrenches a politics of insecurity but also prevents us from seeing security as a broader issue and from locating sources of change that could be essential for the construction of a more peaceful peninsula. Indeed, the state's almost total control of security is perhaps the most crucial reason why the artificially constructed images of the enemy persist and continue to cause tension. There is virtually no travel and communication across the thirty-eighth parallel. The few contacts that exist are largely limited to state-based interactions, such as diplomatic negotiations. Neither North nor South Korean people have a realistic idea of what everyday life looks like in the vilified other half. For decades the two regimes have shielded their populations from "subversive" influences stemming from the other side. The consequences are manifold. In the absence of face-to-face encounters, people on the other side of the Demilitarized Zone can easily be constructed as evil and inherently antagonistic. It is thus hardly surprising that signs of progress and rapprochement are usually followed by a regression into the old patterns of hatred and mistrust.

THE INTERNATIONAL CONTEXT

A similar rethinking is needed to understand the international context of Korean security. This is the main task of chapter 3. And it is a crucial task, for the dilemmas on the Korean peninsula cannot be solved, or even understood, in a purely domestic context. The fate of Korea is intrinsically linked to the intersection on the peninsula of the strategic, economic, and ideological interests of the great powers. The United States, Japan, Russia, and China all consider Korea to be of key importance to their own political calculations.

Particular attention must be given to the role of the United States and not only because it is the only superpower left in a post–Cold War world. Ever since the withdrawal of Japanese occupation forces from the peninsula, the fate of Korea has been intrinsically linked to the United States, and this is unlikely to change any time soon. U.S. policy toward Korea has, of course, changed over the years. Washington has, for instance, oscillated in its willingness to negotiate with North Korea. But despite many policy changes, there is a clear pattern, one that constitutes the North first and foremost as a threat that necessitates a constant degree of high military readiness. At times such a posture may indeed be justified, for the authoritarian regime in North Korea has engaged in countless military provocations. But just as often such a position does not reflect factual evidence. This is why some scholars have lamented that U.S. policy is severely limited by a "securitization paradigm" that is unable to see North Korea as anything but a dangerous and unpredictable "rogue state."[9]

But even rogue states change. And not least in response to those states that constitute them as rogue. North Korea does not exist in a vacuum. It reacts to both internal and external factors. Look at how Pyongyang introduced various significant policy changes during the late 1990s. In response to the near collapse of the official economy, farmers' markets emerged in many parts of the country. The government further reinforced this trend through incentive-based agricultural principles. Similar patterns of action and reaction can be seen in foreign policy. Consider the result of an extensive study by Leon Sigal of U.S. nuclear diplomacy toward North Korea between 1988 and 1995. He reveals a consistent and rather striking pattern: whenever the United States resorted to an aggressive policy, Pyongyang responded in kind. By contrast, a more tolerant attitude led to significant North Korean concessions. As a result the security situation on the peninsula improved only when the United States embarked on a "give-and-take" diplomacy that recognized that Pyongyang's seemingly erratic behavior is in fact a rather consistent bargaining tactic designed to gain specific benefits in exchange for giving up the nuclear option.[10]

The inability to see political trends that contradict prevailing stereotypical images is linked to the overall representational practices that prevail in much of the Western world. Sigal demonstrates, for instance, that the United States often did not hear signs of compromise emanating from Pyongyang because the prevalent story line about North Korea, the one that revolves around an image of an aggressive Communist state incapable of compromising, was simply too strong and too deeply entrenched. North Korea's own views and policy statements, he stresses, were rarely reported in the Western press. This is why key parts of the "story" did not actually appear in the news and could thus never enter the realm of dialogue.[11] Bruce Cumings goes so far as to argue that the state of American media coverage of Korean security affairs was so inadequate that "often one had to read North Korea's tightly controlled press to figure out what was going on between Washington and Pyongyang."[12] Look at U.S. media representations of the North Korean famine. According to Yuh Ji-Yeon, the coverage says far more about U.S. preconceptions and strategic interests than it does about the actual events that took place in the wake of the devastating 1995 floods. Thus the inability to prevent a widespread famine could be attributed only to flawed (Communist) economic policies, even though plenty of evidence showed that a series of other factors, including the dramatic loss of historic trading partners, exacerbated the problem.[13]

The dangers of a militarized foreign policy and public discourse have intensified during Bush's tenure. His policies signal a strong desire to return to the familiarity of dualistic Cold War thinking patterns, except that "evil rogue states" replaced communism as the ultimate threat in world politics. Such an ideological stance cannot sufficiently recognize and react to the interactive dynamic of security relations. For one, the very term *evil* prevents serious investigation into security dilemmas and, more important, into innovative solutions to them. Various authors stress that *evil* is a term of condemnation for an inherently irrational and perhaps even incomprehensible phenomenon.[14] The consequences of such attitudes go far beyond the domain of military policy, for the dominant approach to security also provides, as Hazel Smith stresses, the framework through which social, economic, and humanitarian issues are perceived in Korea. The result is not only paralysis—the belief that when a crisis occurs nothing can be done except reinforce military-based defense—but also, and more important, an inability to appreciate nuances and detect changes when they occur.[15]

PRODUCING DANGER: THE NEED FOR ALTERNATIVES

While the pattern of recurring crises in Korea makes a fundamental rethinking of security an imperative, it is far from clear how such a process could lead to more peaceful alternatives. Before sketching out my suggestions, I want to specify what exactly is involved in a process of rethinking. Central here is awareness of the problematic dimension entailed in the representation of North Korea through conventional security approaches.

Journalists, academics, and policy makers tend to stress that the so-called hermit kingdom of North Korea is so secretive that it is virtually impossible to obtain objective information about how it makes policy. "We are completely ignorant of what is happening in that part of Korea," summarizes one observer.[16] Economists emphasize similar themes, stressing, for instance, that the North is a "statistical wasteland."[17] The refrain of an unknowable hermit kingdom is equally central to newspaper representations of North Korea, which tend to emphasize, or at least imply, how rare it is for a journalist to be allowed to report from this reclusive country.[18] North Korea is, indeed, one of the world's most secluded states. Much about the decision making that occurs is impossible to re-trace. But more details about North Korea are becoming known to the outside world. There are increasingly numerous and detailed studies on society and politics, including Pyongyang's foreign policy and negotiating behavior.[19] Moreover, as a result of the famines that followed the floods of 1995, various representatives of foreign humanitarian organizations took up residence in North Korea. They were given more and more access to the country, something that had hitherto been inconceivable. Some say they have access to 75 percent of the country or 80 percent of the population.[20] Clearly, the hermit kingdom is no longer quite as reclusive as its reputation has it. Hazel Smith goes so far as to speak of a "*de facto* opening up of the country to the outside world." She stresses that many of the nongovernmental organizations (NGOs) active in the North have been able to get access to significant information about the country, often with the assistance of government authorities. But the reports that document these experiences and insights seem to have little influence in the West.[21] Cumings, likewise, argues that a wealth of information is now available about many crucial aspects of North Korea's history, but Western policy analysts hardly ever consult this data.[22]

Even as they perpetuate the image of an unknowable hermit kingdom, many influential academic and policy approaches toward North Korea advance strong claims to objectivity. This practice is as widespread as it is paradoxical. Consider a South Korean report on human rights in North Korea. The authors readily admit that there is a "lack of verifiable or corroborating evidence." But that does not prevent them from stressing that their study is "based on facts."[23] This tendency is particularly fateful in the domain of foreign and security policy. Look at how the otherwise nuanced Perry report, commissioned by President Bill Clinton, insisted that the United States should deal with North Korea "as it is, not as we might wish it to be." It advocated a "realist view, a hard-headed understanding of military realities."[24]

There is no such thing as an "objective reality," especially not in the domain of security policy, which revolves not only around factual occurrences but also, and above all, around the projection and evaluation of threats. The latter are inevitably matters of perception and judgment. This is particularly the case in Korea, where there has been far too much destruction and antagonistic rhetoric to allow for observations that are even remotely objective. Several prominent authors have indeed acknowledged that it is impossible to advance value-free judgments on Korean politics and history.[25] An extensive empirical survey of newspaper articles in South Korea confirms this impression. It demonstrated that explicit "value-oriented" reporting is much more frequent in coverage of North Korea than any other topic. Basing their analyses on a survey of two "conservative" (*Donga Ilbo* and *Seoul Sinmun*) and one "progressive" *(Hankyorae Sinmun)* newspaper, the researchers categorized stories as being "factual," "value-oriented," or "normative." They considered the vast majority of reports to be factual, but value-oriented and normative attitudes were most common in stories relating to North Korean politics. The authors also stress how much this form of reporting, which is mostly negative, has influenced public perceptions over the past decades.[26]

Strategic "reality" in Korea is the reality seen through the lenses of the strategic studies paradigm. This paradigm filters or selects information in a way that sets limits on what can and cannot be recognized as "real" and "realistic." The policy perspectives that are based on realist ideology can thus be presented as "hard-headed" understandings of "military realities," even though (or, precisely because) next to nothing is known (or being acknowledged) about the actual realities of North Korea. But because the realist ideology is articulated from the privileged position of the state, any opposing perspective can relatively easily be dismissed as unreasonable or unrealistic.

A more adequate understanding of the nature and function of security policy in Korea must thus problematize approaches that seek to legitimize themselves through an uncritical reference to "reality." One must ask: whose reality? For what purpose? In whose interest? With what consequences? Needed, then, are not only policy approaches based on an understanding of North Korea "as it is" but also, and above all, attempts to understand how the current security dilemmas "have become what they are."

THE NATURE OF CRISES AND THE VALUES THAT PRODUCE THEM

One must recognize both the values that are entailed in prevailing approaches to security and the interactive role that these values play in the production of political crises. The latter do not occur naturally. They are a product of human interaction. The existence of weapons alone is not enough for a political disagreement to escalate. For a crisis to become a crisis, as in Korea in 1994 and 2003, "military realities" must intersect with certain projections and perceptions of threats. When that is not the case, even a potentially volatile situation does not turn into a crisis or at least is not seen as such. This was the case, for instance, with the introduction of U.S. missiles into Turkey during the Cold War. Such an act could easily have triggered a Soviet reaction along the lines of the U.S. response to the stationing of Moscow's missiles in Cuba, which precipitated a highly precarious military standoff that almost ended in nuclear war.[27]

A crisis is an inherently political event, with rather arbitrary beginnings and ends that mark shifts in political perception. Consider the latest crisis on the Korean peninsula. According to press reports and policy statements in the Western world, it "broke out" sometime in late 2002, when North Korea started to make public its intention to withdraw from the Nuclear Nonproliferation Treaty. The conventional interpretation holds that Pyongyang sought to use "nuclear brinkmanship" to put pressure on the international community, most notably the United States. In a last ditch effort to avoid economic collapse, Kim Jong Il is thus said to have "manufactured a crisis to win concessions."[28] But one could just as easily advance a fundamentally different understanding of the crisis. One could, for instance, locate its beginning earlier in the year, at the moment when the United States declared North Korea to be an evil "rogue state," when it identified the country as a potential target for a preemptive nuclear strike, or when it suspended the promised shipment of much-needed fuel oil to the North.[29] Or one could simply note that a crisis is always already contained in the militaristic culture of insecurity that prevails in Korea. The question is simply when the crisis becomes manifest and recognized as such.

Drawing attention to the socially constructed dimensions of crises is, of course, not to argue that they are not real or dangerous. Rather, the point is to avoid making the mistake of seeing crises as factually given, thereby missing the key political processes that led to their emergence. Central attention must thus be paid to what David Campbell called the "representation of danger."[30]

If one accepts that dangers do not occur naturally but result from a clash of different representations, then an inquiry into the values of these representations becomes central. That such a task must above all scrutinize the role of realism is equally obvious, for realism is, as exemplified by the Perry report, by far the most influential ideology in the domain of foreign and security policy.[31] To be more precise, it is probably a combination of liberal and realist values. But some key underlying features of these two ideologies are rather similar anyway. They revolve around an image of international politics as dominated by nation-states and one key structural feature, anarchy: the absence of a central regulatory authority. The international is thus portrayed as a realm of threats and dangers.[32] While liberals believe that some of these perils can be mediated through international cooperation, the standard realist response is to protect state sovereignty, order, and civility at the domestic level by promoting policies that maximize the state's military capacity and, so it is assumed, its security.[33]

Although some analysts see a gradual weakening of realist doctrines in East Asian politics in favor of more cooperative liberal approaches,[34] many of the most fundamental realist values continue to guide foreign policy decisions, even when they reflect seemingly liberal principles. That realist defense postures only increase everyone else's insecurity is evident, not least through extensive realist attempts to theorize the respective dilemmas. Far less certain, though, and what I dispute here, is whether realist theories and policies remain adequate, and ethical, to deal with the increasingly complex and interactive security situation on the Korean peninsula. Few experts on Korean security have sought to address these normative challenges. Moon Chung-in and Judy E. Chung are among the rare exceptions. They stress that neither realist nor liberal approaches can offer a comprehensive explanation of war and peace in East Asia. Missing from these analyses is "the formation of national identity and the nature of mutual perception among contesting parties." Understanding the realm of identity formation is central, Moon and Chung insist, because "at a very deep level, state behavior is shaped by what states are—and what they are is socially constructed."[35] While basing my inquiry on similar assumptions, I try to take the issue one step further by demonstrating that the inside-outside (il)logic that lies at the heart of realist defense postures generates and entrenches the very antagonistic identity constructs that have been identified as the key source of tension on the Korean peninsula.

SECURITY AS POLITICAL IMAGINATION

To problematize realist approaches to conflict on the Korean peninsula is, of course, not to declare security policy obsolete or to question the need for military-based defense. Nor is it meant to legitimize the highly repressive political regime in Pyongyang, whose brinkmanship tactics pose grave risks to world peace. The point, rather, is to search for new ways of understanding and dealing with the highly volatile security situation. But such approaches can emerge only if one supplements state-based security policies with more innovative *political* approaches to inter-Korean relations.

A major task of rethinking conflict in Korea thus consists of advancing a broader understanding of security. Security should no longer be viewed solely as a protection of the state apparatus, based on realist assessments of allegedly objective "military realities." Rather, security must also be seen as a much wider political project that seeks to secure stability, subsistence, dignity, basic human rights, and freedom from fear. This is why a willingness to forgive and overcome the pains of the past is just as essential to an adequate security regime as are conventional military strategies. A broader political approach to security could not only reduce many of the present tensions but also be of crucial importance in case of North Korea's collapse, which remains a constant possibility and one of the most unpredictable sources of destabilization in northeast Asia.

Security policy, expressed in other words, is about the political imaginary as much as it is about facing threats. Although generally presented as a pragmatic response to external circumstances, security is (and has always been) just as much about defining the values and boundaries of political communities, about separating the inside from the outside. In short, security lies at the heart of modern life. This is why questions of identity are essential for understanding the larger political dynamics that are intertwined with security policy.

Once one appreciates the central link between security, identity, and society, one must also recognize that security not only delineates the limits of politics but also encompasses the possibilities of reaching beyond them. This is why Michael Dillon stresses that security should be seen as a political project that explores how new and more peaceful political constellations may emerge from "the unstable, unjust and violently defended sediment of modern political existence." Security, as he puts it, becomes "a possibility rather than a fixed and determined actuality."[36] To argue that this is so is, of course, not to equate alternative security arrangements with utopia. Dangerous weapons exist on both sides of the divided Korean peninsula. They are used to project and underline political threats. Thus one must never forget that an escalation is possible at any moment and could cause an immense human tragedy. This is why political transformations must be grounded in what is realistically possible, given the prevailing security dilemmas. But the very existence of serious escalatory dangers is also the main reason why one must seek to transcend them. Doing so is the major purpose of the second part of this book. It revolves around an attempt to combine an ethics of dialogue with an ethics of difference.

THE IMPORTANCE OF DIALOGUE

Dialogue is undoubtedly one of the most needed and, until recently, least practiced features that could generate a more peaceful political environment in Korea. Dialogue is essential for defusing tension and preventing the risk of violence. Significant progress has been made in recent years. Kim Dae-jung's Sunshine Policy sought to promote "reconciliation and co-operation between the South and North."[37] This stance, strongly supported by the Clinton administration, created the conditions for a series of historic events that culminated in June 2000 with the summit meeting between the two Korean heads of state. But the ensuing atmosphere of hope did not, as I have already mentioned, last long. Less than two years later the Korean peninsula experienced one of the most dangerous situations since the end of the war.

The verdict is clear: more than diplomatic summits are needed to break the impasse on the Korean peninsula. State-based dialogue is important but not enough. As long as the underlying logic of conflict prevails, high-level politics will not be able to achieve a lasting breakthrough.

Face-to-face contacts between average Korean people offer perhaps the best way out of the current security dilemmas, for they have the potential to dismantle the antagonisms that continue to fuel the Korean conflict. Compromise needs confidence, and the emergence of confidence requires personal encounters that can build trust over time. This is why the most radical but often underestimated element of the Sunshine Policy is its attempt to loosen state control over security by promoting more interaction, communication, and information exchanges between the two parts of the divided peninsula.

Chapter 4 examines the significance of these still very limited but growing nonstate interactions, which have either gone unnoticed or been grossly underestimated by most security experts. Relying on a human security framework, I explore the potential and limits of several features, such as the role of tourism, business, humanitarian assistance, and information flow as well as family and cultural exchanges. Not all of these and other initiatives have been successful, but they are more significant than their seemingly mundane and apolitical nature suggests. Look at how, in 2001 alone, more than eight thousand South Korean businesspeople visited the North. In an international comparison this number may appear insignificant. In the context of the hermetically divided Korean peninsula, it is simply spectacular.

It is, of course, not easy to establish dialogue and tolerance in a political environment whose contours have emerged from national division, violence, and death. So far, breakthroughs in nonstate contacts between the North and South are the exception rather than the rule in intra-Korean politics. Chapter 5 thus examines in detail some of the most challenging obstacles to a promising engagement policy. The South, despite its more open policy of engagement, is still insisting on maintaining a state-controlled unification policy that constitutes any unauthorized private contact with the North as a criminal act. The government continues to use the notorious National Security Law to crack down on dissidents who show sympathy for the archenemy in the North. Roh Moo-hyun, who replaced Kim Dae-jung as president in early 2003, promised to continue the Sunshine Policy. But engagement with the North no longer has strong support from South Korea's traditional ally, the United States, which favors a much more confrontational approach.

Obstacles to dialogue are even greater in the North, where the government is unlikely to soften its nearly total control of civil society. The type of openings that occurred in the late 1990s were more likely a reflection of the desperate economic situation than an expression of genuine desire for engagement. The survival of the political order may well be contingent on the regime's ability to shield the population from subversive outside influences. These constraints will influence all attempts to promote face-to-face interactions between ordinary citizens. The North Korean government will inevitably be torn between, on the one hand, having to open up in order to attract badly needed economic assistance and, on the other hand, trying to stay in power by retaining as much control as possible over the flow of information.

THE IMPORTANCE OF ACCEPTING DIFFERENCE

More than dialogue is needed to deal with North Korea's fear of the outside world and the ensuing potential for conflict. An articulation of a viable alternative security framework must revolve around combining the ongoing search for dialogue with a new and more radical willingness to accept that the other's sense of identity and politics

may be inherently incommensurable with one's own. Differences between the two Koreas are simply too deeply rooted to be merged
into one common form of identity, at least in the near future. One
of the most symbolic manifestations of these diverging identities is
the extreme difficulty that most North Korean defectors encounter,
despite being offered generous financial aid, job training, and other
assistance in the South, in adapting to life in an environment that
espouses values very different from those of their youth.[38]

Accepting the other's sense of identity involves a certain level of
tolerance, even forgiveness. Any successful reconciliation process
will have to mix the search for justice with the ability to forgive.
Both Korean states have taken first, albeit timid, steps toward an acceptance of difference. Starting in the late 1990s, the North began
to display some willingness to engage in dialogue and to open up.
But the regime remains highly repressive and has not fundamentally
altered its hostile rhetoric or, for that matter, its constitutionally
entrenched objective of "communizing" the entire peninsula. The
South has been somewhat more forthcoming. One of the most significant steps toward an acceptance of difference is Kim Dae-jung's
repeated declaration that the South has no "intention to undermine
or absorb North Korea," which remains one of the key fears in
Pyongyang.[39] But at the same time there are few signs that South
Korea is willing to accept the North on its own terms. Countless
government policies and documents call for a peaceful construction of a unified nation but one that is carried out on South Korean
terms. The Communist identity that has permeated the North for
more than half a century is to give way to an "open society with a
free market economy."[40] Desirable as this objective may be, it does
not rest upon a willingness to contemplate and discuss different
models of social, political, and economic interactions.

In chapter 6, I explore the potential and limits of applying an
ethics of difference to the security situation on the Korean peninsula. Key here is a genuine attempt to understand the position of the
enemy, the vantage point of the vilified other, so to speak. For instance, Western policy makers and journalists often stress that North
Korea now has missiles capable of reaching the western part of the
U.S. mainland.[41] But who ever contemplates how many American
nuclear missiles have the potential of hitting North Korea? A variety
of studies have already sought to demonstrate how the actions and

the negotiation behavior of the government in Pyongyang can be seen as rational and predictable if one makes the effort to understand how the world, and its security threats, appear from a North Korean perspective.[42] To imagine and analyze such perceptions is not to legitimize North Korean foreign policy decisions or to endorse its authoritarian governing style. Rather, the point is to understand the interactive dynamics entailed in security dilemmas. Imagining the other does not mean that one needs to agree or become implicated with its worldview.

Dealing with difference is essential not only to attenuate the present culture of insecurity but also, and perhaps even more important, to prepare for the conflicts that could emerge if North Korea collapses. Such an event cannot be predicted. But it cannot be excluded, either. Current approaches to security are particularly ill equipped to deal with this potentially significant challenge. This is the case even though some commentators now speak of a significant policy shift, one that interprets the North Korean threat as no longer stemming solely from a conventional military attack but also from the potentially disastrous consequences of an uncontrolled regime collapse, such as a refugee crisis or even a potential civil war.[43] As a result, the so-called soft landing scenario has become the preferred policy option of all great powers concerned with Korea. It is based on the assumption that a gradual, step-by-step rapprochement can prevent a regime collapse. Such a position is undoubtedly desirable. Whether it is feasible is an entirely different question. For one, a successful rapprochement would require a fundamental rethinking of security policy, including an acceptance of difference, which is so far lacking. But even if that were the case, a soft landing scenario may not actually work. North Korea may simply implode one day, particularly if it further opens up to the outside world. It is thus essential that the antagonistic identity constructs that persist at the moment, and that would be among the most dangerous sources of conflict in a chaotically unified Korea, are eliminated or at least attenuated while there is time to do so.

ETHICAL DILEMMAS IN THE ARTICULATION OF SECURITY POLICY

The dilemmas identified in the previous sections give rise to some of the most difficult policy challenges in current global politics. Should one support North Korea with humanitarian aid and other forms of economic assistance to avoid a famine or a collapse? Would such assistance not also sustain and perhaps even legitimize the authoritarian regime, facilitate human rights abuses, and prevent important social change from occurring? And would a conciliatory approach in general not allow North Korea to pursue its nuclear weapons program, either secretly or in the open, thereby creating one of the most dangerous security risks in the world today? Is it thus, by contrast, more ethical to refuse assistance to the authoritarian government in Pyongyang, perhaps even impose sanctions, as the United States was contemplating in February 2003?[44] But would such a position not risk causing massive starvation, either without effecting any regime change or by precipitating an uncontrolled collapse? And would this policy not give reasons to North Korea to acquire nuclear weapons in an effort to deter an attack on its sovereignty?

Finding ethical and politically acceptable approaches to these dilemmas is neither obvious nor easy. The debates are correspondingly polarized. On one end of the spectrum are advocates of a hard-line policy toward the North that aims to undermine the authoritarian regime as fast as possible, leading to a quick disintegration and subsequent absorption.[45] The second and more widely accepted approach is based on the soft landing scenario that I mentioned earlier.[46] With the reemergence of major tensions in 2003 over North Korea's nuclear program, the front lines of these debates became even more polarized. Some believe that a firmer stance toward North Korea, as advocated by the U.S. administration, was long overdue and is, indeed, essential for dealing with the challenges ahead.[47] Others stress that precisely at such a moment of crisis it is crucial to hold on to the more tolerant approach favored by the subsequent South Korean presidents Kim Dae-jung and Roh Moo-hyun.[48]

The task of this book is not to search for and develop a position somewhere along this spectrum of policy approaches to North Korea. Doing so could hardly add substance to a debate that is already as extensive as it is polarized. The point of rethinking security is, rather, to understand and investigate why this debate has come to be framed in this particularly polarized manner in the first place. The need for a reframing of debates becomes clearer if we recall an argument that Robert Cox once made in the general context of international politics. He distinguished between two types of approaches: problem-solving approaches and those that are critical.[49] Problem-solving theories consider the prevailing structures of the world as the given framework for action. They study the workings and influences of a political system or address the problems that it creates. They assume, as is the case of the realist ideology, that one can and should "deal with human nature as it is and not as it ought to be."[50] But such theories not only accept the existing political dilemmas as given but also, intentionally or unintentionally, sustain them. Critical theories, by contrast, attempt to transcend the existing order with the objective of comprehending how it was created and how it could give way to less violent alternative political constellations. Doing so is the task of a rethinking process, and it inevitably entails deemphasizing some political issues hitherto perceived as central while moving other, more marginal, concerns to a prominent position. Among the issues that move to the background are diplomatic negotiations or debates about the nuclear issue, which have so far preoccupied analysts of Korean security. This is not to say that they are not important or that a potential military escalation should not be of utmost concern. The point, rather, is that these dangers must be seen as symptoms, rather than causes. The nuclear threat, for instance, does not exist primarily because of the proliferation of weapons. The threat has emerged and persists to a large extent because the underlying political discourse led the two Korean states into a situation in which conflict has become the modus operandi of political interactions.

What, then, are the potentials and limits of a critical rethinking of Korea security? How, exactly, is such an effort different from prevailing problem-solving approaches? First, let me address the limits of this study. It offers neither a comprehensive review of the Korean security situation nor a detailed engagement with the most current events. There will be no systematic survey of great power policies toward the Korean peninsula, no thorough analysis of the technicalities and negotiation tactics surrounding the latest nuclear crisis. Various monographs and articles have done this already in a highly competent manner. I seek to chart a different route, identifying broad patterns of conflict and possibilities for peace that emerge from rethinking the policies that sustain these patterns.

Focusing on underlying trends and conceptual challenges inevitably entails glancing past nuances at times. As a result it will be easy to find certain political events or perspectives that seem to contradict the book's central arguments: moments when identity differences are overcome in a passionate display of Korean national unity, for instance, or policy positions that show willingness to compromise. Consider that even while the 2003 nuclear crisis escalated, the United States sought to solve the issue through negotiations. President Bush stressed that "I believe this is not a military showdown, this is a diplomatic showdown."[51] When the crisis escalated further, U.S. Secretary of State Colin Powell reiterated that there were "no armies on the march" and further pledged 100,000 tons of food aid to the North.[52] Much has been made about the difference between this seemingly conciliatory U.S. stance toward North Korea and Washington's far more aggressive opposition to Iraq's weapons of mass destruction, where war was presented as virtually the only way to halt a dangerous escalation. The situation was particularly paradoxical since Pyongyang publicly withdrew from the Nuclear Nonproliferation Treaty and asked the International Atomic Energy Agency (IAEA) to leave the country. Baghdad, by contrast, denied possessing weapons of mass destruction and permitted IAEA inspectors to verify its claims.[53]

Washington's apparently tolerant attitude toward the 2003 crisis in Korea does not change the more significant and basic fact that the United States consistently represents and treats North Korea as a dangerous "rogue state." That war was not advocated as a main option in Korea, as in Iraq, is a reflection of diplomatic constraints and, above all, strategic calculations. South Korea's then newly elected president, Roh Moo-hyun, strongly opposed a military solution to the problem. And so did the neighboring states, most notably China. Perhaps even more important, the consequences of an escalation in Korea would be hard to contain. One of the world's biggest cities, Seoul, is only about thirty miles from the border. Even if preemptive strikes were to neutralize any nuclear arsenal that North Korea might possess, they would not be able to destroy all conventional weapons. The latter alone could easily trigger a second Korean war with disastrous consequences on all sides. Negotiations are thus simply imperative, even for a U.S. government that advocates a policy stance predicated on "no bargaining with rogues and terrorists."[54]

Diplomatic initiatives, even if they are well intended and even if they seemingly reflect a momentary lapse from realpolitical entrenchment of security dilemmas, neither replace nor challenge the central patterns of conflict on the peninsula. They confirm them. Drawing attention to these entrenched patterns of conflict is just as important as understanding the strategic maneuverings that take place within them. Both tasks cannot be pursued at the same time, which is why the following ruminations clearly opt for the former.

Thus the key question a reader must ask of this book is not whether its arguments are true. Far more important is whether it presents old dilemmas in a new light.[55] I search not for new facts but for new visions. I seek not new evidence but new perspectives. I hope not for discoveries but for uncoveries.[56] To pursue this line of inquiry is, of course, not to say that the material I present in this book is fabricated or that its arguments are merely utopian. Rather, the point is to stress that a rethinking process has primarily conceptual, rather than empirical, objectives.

THE POLICY RELEVANCE OF RETHINKING SECURITY

Can a book that favors a critical and conceptual rethinking over a problem-solving approach still be relevant to policy makers? The answer is yes, but I need to elaborate. The lack of communication between academics and practitioners is, of course, notorious. Andrew Mack stresses that the institutional and disciplinary structures of academia award scholars not for making policy recommendations but for advancing theoretical contributions.[57] When urged to comment on the key political challenges of his day, Martin Heidegger, for instance, responded that he could not help, that it is not the task of thinking to make public statements on moral and practical issues.[58] Obstacles from the other side are equally high because, as Mack points out, policy makers rarely have the time for extensive reading. And if they do read, they often feel alienated by the abstract theoretical language that permeates many academic analyses. William Tow, an experienced analyst of East Asian security policy, stresses that many policy makers in the region view theoretical debates emanating from the West as "intellectually elegant but distant from their own immediate interests and agendas." Rather than participating in academic debates, Asian policy makers base their strategic decisions mostly on intelligence assessments, cables dispatched from foreign missions, and discussions within their own policy community.[59] The problem is, of course, that all these discussions, briefs, and dispatches are framed, as Tow acknowledges, by the prevailing statecentric and realist approach that I have identified as the main obstacle to a more peaceful security arrangement in

Korea. This tendency is even more problematic because realist perspectives are not presented as the ideological positions that they are but as detached and factual assessments of strategic reality. Realist approaches to foreign policy have been around for so long and have become so influential that their political origin appears more and more real until the ensuing worldviews, and the conflicts that they generate, seem inevitable, even natural. We begin to "lie herd-like in a style obligatory for all," Nietzsche would say.[60]

A more adequate security policy must, as I argued earlier, challenge the equation of realist ideology with objectivity and common sense. A major purpose of rethinking security policies is thus to question their taken-for-granted nature. This cannot be done without a certain distancing from the way in which security issues have conventionally been portrayed. Some speak of a need to "defamiliarize commonsense understandings" of security to make their constructed nature apparent.[61] My own attempt at doing so is based primarily on two strategies.

First, I rely on an interdisciplinary approach in an attempt to problematize security dilemmas that may not be visible from within the relatively narrow disciplinary debates of security studies. I draw upon a range of different sources, such as anthropology, sociology, philosophy, psychology, linguistics, and literature, which are not usually taken into account by experts in defense policy. Lack of communication among academic disciplines is one of the major obstacles to a more insightful approach to Korea's political dilemmas. For instance, psychologists and anthropologists have long drawn attention to problems that emerge from the development of two different identities in the North and South. But virtually none of these insights, well developed and convincing as they are, have penetrated security studies, which remains one of the most insular domains of intellectual exchange, in both its academic and policy-oriented versions. This is not necessarily surprising, for academic disciplines are powerful mechanisms to direct and control the production and diffusion of knowledge. They establish the rules of intellectual exchange and define the methods, techniques, and instruments that are considered proper for the pursuit of knowledge.[62] Thus a major methodological task of this book is to break through these disciplinary boundaries in order to bring new perspective and insights to the study of Korean security.

Second, I try to defamiliarize security dilemmas in Korea by comparing them with the division and unification of Germany. Numerous studies of this nature already exist, but they have focused almost exclusively on geopolitical and economic issues. A focus on identity can, by contrast, open up new and highly informative perspectives on the Korean dilemmas. Here too my study is not comprehensive, in part because many of the dynamics are intrinsically linked to their unique political and cultural environment. Rather, I will draw on this comparison when it can help illuminate problems or potentials that otherwise may remain unnoticed. It is highly revealing, for instance, that identity constructs that developed in divided Germany continue to pose significant problems more than a decade after unification. In Korea these identity constructs are far more volatile and dangerous than in Germany, for Germans have never fought a war against each other and regular cross-border contact kept antagonistic stereotypes at much lower levels. The German precedent thus strongly suggests that the success of future efforts toward rapprochement in Korea hinges largely on how successful the political leaders and their societies are in dealing with the legacy of half a century of division, hostility, and grief.

The call for an interdisciplinary and comparative approach brings us back to the lack of meaningful communication between academics and policy makers. Addressing this challenge is not easy, for defamiliarizing entails breaking with the way in which conventional approaches have represented the dilemmas. It requires drawing on different sources of evidence and different concepts. Essential as it is, this process of challenging the problematic presentation of common sense also runs into major difficulties, for any text that breaks with established conventions risks appearing obscure and unrelated to the "real" problems that decision makers are facing. But an alternative security framework can become viable only if it manages to break out of intellectual obscurity, if it is able to reach people and change the way they think about the issues in question.

My attempt to rethink Korean security enters the ongoing struggle over politically relevant debates in a particular manner. I do not try to provide clear and indisputable policy recommendations. I do not suggest what country X should do vis-à-vis country Y. Doing so is the task of politicians and diplomats. It requires assessing the unique circumstances that surround each decision. The task of a rethinking process consists, rather, of identifying and exploring the type of mind-set with which the existing security dilemmas can be approached more productively. It explores the preconditions necessary for more nuanced political judgments.[63]

A rethinking process is inevitably a long-term affair, for it revolves around challenging notions of security that are deeply entrenched in political practice and societal consciousness, not just in Korea but in international politics in general. Some aspects of an alternative approach to security may, it is hoped, come across, even in a political context that remains dominated by the powerful conceptual grip of realist ideologies. Other elements will undoubtedly be dismissed as irrational or obscure by a policy discourse that has managed to present its own, politically motivated, interpretations of security dilemmas as "hard-headed understandings of reality." But the marginalized perspectives are neither unimportant nor lost. They can perhaps be compared to how Paul Celan described the function of poems. They are "messages in a bottle": pleas that are sent out with the hope that they will be recovered at some stage in the future. The message may not be picked up immediately. At the moment of its release there may be no language to appreciate the bottled plea for dialogue and a more peaceful future. But one day it will be washed onto a shore, onto something open: a policy maker longing for alternatives, a situation requiring dialogue, a receptive reality.[64]

Existing Security Dilemmas in Korea

In this first part, I rethink existing security dilemmas on the peninsula. This process starts with recognizing that identities are historically constructed and that these constructs are intertwined with current security dilemmas. By focusing on linkages between individual, collective, and state identity, I provide an understanding of security that goes beyond conventional realist and statecentric approaches. Or, rather, I seek to show how these approaches are manifestations of a more deeply seated and highly problematic practice of defining security as an attempt to defend a safe inside from a hostile outside. The resulting mind-set creates a culture of insecurity that makes conflict on the Korean peninsula virtually inevitable. It also prevents us from recognizing the interactive dimensions of security dilemmas, making it easy to put all blame for the repeatedly recurring crises on the vilified other, in this case the rogue state of North Korea. By revealing the historically constructed nature of identity and difference, I provide in Part I the foundation for my subsequent attempt to outline the contours of an alternative security framework for the peninsula. Once the socially constructed dimensions of identity are recognized, they no longer appear solely as a cause of conflict. The relationship between identity and difference can then be used as a crucial source of hope for a more peaceful future.

The Emergence of Antagonistic Identities

Rare human rubbish . . . human butcher . . . chieftain of irregularities and corruption and human scum . . . pro-U.S. flunkeyist traitor . . . chieftain of tyranny and murder . . . bloodstained master of torture policy . . . war-maniac . . . political charlatan without parallel in history
—DESCRIPTIONS IN THE NORTH KOREAN PRESS
OF SOUTH KOREAN PRESIDENTS,
JANUARY–FEBRUARY 1988

In speech, do not say things that are untrue or fabricated. . . . What is valued in speech is clarity, meticulousness, simplicity: hence avoid abstruseness, exaggeration, and clutter.
—*SMALL MANNERS FOR SCHOLARS*, CHOSON DYNASTY, 1775

The honorific attributes in the first epigraph were bestowed by North Korea's official press upon the outgoing and incoming South Korean presidents Chun Doo-hwan and Roh Tae-woo. The year was 1988. In the South, hatred of North Korea's Communist leadership was widespread too, although articulated in slightly less colorful ways. According to the Tae Sung Dong Primary School, a nationally designated model village located within the Southern part of the DMZ, the primary aim of education was "love your country and lead the way in anti-communism."[1] One does not need to be a trained psychologist to realize that children who grow up with such educational leitmotifs, or with the type of antagonistic rhetoric prevalent in North Korea's press, contribute to the dissemination of a societal self-awareness that is articulated through a stark opposition between identity and difference.

During the last few years both sides have tried to tone down at least some of these antagonistic rhetorical practices. Officers of the South Korean Armed Forces, for instance, have been encouraged to use military jargon that allows soldiers to distinguish between the evil North Korean system (the "main enemy") and their innocent brothers and sisters in the North (the "anti-enemy").[2] This distinction has also penetrated many public discourses. Textual analyses of South Korean newspapers, for instance, reveal that the media have presented a view of national identity that stands in direct opposition to "Northern" values. But most reports still have managed to convey that the main enemy is North Korea's "odious system, rather than the country itself."[3] Such differentiations have increased under the governments of Kim Dae-jung and Roh Moo-hyun. But one cannot easily uproot deeply entrenched antagonistic identity constructs and the demonizing images that are associated with them. They permeate all aspects of society, from diplomacy to everyday life. They become internalized in language, school curricula, political institutions, and moral discourses. Consider, for instance, how President Kim Dae-jung created a major political controversy when describing Kim Jong Il, the North Korean leader, not in the usual negative terms (as a brutal, insane, licentious, and impetuous drunk and playboy) but as "a pragmatic leader with good judgment and knowledge."[4] A highly experienced political commentator stressed that many South Koreans "cannot easily accept the rhetoric that the North's dictatorial leader has become suddenly a trustworthy partner."[5] Public surveys tend to portray a similar picture of entrenched stereotypes and antagonisms. In May 2000, for instance, the image of Kim Jong Il was still overwhelmingly negative. When pollsters asked South Koreans what first comes to their mind when thinking of the North Korean leader, the most common answers were "dictator" (34.6 percent), "Communism" (6.1 percent), "bastard" (5.5 percent), "war" (3.5 percent), and "savage" (3.2 percent).[6]

In this chapter I examine how antagonistic identity patterns emerged historically and how they have become intertwined with the current culture of insecurity. Such an endeavor can, of course, not be exhaustive. A thorough investigation into the nature and function of identities would need to scrutinize in detail the developments of each Korean state, drawing attention to moral discourses, policy shifts, media representations, educational practices, and a wide range of other factors essential to the process of nation building. Doing so would go far beyond what is possible in the context of a brief chapter. The focus of my inquiry will thus be limited to identifying broad patterns that arose during key periods of Korean history, such as the Japanese colonial occupation, the Korean War, and the ongoing Cold War confrontation. It is evident that such an abbreviated intellectual endeavor requires glossing over some nuances that inevitably occur within these larger patterns.[7] But locating underlying trends is nevertheless crucial, for it can reveal how identity patterns that formed during the last half-century of Korea's national division are essential to understanding and dealing with the security challenges that lie ahead. To be more specific, the key security dilemmas of today are intrinsically linked to identity constructs that portray the political system at the opposite side of the divided peninsula as threatening, perhaps even inherently evil. The constructed nature of these dilemmas is all the more evident because the boundaries of identity in Korea are drawn not along "natural" lines, such as race, ethnicity, language, or religion. They are based above all on two artificially created and diametrically opposed ideological images of the world.

Most discussions of Korean security make little or no mention of identity issues, even though they shape virtually all aspects of defense policy. An essay by Chun Chae-sung is one of the rare systematic attempts to examine the specific links between identity and foreign policy during different periods of South Korea's history.[8] But his analysis, which draws upon a constructivist methodology and challenges the idea of identities being fixed and immutable, focuses primarily on state-level actions, rather than the more deeply rooted individual and collective identities that I seek to examine in this chapter. By focusing on multiple levels of analyses, I draw upon a number of international relations scholars who have theorized identity and security. They argue that "security cannot be severed from the claims of group and collective structures within which individuals find their identity and through which they undertake collective projects."[9]

I am also writing in the wake of a long tradition of examining the role of culture in Korean politics, a tradition that has had next to no influence on security analyses. This body of literature explores links between specific cultural traits, most notably the hierarchical values of Confucian thought and the tendency toward authoritarian rule in both parts of divided Korea. Shaped by the so-called modernization paradigm, these scholarly debates are waged in the wake of two influential concepts, Karl Wittfogel's "hydraulic theory" and Gregory Henderson's "politics of the vortex."[10] While political forays into culture offer revealing insight, a methodological word of caution is in order, for they can easily lead to problematic forms of essentialism: attempts to superimpose stereotypical cultural images upon far more complex personal and political realities. Various features, most notably the historically weak role of the Korean state and the existence not only of old democratic roots but also of a largely successful transition to democracy in the South, clearly contradict the assertion that there is a link between cultural values and authoritarianism in Korea.[11] Thus I advance my inquiry into identity and security with corresponding scholarly caution. But I also advance it with the knowledge that seemingly soft analytical categories, like identity or culture, can shape a range of hard political dilemmas. Consider North Korea's constitutionally entrenched objective of "communizing" the entire peninsula. It is one of many manifestations where identity has direct and far-reaching political consequences. The situation in the South is not much different. Here too the constitution promises to "destroy all vices and injustice." It holds that its territory "shall consist of the Korean peninsula and its adjacent islands."[12]

THE HISTORICAL LEGACY OF COLONIALISM AND WAR

The metaphor of a hermit kingdom, which the Western press frequently applies to North Korea, has earlier roots. Until the late nineteenth century Korea lived a relatively isolated existence. The first extensive and recorded modern contact with the West occurred in 1653, when the Dutch merchant ship *De Sperwer,* or Sparrowhawk, was shipwrecked on the southern tip of Jeju Island. Hendrik Hamel, the ship's bookkeeper, later described how he and thirty-five other survivors spent ten months interned on Jeju and were then taken to the Jeolla region and later to Seoul, where they were forcibly retained for the next thirteen years. On a September night in 1666

Hamel and some of his friends eventually escaped by boat to Japan.[13] Subsequent visitors fared only slightly better. Although they were no longer retained, they were strongly encouraged to leave. Basil Hall, a captain of the British army, arrived in 1816. He noted that Koreans took little interest in him and that their "chief anxiety was to get rid of us as soon as possible."[14] Korea's hostility toward the outside world grew in direct relation to the West's determination to open up the country. The introduction of Christianity, for instance, was strongly resisted by Korea's rulers, who had thousands of converts killed. The same fate met the crew of the American merchant ship *General Sherman* when it sailed up the Taedong River toward Pyong-yang in 1866.[15]

An antagonistic sense of identity clearly existed during Korea's long reclusive period. But it revolved around cultural and ethnic features rather than ideological values. It reflected a strong desire to protect Korean identity against pressures from the outside world. This identity did indeed become increasingly threatened soon after Korea was finally forced to open up, in the mid-1870s. The United States was one of the first Western powers to sign a treaty with Korea, in 1882. A decade later Japanese influence over the peninsula started to become more menacing, particularly when the Japanese minister of war, Yamagata Aritomo, linked Japan's independence to a dual defense strategy. He argued that in addition to its traditional boundaries of sovereignty, Japan had to defend a broader sphere of interest. The Korean peninsula, Yamagata continued, was within this sphere of interest because whoever occupied it would wield enormous control over East Asia.[16] As a result Japan fought two wars for the control of Korea, one in 1894–1895 against China, the other in 1904–1905 against czarist Russia. The outcome of these conflicts was the basis for Korea's annexation into the Japanese colonial empire in 1910, and it lasted until the end of the Second World War. During this time the occupation forces tried everything possible to eradicate Korean identity, to the point that schools were not allowed to teach Korean history, culture, or language.

Half a century of colonial occupation may have created a certain vacuum of Korean political identity, which could have facilitated the subsequent imposition of ideological conceptions of self and other that were entirely alien to the Korean tradition. Be that as it may, the current division of the peninsula into two ideologically opposed states is the direct result of external impositions on Korea at the end of World War II.

In the process of dismantling the Japanese colonial empire, American and Soviet troops occupied the peninsula, dividing it into two parts along the thirty-eighth parallel. American officials drew this line in August 1945, hastily, arbitrarily, and without consulting any Koreans.[17] The Soviet Union then accepted the unilateral U.S. move. Separate political regimes were established on each side, reflecting the ideological standpoints of the two superpowers. In August 1948 the Republic of Korea was formed in the South, with the Korean expatriate Syngman Rhee installed as its first president. The following month Kim Il Sung, an anti-Japanese guerrilla fighter, became the first premier of the newly proclaimed Democratic People's Republic of Korea in the North.

What happened between then and the outbreak of the Korean War is much debated. The most neutral descriptions, to the extent that this is possible, given the highly emotional issues at stake, hold that "tension along the thirty-eighth parallel flared up in intermittent military clashes until a full-scale war broke out in June 1950, when North Korea launched a general invasion against South Korea in an attempt to bring all of Korea under its rule."[18] The two Korean governments have, however, sponsored accounts of the war that are much more black-and-white: they put all blame for the conflict on the other side. The respective narratives then became essential elements in the creation of two diametrically opposed notions of nationhood. For instance, Park Chung Hee, South Korea's president during the 1960s and 1970s, argued that "the north Korean Communists villainously unleashed an unwarranted armed invasion of the south with a view to communizing the entire Korean peninsula."[19] The North, by contrast, sees these events as a heroic attempt to "liberate the homeland" and "drive out the beast-like American imperialists."[20]

The juxtaposed interpretations of history are so deeply rooted in the respective state mythologies that it is virtually impossible, as a senior scholar acknowledges, "to venture a balanced account of Korea's recent history."[21] But an increasing number of revisionist historians are trying to see beyond the black-and-white images that make up most accounts of conflict on the peninsula. Bruce Cumings, for instance, stresses that the Korean War "did not begin

on June 25, 1950, much special pleading and argument to the contrary." He points out that intense fighting had already taken place
for the nine preceding months. Without denying Kim Il Sung's "grave
responsibility," Cumings presents the war as a complex and inter-
connected set of events. He stresses that the war "originate[d] in
multiple causes, with blame enough to go around for everyone—
and blame enough to include Americans who thoughtlessly divided
Korea and then reestablished the colonial government machinery."[22]
This revisionist position has led to much opposition in South Korea
and the West, including factual critiques related to recently released
Soviet material,[23] regrets about an "unappealing . . . bias towards
the Communists,"[24] and even accusations of irresponsible scholarship, subjective teleology, and pro–North Korea propaganda.[25]

Less debatable than these scholarly disputes is the far-reaching
effect of the war itself. It started as a civil war but then involved
two great powers on opposing sides: first, the United States, which
intervened, together with other nations through a U.N. mandate designed to roll back the Northern occupation of the South; and then
China, whose involvement saved the North from defeat and secured
a military stalemate along the original dividing line at the thirty-
eighth parallel. Documents released in the 1990s also reveal limited
involvement by the Soviet Union.[26] In all, the conflict claimed the
lives of more than a million people. Half a century after the events,
an estimated ten million individuals are still separated from their
families.[27]

Less debatable as well is that the Korean War "became the point
of departure for all post-war Korean politics."[28] At its most basic
level the war resulted, as Park Myung-Lim notes, "from efforts to
break the status quo of the peninsular division."[29] In this sense the
war could have solved, as many civil wars do, some of the political
tensions that existed in Korea during the 1940s and early 1950s,
tensions that were unusually high and linked to such issues as colonial legacies, foreign intervention, and national division. But "the
war solved nothing," Cumings stresses, for all it did was restore the
status quo ante.[30] Indeed, the Korean Armistice Agreement of July
1953, which was never signed by South Korea, constitutes only a
cease-fire. A clause called for a political conference, during which
the terms of a peace treaty were supposed to have been discussed.
This conference, which took place in Geneva in 1954, failed in its

prime task. In juridical terms the two Koreas have thus remained in a state of war ever since.[31]

THE SOCIAL CONSTRUCTION OF ANTAGONISTIC IDENTITIES

The legacy of the Korean War has decisively shaped the last fifty years of political discourses and practices on the peninsula. Much can be said, and countless books have been written, about the highly volatile competition between the two Korean states. Particularly revealing, but not sufficiently acknowledged, is the role of identities in this process. The identities that developed during the long period of Cold War tensions on the peninsula are not only deeply entrenched but also lie at the heart of current security dilemmas. This is why a closer look at the emergence and nature of these identities is in order.

To start with a simplification: identities in Korea are articulated largely in negative terms. To be South Korean means, above all, not to be Communist. To be North Korean means not to be part of a capitalist and imperialist order. Each state bases its legitimacy, as Leon Sigal puts it, "on being the antithesis and antagonist of the other."[32] Or, as the South Korean president Park Chung Hee once said: "Unfortunately, the north Korean communists have chosen a path diametrically opposed to what we have been pursuing."[33] The situation is, of course, not quite as straightforward. Koreans derive their identity from a variety of sources. Depending on the situation, a person may, for instance, be identified primarily as a man or a woman, an elder or a youth, a manager or a peasant.[34] These and many other forms of identification are embedded in the Korean language, which possesses verb and noun suffixes that structurally force a speaker to identify specific hierarchy relationships in all verbal interactions. The Cold War did not eradicate these aspects of Korean culture. Rather, it created a situation in which a very specific, externally imposed, and ideological identification has come to prevail over all others. Whereas gender, age, education, or regional affiliation continue to be key factors in determining a person's social status and possibilities, his or her ideological identification has literally turned into a matter of life and death, or at least freedom and imprisonment. As Chun Chae-sung observes: "The Korean war put an end to multi-identity competition at various levels only to make the Cold War identity the most dominant one."[35]

The domain of education is particularly illustrative of how the two Korean states managed to infuse their populations with their respective ideological mind-sets. By examining North and South Korean school textbooks, Denis Hart notes how essential the process of incorporation of a "national other" has become to the construction of identity on each side. Preoccupied with the need to present itself as the only legitimate government on the peninsula, with the desire to win the "hearts and minds" of its people, each side promotes ideologically based historical narratives aimed at discrediting the legitimacy of its national rival. As a result many aspects of the educational system in both parts of the peninsula have encouraged students to feel estranged from their brothers and sisters on the other side.[36]

Education is one of the most central societal mechanisms through which histories and political identities are being produced, reproduced, and entrenched. Laura Hein and Mark Selden stress that "schools and textbooks are important vehicles through which contemporary societies transmit ideas of citizenship and both the idealized past and the promised future of a community."[37] What students learn during the first few years of their lives inevitably influences their political and social attitudes for decades to come. While narratives of nationhood create boundaries between self and other from the very beginning of the educational cycle, secondary school education plays a particularly crucial political role. It is at this level that historical narratives are first taught, thereby providing a detailed interpretative and factual foundation for the previously established sense of identity.[38] School education is thus one of the most powerful ways of promoting a particular form of political socialization. The objectives of a state can in fact often be achieved most effectively "at a distance," through various mechanisms that seem, at first sight, to be of an apolitical nature. They include not only education but also the organization of welfare, health, urban planning, and the regulation of crime and the economy.[39]

Given the intense conflict on the Korean peninsula, it is not surprising that both states have exerted an unusually high degree of control over the process through which historical awareness is taught in schools. In North Korea textbooks are, predictably, published by the government, which also controls all aspects of the teaching process. But in the South too, many aspects of education are state controlled. There are two systems for publishing textbooks. Under the first system textbooks are published by the South Korean Ministry of Education itself. The second system allows private companies to publish textbooks. But the publication process is still strongly regulated by the Ministry of Education, ensuring government control over the teaching of history. During its five decades of existence South Korea has oscillated between direct governmental publication of textbooks (especially during the more authoritarian periods, when nation building was considered a direct state-sponsored project) and a more decentralized and privatized phase.[40] At the moment the latter system is being promoted. Each school can choose from among several state or privately published textbooks (currently about five versions), but, given the tight governmental control of the publication process, this amounts to little substantive influence.

The political appropriation of education in Korea is as obvious as the control of textbooks and curriculum design. Denis Hart stresses that school textbooks present "tales of national identity" that reflect, above all, the specific and politically motivated preferences of each Korean state. The so-sponsored historical narratives are thus not authentic representations of the past. They "tell that nation what their memories are supposed to be."[41] Each state, he points out, "felt free to teach its citizens to forget the past and instead learn history."[42] This, of course, amounts to a very particular, ideologically driven notion of history. Both Korean states do indeed openly admit that they use education for political purposes. The North Korean dictionary, for instance, defines *education* as "something that produces revolutionaries, who . . . [uphold] the communist principle of one for all, all for one."[43] Kim Il Sung repeatedly reinforced this position in public, pointing out that the purpose of education is "to influence people so that they serve the societal order."[44] And a few years later he stressed that "we must intensify the political-ideological education of pupils and thus make all of them workers and revolutionaries who . . . fight vigorously for socialism and communism."[45] Things are no less explicit in South Korea, as illustrated by the earlier example of education at the Tae Sung Dong Primary School: "love your country and lead the way in anti-communism."

IDENTITY PATTERNS IN NORTH AND SOUTH KOREA

How, exactly, have these political and educational manipulations shaped contemporary Korean identity?

Anticommunism clearly was the leitmotif of each South Korean government. No alternative visions were allowed, to the point that "socialist discourse was legally forbidden."[46] At some stage North Korea was actually seen as not belonging to the same nation. Park Chung Hee, who gained power through a military coup in 1961 and ruled the country until his assassination in 1979, literally believed that the North lost its Korean national identity because communism is an ideology "wholly alien to the tradition and history of our nation."[47]

Anticommunism has become far more than a government policy. It has penetrated every aspect of South Korea's national consciousness, to the point that it reached, as one commentator puts it, "a hegemonic hold over civil society."[48] Choi Chungmoo stresses how, "for more than two decades after national partition, South Korean schoolchildren visually depicted North Koreans literally to be red-bodied demons with horns and long fingernails on their hairy, grabbing hands, as represented in anti-communist posters."[49] Hart's extensive study of South Korean primary school textbooks identifies roughly one-fifth of the material as explicitly anti-Northern. He examines a range of stories, some quite graphic and violent, that represent the North in a dehumanized way and as a direct threat to Southern safety. Stories such as "The Beastlike Communist Spy" or "I Hate Communists" implicitly suggest the need to free the people of the North from the Communist demons that have taken hold of their government.[50] The anticommunism that pervades school textbooks is so exhaustive that various important historical features, such as the role of Korean Communist guerillas in the struggle against the Japanese colonial occupation, are simply left out.[51] Anticommunism penetrates not only the teaching of history but virtually all domains of study, from biology (the need for democracy to develop a healthy mind and body) to mathematics (using numbers of Communist infiltrators to illustrate numerical puzzles).[52]

The situation in the North is comparable, for an anti-imperialist and anticapitalist discourse prevails in an equally strong manner. "In order to understand North Korea," one commentator argues, "one only needs to look at the South, for whatever characterizes the South is denounced and demonized in the North."[53] One key difference, though, is that North Korea's *Juche*, or self-reliance ideology, is based as much on anti-imperialist values as it is on an opposition to South Korea. Here too an analysis of school textbooks is highly revealing. Hart speaks of "multiple others," consisting mostly of

Japan, the former colonial occupant, and, with increasing vigor during the last few years, the United States. A journalist who visited the North in 2003 remarked that "the fixation on everything American is stunning."[54] Both the United States and Japan are represented as evil imperial forces that constitute a direct threat to Korean people. The North Korean press, distinguished by its extraordinary rhetorical flourish, then supplements these images with corresponding metaphors, ranging from "warhawks," to "warmongers," "fascists," "imperialists," and "reactionaries."[55] When the North Korean press is speaking of South Korea, it too makes a distinction between the government and its people. The latter are seen as victims to be liberated from colonial occupation, the former as a corrupt and dangerous "puppet regime."

Juche is perhaps the most central element of North Korea's attempt to define its identity with reference to threats from the outside world. Often interpreted as "self-reliance" in all aspects of life, *Juche* emerged in the mid-1950s. It became the state's leitmotif a decade later, when Kim Il Sung sought to pursue an increasingly independent position from both of North Korea's key Communist allies, the Soviet Union and China. *Juche,* then, is above all a form of nationalism, an attempt to place "Korean things first," as Cumings puts it.[56] Its three core elements do indeed contain strong nationalistic tones: political independence, economic self-sustenance, and military self-defense.[57] The compulsion to construct an authentic and self-contained national discourse included minimizing the central influence that China exerted on Korea. This is illustrated, for instance, by archeological efforts to deny the existence of Han commanderies on the peninsula[58] or by Pyongyang's "language purification movement." The latter was introduced in 1949 and abolished the use of Chinese characters in favor of an exclusive reliance on Korea's own hangul script. Meant as a way of cleansing Korean society of foreign elements, this practice is seen by some as a prime example of a state's use of language planning to promote a particular political ideology.[59] These practices are part of a larger pattern, visible, for instance, in how both Korean states have tightly controlled the collection and display of archaeological artifacts in an attempt to construct a nationalist version of a pure and authentic Korean identity.[60]

Many commentators, such as Oh Kongdan and Ralph Hassig, stress that *Juche* ideology is "riddled with falsehood and lies."[61]

Self-sufficiency is, indeed, hardly the order of the day in North Korea, where humanitarian aid is needed to feed a significant part of the populace today. But that does not detract from the centrality of *Juche* to North Korea's understanding of itself and the outside world. Oh and Hassig recognize that Pyongyang's attempt to establish a strong and reclusive "fortress" and a unitary ideology, as absurd and anachronistic as it may appear, is nevertheless hardly surprising, given Korea's history as a victim of foreign aggression, subjugation, and conquest.[62]

Antagonistic identity patterns pose one of the most difficult challenges to politics and security in Korea. My intention in this chapter was to retrace their emergence and understand their influence on the current political climate. Superpower rivalry divided the peninsula at the end of the Second World War and set the stage for a sustained ideological confrontation. The devastating Korean War then created wounds that still influence politics on the peninsula half a century later. On each side an unusually strong state emerged and was able to promote a particular ideological vision of politics and society, a vision that constructs the other side of the dividing line as an enemy and a source of fear and instability. A virulent anti-Communist discourse has acquired a quasi-hegemonic status in the South, while an equally pronounced anticapitalist and anti-imperialist attitude prevails in the reclusive North.

The construction of antagonistic identities, and the threat perceptions that are associated with them, have decisively shaped the domestic political atmosphere in both North and South Korea. The same can also be said in regard to foreign policy, as I will demonstrate in subsequent chapters. In an extensive study Moon Chung-in has shown how existing threat perceptions, which are based on antagonistic identity constructs, are among the most difficult obstacles to the successful negotiation of arms control. "Both parties," he stresses, "are entrenched in their perceptual vortex of mutual denial, mistrust, and tunnel vision."[63] Over the years these antagonistic forms of identity have become so deeply entrenched in societal consciousness that the current politics of insecurity appears virtually inevitable. Indeed, the prevailing identity constructs have helped to legitimize the very militarized approaches to security that have contributed to the emergence of tension in the first place.

2

The Persistence of Cold War Antagonisms

I am living in a country where the people look like me and speak the same language, but their lifestyle and mentality are so vastly different that I feel like an alien.

—A NORTH KOREAN DEFECTOR IN SOUTH KOREA

One would think that ideological antagonisms substantially subsided with the collapse of the Berlin Wall in 1989 and the subsequent disintegration of the Soviet Union. But in Korea it is striking how much remains the same. The peninsula has become an anachronism in international relations: a small but highly volatile Cold War enclave surrounded by a world that has long moved away from a dualistic ideological standoff. What Kihl Young Hwan noted two decades ago thus remains by and large true today: the level of ideological hostility in Korea is so intense that it leads to the perception, and actual enactment, of a "zero sum game of politics."[1]

In this chapter I want to examine the reasons for the striking resilience not only of Cold War political structures but also of the antagonistic identity constructs that sustain them. Key here is to understand how two exceptionally strong Korean states have dominated virtually all aspects of cross-border relations, making it all but impossible for alternative discourses to challenge the existing Cold War attitudes. There are, of course, major differences between the South and North Korean state apparatuses. But there are many similarities too. In both parts of the peninsula the state has, at least until recently, exercised the exclusive right to deal with the enemy on the other side of the dividing line. For decades the DMZ has been one of the world's most tightly sealed borders, suppressing not only the movement of people but also the exchange of information and communication. As a result both states have been able to promote and legitimize an unusually narrow approach to security issues, one that revolves almost exclusively around a military-based protection of the state apparatus. Given the absence of meaningful cross-national interactions for almost half a century, the two Korean states have been quite successful in promoting the type of antagonistic identity practices that I presented in chapter 1 as the main source of tension on the peninsula. In the absence of objective knowledge about the other side, there is no possibility to challenge the demonization of the archenemy, Moon Chung-in stresses, and "so the antagonism is perpetuated and the conflict reinforced."[2] This is why antagonistic identity constructs, born out of death, fear, and longing for revenge, continue to fuel ideological tensions and militarized policies, even more than a dozen years after the dissolution of global Cold War power structures.

Problems emerging from the tension between identity and difference tend to be either minimized or downright ignored in Korea. Security experts in particular do not consider questions of identity to be relevant. They rely instead on well-rehearsed strategic and geopolitical frameworks to understand the challenges ahead. Equally widespread is the tendency that Roy Richard Grinker refers to as the "master narrative of homogeneity": the belief that the division of the peninsula was imposed from the outside and that unification would immediately recover the lost national unity.[3] Such a quest for national cohesion is understandable, both emotionally and historically. Many commentators draw attention to the remarkable degree of cultural homogeneity in Korea. They argue, for instance, that "the common language, culture, and history of the two Koreas, along with growing re-acquaintance and familiarity, are likely to predominate over the 50-year interlude of separation."[4] Some even go so far as to present existing identity differences as "trivial compared to the amount and depth of the homogeneity accumulated for 1,000 years in the past."[5] The common aspects of Korean culture will undoubtedly prevail in the long run. But major problems will persist if differences that have emerged since the 1950s continue to be downplayed or ignored.

I also draw attention to two domains that can further underline how problematic and deeply entrenched the identity differences are: the experience of North Korean defectors in the South and a comparison with a dozen years of German unification. Entering these domains of inquiry is to embark on a brief detour from the immediate concerns of security policy. But doing so is important, for insights from defectors and from Germany clearly demonstrate not only that significant identity differences exist but also, and perhaps more important, that they persist far beyond the ideological and political structures that set them up in the first place.

STATE CONTROL OVER CROSS-BORDER RELATIONS

One of the most striking features of politics in Korea is the almost total state control of cross-border relations. Nowhere is this influence more pronounced and more consequential than in the articulation of security policy, which already is the least democratic of all decision-making domains. Both Korean states have gone to great lengths to monopolize all aspects of security. Travel, mail, and telecommunications links between North and South have been entirely cut off. For fifty years the Demilitarized Zone has been perhaps the world's most hermetically sealed border.

In the case of North Korea state control of civil society is particularly pronounced. One could, indeed, speak of an annihilation of civil society. Oh Kongdan and Ralph Hassig stress that North Korea is "the most closed society on earth" and that it has been more successful than any other modern government in cutting its people off from the outside world.[6] Average citizens have no access to foreign television programs, radio broadcasts, or newspapers. The country's official and only media are completely controlled by the state and geared toward one objective: the mythological legitimization of the state and its leaders. This process is based less on traditional Communist themes and more on the central idea of *Juche*, or self-reliance, and on an extreme personality cult surrounding the country's only two heads of state, Kim Il Sung and his son, Kim Jong Il. The former ruled North Korea with an iron grip for its first four decades. Kim Il Sung's leadership was rooted in his allegedly heroic involvement in anti-Japanese guerrilla activities. Given the centrality of Kim Il Sung to the legitimization of the state, many commentators believed that he failed to establish and refine a political system that will survive his personal rule.[7] They stressed that Kim's effort to designate his son, Kim Jong Il, as his official political heir was unlikely to succeed. But the North Korean system proved far more resilient than the commentators expected. Kim Il Sung's death in 1994 did not mark the end of the regime but signified a remarkably smooth transition to a new era of governance, one that is as tightly controlled by Kim Jong Il as the previous one was by his father.

The North Korean state has managed to survive in a surprisingly stable manner for more than fifty years, not least because the state has penetrated and controlled essentially all domestic societal aspects, providing the populace with an exclusive and unchallenged view of the world. In the absence of information from abroad, verifying these mythological constructions becomes very difficult. And if challenges did occur, even if ever so minuscule, an extraordinarily ruthless police apparatus immediately repressed them.

State control over inter-Korean relations has been unusually high in South Korea too. For decades ordinary citizens had no access to any form of news from the North. Even photographs of the North Korean leaders were banned. State control of civil society has varied throughout South Korea's history, whose first four decades were characterized by a succession of authoritarian regimes. If a civil society existed during this period, it was certainly depoliticized, unable to challenge the dominance of the state. With the gradual move toward democratization that began in the late 1980s, the state lost some of its dominance. But what Hagen Koo noted in the early 1990s has by and large remained valid: that "hardly anything socially consequential in South Korea is left untouched by the regulatory actions of the state."[8] This is particularly the case with regard to cross-border relations. Every nongovernmental contact with the North still requires prior approval by the Ministry of Unification. On various occasions South Korean citizens visiting Pyongyang without permission were charged with violating the National Security Law and given jail sentences as long as ten years.[9] Indeed, ever since its introduction by Syngman Rhee in 1948, the National Security Law has been one of the state's key instruments for maintaining order and repressing dissent. It led to the arrest of 188,621 people in its first year of enactment alone.[10] The scale of repression subsequently diminished, but the practice itself has remained intact, even during the more tolerant Sunshine Policy. In August 2001, for instance, seven South Koreans were arrested upon their return from an unauthorized attendance at an "inter-Korean" festival in Pyongyang. They were imprisoned for "expressing pro-North sentiments and fraternizing with North Koreans."[11]

For decades North and South Korean authorities have attempted to undermine each other's control of civil society. But each regime has been highly successful in filtering counterindoctrination. Because North and South Korea use different television systems (PAL and NTS, respectively), broadcasts from the other side can be received only with the help of a special television set that is not available to the average citizen. Not even shortwave radio broadcasts have been able to reach the population. Shortwave radios are unavailable to most North Koreans, and South Korea has imposed prison sentences for possessing them and tuning in to North Korean broadcast frequencies. Other forms of counterindoctrination that each regime has used include loudspeakers along the Demilitarized Zone to spout ideological messages and balloons to drop flyers in the opposition's territory. Yet these messages rarely reach either population because they are picked up and filtered by military authorities.

Various consequences emerge from the strong statecentric patterns and the absence of communication between the two sides. The state is always in a privileged position. It has access to information that other actors or individuals do not have. Its viewpoints, even if subjective or simply wrong, can be made to appear credible because they come from an established authority and can be backed up by force.[12] In addition, the practice of imprisoning those who think differently, which is automatic in the North and still practiced in the South, perfectly illustrates what Michel Foucault also identified as a key feature of Western modernity: a penal system that is part of a larger state-directed set of technologies designed to observe, control, and discipline individuals: to make them "obedient and useful at the same time."[13]

Both Korean states have used their power to promote and legitimize their particular worldviews. Through a variety of mechanisms, from ideology-based education to a tightly controlled media environment, both states were highly successful in disseminating a very peculiar form of nationalism that portrays the political system on the opposite side of the divided peninsula as threatening, perhaps even inherently evil. What Bruce Cumings wrote of the immediate postwar period has remained valid for the decades that followed: not one good thing could be said about the leader on the other side of the dividing line. "To do so was to get a jail sentence."[14] Little does it matter, of course, that in the almost total absence of interactions between North and South, the construction of hostile perceptions is based far more on fiction than on fact. Indeed, the practice of constructing a threatening other is greatly facilitated by the unusually hermetic Demilitarized Zone that separates the two Koreas, for average citizens cannot verify what everyday life looks like in the vilified other half.[15]

It is not unusual for states to use their privileged position to advance particular political objectives. For centuries states all over the world have promoted, legitimized, and protected identity constructs, particularly those essential for the process of nation building. The state provides mythological and institutional frameworks that separate self from other, inside from outside, safe from threatening.[16] But these constructions are particularly fateful in Korea, where the state is unusually dominant, where identities are unusually antagonistic, and where the presence of a large arsenal of weapons on both sides creates a constant danger of a military escalation.

TAKING IDENTITY SERIOUSLY

Time does not stand still. Nor does Korea. With South Korea's gradual move to democracy some of the hostile attitudes toward the North have come under challenge. During the 1980s, for instance, a radical protest movement espoused anti-American values and questioned the deep-seated anti-Communist attitudes. But this and other comparable movements remained marginal and were never able to change the prevailing sense of identity.[17] The push toward a more conciliatory, or at least more nuanced, approach to the North intensified with the introduction of President Kim Dae-jung's Sunshine Policy in 1998. Television stations started to (carefully) broadcast selected programs from the North. Some North Korean items, such as ginseng wine and cigarettes, became available for sale in special stores in the South. Art exhibitions could now feature works that represent North Korean themes.[18] This new openness intensified in the wake of the historic summit meeting of June 2000 between Kim Jong Il and Kim Dae-jung. That the two heads of state publicly embraced and used a complimentary vocabulary to describe each other constituted a major divergence from deeply entrenched patterns. The day after the summit meeting, and in response to a similar move by the North, South Korea stopped its anti-Communist propaganda broadcasts, which had been transmitted for decades from giant loudspeakers across the DMZ. The media in both North and South began to use a substantially less antagonistic style of reporting in the weeks following the summit. It is thus not surprising that public opinion surveys increasingly reveal that South Korean people have an inherently ambivalent attitude toward the North: the image of an "enemy" prevails in realist security policy, while the image of a "brother" dominates the more nationalistic attitudes toward unification.[19]

In later chapters I will examine the significance of these and other political changes. But for now it is important to stress that deeply entrenched antagonistic identity constructs cannot be changed overnight. They have penetrated virtually all aspects of life. They have long passed the stage of being mere ideology and propaganda. Categorizing people into friends and foes is a type of pathological illness that persists even if external images and circumstances change.[20] It is not surprising, then, that right after the summit meeting Kim Dae-jung declared in a public statement that "we must not let our guard down and should strengthen our defense posture. Only those who are well prepared for war can enjoy peace."[21] Or consider how a textbook for fifth-graders that was released at the same time still featured countless negative images of the North, such as statements that "North Korea has reinforced its control of the masses" and "North Korea continues to build up its military." A pictorial for third-grade students shows North Korean students "mobilized for mass calisthenics" and "gun-handling training for primary school students."[22] Even simple and seemingly harmless linguistic nuances can reveal underlying pathological patterns. Note, for instance, how an otherwise conciliatory author portrays the augmentation of each state's weapons arsenal: in the case of the North he refers to an "increase" of military power, which implies a threatening tendency. With regard to the South his terminology changes to the much more defensive and positive "modernization of military power."[23]

Recognizing the often-neglected role that identity plays in the context of Korean security dilemmas is one of the most important challenges today. Identity contains both the key to understanding the persistently recurring patterns of conflict and the potential to replace them with a more adequate and peaceful security arrangement. To underline the significance of identity I now will embark on a brief detour, for an adequate analysis of security dilemmas can emerge only by moving between different levels of analysis, from the individual to the international. Before going on to examine the international dimensions of the Korean security dilemmas, it is necessary to take a step back from the immediate realm of security policy, even of national policy, and contemplate the level of importance that should be given to individual and collective identities. This is why I now turn to two relatively unusual domains of inquiry: the German precedent and the experience of North Korean defectors in the South.

INSIGHTS FROM NORTH KOREAN DEFECTORS

A small number of North Koreans have been able to make their way to the South in the last decades. The exact figures vary depending on the source, but average estimates indicate that during the 1970s about twenty-five defectors arrived per year. This number increased to about fifty during the 1980s and then to more than a hundred in the early 1990s. By the mid-1990s the number of defectors for the first time reached more than one thousand per year.[24] But this figure is still minuscule compared to a population of twenty-two million in the North Korean and forty-eight million in the South.

What, exactly, can one learn from the experiences of these North Korean defectors in the South? Generalizing from a few thousand people is, of course, problematic. This is all the more the case since the reaction of defectors depends to a large extent on the positions that they held in North Korean society. Methodological caution is thus in order. Nevertheless, the resulting insights can, at least to some extent, serve as a device for measuring how effective the control of information has been in the North. Such insights can reveal the significance of identity differences between North and South and how they manifest themselves in a direct encounter that takes place outside the realm of state control.

Meanwhile, many surveys have been conducted about the life of

North Korean defectors in the South. Virtually all, including an official study conducted by South Korea's Ministry of Unification, stress one key theme: that many defectors, despite being offered generous financial aid, job training, and other assistance in the South, find it extremely hard to adapt to life in an environment that espouses very different values from the ones in which they grew up. Maladjustment and marginalization are clearly the norm.[25] But before exploring these difficulties I need to explain, at least briefly, the context within which defectors arrive in the South.

The South Korean state is, not surprisingly, closely managing the integration of Northern refugees. Upon their arrival they are immediately taken to a facility operated by the National Intelligence Command of the Ministry of National Defense. A one-month security check follows, along with a further intelligence investigation that can last as long as five months. In 1999 the latter procedure was replaced by a few months' training in a specific "rehabilitation and education facility."[26] Only after six to eight months of investigation and reeducation are defectors released into society, where various counseling services help them further with the process of adjustment. During the initial years, when defectors were few and anti-Communist rhetoric was central to regime survival, the newly arrived citizens from the North were celebrated as national heroes. They were provided with a relatively generous "resettlement" allowance, consisting of 100 million won in cash, a spacious apartment, and an "extra" bonus, depending on the value of the intelligence that they could provide about the North.[27] The status of defectors rapidly decreased when more of them arrived and regime legitimization was gradually shifting toward a democratic electoral process. In 1993 the allowance was reduced to 15 million won but was raised again in 1999 to 37 million won when it became evident that many defectors had great difficulties integrating into South Korea's society.[28]

The change for defectors is, of course, dramatic: they move from a totalitarian and often highly regulated society right into a chaotic free-market system. Many encounter great difficulties, particularly when facing a competitive labor market in which they have to promote their capabilities. They lack the family and alumni ties that are often essential for success. The education that they had in the North does not always provide them with what they need to land a job in the South, such as computer skills or fluency in English. Many even have difficulties with the Korean language, particularly with imported English words and the frequent use of Chinese characters, which have been banned in North Korea since 1949. Grammatologists do indeed stress that the divergence between standard North and South Korean languages is "far greater than one would normally expect after the passage of a mere four decades."[29] Difficulties can persist even after defectors manage to get jobs. The experience of one young woman is instructive here. She insists that she was fired from three positions because she lacked initiative, which was precisely what had always been required of her in the North: to strictly obey orders and do no more than what was asked of her.[30] Not surprisingly, then, the unemployment rate for defectors is unusually high and their income unusually low, far below the national average.[31]

Even more indicative of identity-related difficulties are the psychological and sociocultural obstacles that many defectors experience in their attempt to integrate into South Korean society. They range from specific challenges, such as difficulties in the realm of sexual relations, where North Koreans are used to far more conservative norms,[32] to more general psychosomatic illnesses, such as inferiority complexes, depression, stress, and trauma. Particularly revealing is that defectors from the North suffer far more from such psychological problems than do immigrants from other countries.[33] Many defectors criticize South Korean society and its people for being "closed" and "selfish."[34] The defectors tend to feel lonely, alienated, inferior, and powerless, or, as one commentator puts it, they experience a "sense of not belonging to the new society."[35]

Do the psychological difficulties that defectors experience in South Korea indicate that the North Korean system of information control has worked? Have decades of socialization produced people with different identities? Some indicators suggest yes, at least at first sight. Defectors from the North "unanimously agree that the vast majority of North Koreans harbored great love and respect for Kim Il Sung as the man who freed them from the Japanese, defeated the Americans in the Korean War, and built the foundations of the national economy."[36] Equally revealing, though, is that most defectors have no difficulties adjusting to the political dimensions of the South Korean system. That may be the case because, as some suggest, they explicitly decided to defect from the North.[37] But there is more to it. Consider how many participants in a survey of defectors point out that North Korean people do not tend to be particularly concerned with ideology. They stress that an "absolute obedience to ideology is more important than its content." Professing adherence to an ideology, then, becomes more of a survival tool, something that is, in effect, quite removed from the daily lives and beliefs of people.[38] Such interpretations are supported by insights from different cultural contexts. Consider how James Scott, in a study of domination and resistance, draws attention to the differences between "public transcripts" and "hidden transcripts." The latter represent what is visible in public of the interaction between subordinates and those who hold power.[39] By controlling the public transcript, elites can establish an official ideological narrative that depicts how they want subordinates to see them. But this is not the whole story, Scott insists. In addition to this hegemonic public conduct there is "a backstage discourse consisting of what cannot be spoken in the face of power."[40] Scott is particularly critical of what he calls the "thick theory of hegemony." He dismisses as untenable the argument that a dominant ideology is so powerful in concealing its logic of oppression that it persuades subordinate groups to espouse uncritically the values that explain and justify their own subordination. Such a position gravely misjudges the ability of subordinates to learn from their daily material experiences, which allows them to penetrate and demystify the dominant ideology.[41]

Whether Scott's position on hegemony applies to North Korea is open to debate, for the latter is clearly one of history's most totalitarian and reclusive societies. Independent of this debate, it is clear that most defectors have few difficulties adjusting to the ideological surroundings of their new life in South Korea. A 1996 survey, for instance, revealed that defectors believed that the biggest problem after a unification would not be of an ideological nature but would involve more generic value patterns and prejudices. In 2001 a survey of 528 defectors produced a similar picture. When asked if North and South Koreans would be able to live together amicably after unification, only 15 percent of the respondents evaluated this possibility as very high. Most answers were in the "so-so" and "not-so-high" category, while 20 percent had a very pessimistic view. The reasons most cited for this widespread pessimism were "cultural differences in norms, values and living habits."[42]

The clash of values that occurs between North Korean defectors and South Korean citizens does, at least to some extent, reflect stereotypical differences associated with Communist and capitalist societies. Or so several commentators argue. As a result of having lived in an totalitarian society, Northerners are said to lack the experience of making choices, expressing opinions, and assuming responsibility. They are used to a system that distributes privileges according to position and status rather than individual merit. Their attributes are said to include passive acceptance of authority, a strict moral code, importance placed on solidarity and equality, and a tendency to principled black-and-white logic. This contrasts with Southerners, who grew up in a competitive market economy and an increasingly democratizing society. Their attributes are said to include individualism, attachment to material wealth, decay of community solidarity, looser moral codes, and a tendency toward utilitarian "gray logic," designed to further their interests.[43] As with all stereotypes, these differences are partly fiction, partly true. But the experience of defectors does suggest that Northerners are oriented toward collectivism and equality, while Southerners are more characterized by individualism and libertarian notions of freedom.[44] These differences account for major societal difficulties, no matter how constructed and stereotypical they are.

INSIGHTS FROM THE GERMAN PRECEDENT

Before contemplating the relevance of these psychological tensions for security issues, it may help to put the Korean experience in a broader context. I am therefore examining how people in a different cultural and political environment, in Germany, faced similar challenges. In many ways the fundamental features of postwar German and Korean politics were strikingly similar. At the end of World War II both countries were divided into different occupation zones in order to facilitate the transition into a new world order. The emergence of Cold War tension transformed the supposedly temporary partitions of Germany and Korea into sustained national divisions. The big difference is, of course, that Korea remains divided, whereas Germany was unified following the collapse of the Berlin Wall in 1989.

Initially, the precedent of German unification had an encouraging influence on Korea, at least in the South. It raised hopes that Korea too might soon be unified. Countless South Korean study groups, including parliamentary commissions, were sent to Germany. Scholars investigated the events in detail.[45] Prominent Germans, such as Helmut Schmidt, Günter Grass, Jürgen Habermas, Gregor Gysi, and Egon Bahr were invited to visit Korea in order to share their insights about unification.[46] Soon, though, the enthusiasm evaporated. In part this was the case because South Koreans realized they would never have the economic resources to assist the North in the manner that West Germany is trying, with great ongoing difficulties, to rebuild the former East Germany.[47] The North Korean economy is in far worse shape today than East Germany's was in the late 1980s. South Korea has only about twice as many people as the North, whereas the population of West Germany was four times that of the East. Fears of a drastic decline in standards of living in the South thus put a clear damper on the enthusiasm for quick unification.[48] The North was even less enthusiastic about the German precedent, fearing that North Korea would be absorbed by the South just as East Germany was by West Germany. North Korea's official press organ, the *Rodong Shinmun,* went so far as to publicly criticize South Korea for sending "unification-related" experts to Germany. As one commentator put it: "Pyongyang will never forget the cruel lesson of German unification."[49]

While there is widespread consensus that Germany cannot serve as a desirable model for Korean unification,[50] one may still be able to derive valuable insight from the German experience. Such insight must, however, be treated with caution. Many political dynamics are intrinsically linked to their unique historical and cultural environment. They cannot simply be lifted out of one context and into another. Furthermore, there are perhaps more differences between the German and Korean situations than there are similarities. But Korea is nevertheless in a unique situation to learn from the unification of a homogeneous nation that was also divided by the external dictates of Cold War politics. And investigations into identity can perhaps offer the most revealing insight, even though they have received relatively little attention in the countless studies of the German case.

Leaving aside the enormous political, economic, and administrative challenges, one stunning feature characterizes the early days of German unification: the realization that four decades of very different socializations in East and West created rather different identity

patterns. "Every day we are surprised anew that 45 years of separation had a greater impact upon us than we thought it had when
the Wall came down," says Lothar de Mazière, East Germany's
first freely elected prime minister.[51] The mayor of Leipzig, likewise,
stresses that "no one on either side of the Wall had any idea how far
apart we had grown in forty years. Only now are we beginning to
understand it."[52] Particularly revealing is that these differences became manifest only after unification. The realization that "till now
we did not know we had an [East German] identity" was a common
experience.[53] Heiner Meulemann puts this seemingly paradoxical
issue somewhat differently but gets at the same dynamic. In a com-
pelling empirical study he revealed that East Germans did in fact not
identify strongly with the old regime, for it was generally perceived
to be unjust and inefficient. But as soon as it disappeared, people
started to display an emotional attachment to the order that had
vanished. The long process of socialization under the Communist
regime showed its real power only after its demise, because for many
people its worldview was the only one available to interpret and deal
with the new situation.[54]

The "wall in the head" was far more difficult to bring down than
the wall that divided Berlin and the rest of the country. In many
ways the experiences of east Germans after unification mirror the
fate of North Korean defectors in the South. Hans-Joachim Maaz,
a prominent east German psychiatrist, whose book *Behind the Wall*
generated a major public debate soon after unification, stresses that
the demands of the market economy were virtually the opposite of
the attributes that people from a Communist socialization brought
to the new context. What was demanded of East Germans before
was "submission, adjustment, restraint," in short, not to be critical,
creative, not to stick out and take initiative. But these were precisely
the attributes demanded of people after unification. As a result many
felt simply overwhelmed.[55] Maaz describes how people from the east
tended to experience psychological problems after German unification, such as insecurities, anxieties, panic attacks, and depression.
One of the most destabilizing factors was the challenge to individuals of ascertaining who they were and how they could prevail in the
new environment.[56]

The identity problems that emerged with unification were thus
not of an ideological nature but had mostly to do with entrenched

behavior patterns that formed over a long period of socialization, with fundamental assumptions about who one is and how one relates to family, friends, colleagues, the state, and the public realm. Herta Müller, a prominent novelist, goes so far as to argue that although East Germans were German by language, they had in fact much more in common with East European people than with West Germans.[57]

The clash of values in unified Germany produced stereotypes that are strikingly similar to those generated when North Korean refugees encountered the South Korean populace. The images of the *Besserwessi* (know-it-all Westerner) and *Jammerossi* (lamenting east Germans) started to gain widespread currency. Although based on stereotypical perceptions of the other, these images are nevertheless well entrenched. Various opinion polls demonstrate how understandings of self and other vary greatly among Germans. Easterners tend to lean toward values such as equality, collectivity, and solidarity, while westerners are associated with freedom and individualism. Differences also exist with regard to attitudes toward such issues as health care, employment, leisure, and religion.[58]

The most obvious political manifestation of a distinct eastern identity was the remarkable postunification comeback of the old East German Communist Party, now called the PDS, the Party of Democratic Socialism. Thrown out of power in one of the twentieth century's most spectacular revolutions, it soon thrived again and did so on one key source: resentment against the downsides of unification. By advancing a critique of laissez-faire capitalism and stressing themes such as solidarity and community, the PDS attracted those voters who were longing for the secure and stable old times. It was the political voice of *Ostalgia,* so to speak, a longing for the comforting and predictable aspects of the old system. And it regularly attracted about 10 percent of the east German votes.[59] Given this consistent success, the PDS was often seen as an indication of the existence of a distinct "east identity." But the party's survival was at stake in 2002, when it suffered heavy losses during the elections for the Bundestag, the federal parliament. It had held thirty-six seats but managed to retain only two.[60] Some commentators interpreted this development as a sign of diminishing *Ostalgia.* The prominent newspaper *Frankfurter Allgemeine Zeitung,* for instance, argued that "the eastern type, with his special identity, is becoming rarer and rarer."[61] But to suggest this is to misunderstand the nature and staying power of identities, for they are not limited to political parties and institutions. Various polling data do, indeed, suggest that the disparities have, if anything, grown since unification. Comparing data of 1990 with those of a decade later, Meulemann finds that differences in values between east and west Germans have not narrowed at all. They have either stayed constant or have even increased.[62] This is also Maaz's impression. He believes that identities are so deeply embedded in relationship structures, in the approach to life and society, that it will take at least one more generation until tensions between east and west German people give way to a more harmonious common societal identity.[63]

In this chapter I analyzed some reasons for the remarkable and highly problematic resilience of Cold War power structures and thinking patterns in Korea. I emphasized the crucial role that has been played by two strong Korean states that have monopolized virtually all aspects of cross-border relations during the last half-century. Given their dominant positions, both Korean states were able to disseminate and entrench identities that are based on demonizing the ideological position of the archenemy across the dividing line. The controlling mechanisms of the state are so strong that some commentators speak of "the perpetual primacy of the state over civil society."[64] This is particularly striking because the state played a relatively weak role in most parts of the peninsula's history. During the Yi dynasty, for instance, the power of the state was largely overshadowed by the Yangban, an agrarian upper class. The strong Korean state is, above all, a product of Cold War politics, which persist because the sense of identity and political order established in that period has come to be seen as legitimate and natural, no matter how violence-prone it is.

I also examined identity at the individual level, a detour that seems, at least at first sight, of little relevance to Korean security. And yet if one takes identity seriously, one needs to take into account all levels of analysis, from the individual to the national to the international. One must observe how, at all these levels, the resulting identity constructs are implicated in the production of danger and the resulting security dilemmas.

I scrutinized the experience of North Korean defectors in South Korea and the precedent of German unification in an attempt to understand the nature and function of antagonistic identities that developed during decades of national division. A dozen years after the collapse of Communist rule and the unification of Germany, a clear division still exists between east and west, one that goes far beyond the existence of socioeconomic disparities. It has to do with people's understanding of themselves and their role in the world. The Berlin Wall may have crumbled, but the wall in people's heads still stands. This is, of course, not to say that unification was all negative. It engendered far more opportunities and positive features than it did problems. Most Germans, east and west, approve of unification. But that does not change the fact that four decades of antagonistically constituted identity practices proved too entrenched to simply vanish with a sudden ideological turnaround and a subsequent redrawing of political boundaries. Many difficulties that east Germans have experienced since unification mirror the challenges faced by North Korean defectors in South Korea: an inability to adjust to a societal system that revolves around a very different set of values. These values go beyond the ideological tension that characterizes the political division. They are rooted in a much deeper sense of identity, which has to do with people's understanding of themselves and their role in society.

Cultural homogeneity is no guarantee of harmonious identities. Indeed, the German precedent, combined with the experience of North Korean defectors, demonstrates that considerable potential for conflict is entailed in the antagonistic identity constructs that still prevail in Korea. Acknowledging the ensuing problems is not to argue that identities are fixed and immutable or that they necessarily lead to violence. Looking for commonalties across difference is one of the most important tasks, which I pursue later in this book. Identities are in a constant state of flux. Just as they have grown apart, they can grow closer again. Korean psychologists have already started to conceptualize this process of North-South rapprochement. When examining the integration of North Korean defectors into the South, Han Man-gil and his collaborators speak of five stages of adaptation and five periods. The stages are shock at encountering a foreign culture, preparing for basic employment, establishing a life, resocialization, and cultural as well as social integration. The five periods are adaptation, confusion, conflict, adaptation, assimilation, and stability.[65] That the integration process between

North and South Korea is still stuck at stage one does not mean there is no hope. If one is equipped with an awareness of identity problems, one can confront them in an attempt to overcome, or at least attenuate, the security dilemmas that they have generated during half a century of national division.

3

The Geopolitical Production of Danger

We'll kill every son of a bitch north of the forward edge of the battle area, and we won't retreat one inch.
—U.S. LIEUTENANT GENERAL JAMES F. HOLLINGSWORTH
AT THE DMZ, 1974

We're a peaceful people. . . . Traveling south on that road, the people of the North would see not a threat but a miracle of peaceful development.
—U.S. PRESIDENT GEORGE W. BUSH AT THE DMZ, 2002

Constituting a natural link between the Asian mainland and Japan, the Korean peninsula has always been an important factor in the security policy of the surrounding powers. In the nineteenth century two major wars were fought for control of the peninsula, one between Japan and China (1894–1895) and the other between Japan and Russia (1904–1905). With the development of military technology and the increased globalization of the confrontation among the great powers in the twentieth century, the geopolitical importance of Korea increased. The arbitrary partition of Korea in 1945, and the subsequent transformation of this supposedly provisional settlement into a permanent division of the peninsula, must be attributed largely to the strategic and symbolic importance of Korea in the emerging Cold War power struggle between the United States and the Soviet Union. Initially, the competition was largely a rivalry between these two hegemons, but the struggle for influence in Korea did not remain a Soviet-American affair. With the Sino-Soviet split in the early 1960s and the reemergence of Japan as an economic power, the situation in Korea became directly linked to the security and economic interests of the four great powers, the United States, the Soviet Union, China, and Japan.

Acknowledging the importance of geopolitical factors is not as obvious as it seems at first sight. Many studies of Korean politics and society, especially those conducted under the broad influence of the modernization paradigm, paid relatively little attention to geopolitical issues. Consider, for instance, how Gregory Henderson, in one of the most influential early texts on Korean politics, argues that "external factors are for Korea and her internal courses of secondary importance. If this judgment is wrong, I stand most ready to have it proven so."[1]

By scrutinizing the geopolitical context of Korea's security dilemmas, I bring the earlier discussions of individual and national identity back to the locus classicus of security studies, to its object and subject: the state.[2] States have identities just as individual people do. They struggle with a variety of internal dilemmas, which are then projected onto the outside world. Military doctrine, for instance, is just as much about the allocation of power within society as it is about warding off an external threat. This is why Elizabeth Kier believes that it is "counterintuitive to assume that military doctrines respond only to objective conditions in the international arena."[3]

Now I would like to examine how Korea's security dilemmas became intertwined with Cold War international relations and how the ensuing identity constructs continue to shape politics on and toward the peninsula long after the collapse of the Soviet Union. I will give special attention to the two nuclear crises that have haunted the Korean peninsula since the early 1990s. In each case, in 1993–1994 and in 2002–2003, the events were strikingly similar: North Korea made public its ambition to acquire nuclear weapons and withdrew from the Nuclear Nonproliferation Treaty. Then the situation rapidly deteriorated until the peninsula was literally at the brink of war. The dangers of North Korea's actions, often interpreted as nuclear brinkmanship, are evident and much discussed but not so some of the interactive dynamics that have led to the standoff in the first place. In this chapter I seek to shed light on at least some of them.

I will pay particular attention the role of the United States, for nothing about the past and present dilemmas on the peninsula can be addressed or even understood without recourse to the United States. This is why China repeatedly stressed that the latest nuclear crisis was primarily an issue between North Korea and the United States.[4] Kim Dae-jung, in his final speech as South Korea's president, reiterated the same theme: "more than anything, dialogue between North Korea and the United States is the important key to a solution."[5] A solution is, however, far from imminent. Both the United States and North Korea see each other as a threat. And each has good reason for doing so. But each is also implicated in the production of this threat. The problem is that these interactive dynamics are hard to see, for the West tends to project a very one-sided image of North Korea, one that sees it solely as a rogue and thus a source of danger and instability. Nicholas Eberstadt, for instance, stresses that "North Korean policies and practices have accounted for most of the volatility within the Northeast Asian region since the end of the Cold War."[6]

The deeply entrenched image of North Korea as a rogue state is part of an identity-driven political attitude that severely hinders both an adequate understanding and potential resolution of the crisis. The rhetoric of rogue states is indicative of how U.S. foreign policy continues to be dominated by dualistic and militaristic Cold War thinking patterns. The "evil empire" may be gone but not the underlying need to define safety and security with reference to an external threat. Rogues are among the new threat perceptions that serve to demarcate the line between good and evil, identity and difference. As during the Cold War, building up a strong military arsenal is viewed as the key means through which this line is to be defended. In the absence of a global power that matches the United States, this militaristic attitude has, if anything, intensified. Look at Washington's recent promulgation of a preemptive strike policy against rogue states. The consequences of this posture are particularly fateful in Korea, for it reinforces half a century of explicit and repeated nuclear threats against the government in Pyongyang. The effect of these threats has been largely obscured, in part because the highly specialized discourse of security analysis has managed to attribute responsibility for the crisis solely to North Korea's actions, even if the situation is in reality far more complex and interactive.

Drawing attention to the interactive dimension of security dynamics, and the role of the United States in it, is not to absolve North Korea of responsibility. Pyongyang bears perhaps the lion's share for

much of the culture of insecurity that still persists on the peninsula. Over fifty years it has committed at least a dozen terrorist
acts, from bombings of civilian airliners to tunnel and submarine
infiltrations across the DMZ, not to speak of countless other provocations and verbal aggressions. The production of crises has become
a hallmark of North Korean politics, designed both to fortify its
authoritarian rule and to win concessions from the international
community. But this does not mean developments take place in a
vacuum. Indeed, in an almost mirror image of North Korea's vilified brinkmanship tactic, the U.S. administration under President
George W. Bush has embarked on a form of crisis diplomacy that
explicitly generates threats in order to improve its negotiation position and force its opponent into submission.

IDENTITY AND COLD WAR GEOPOLITICS

The overwhelming influence of identity on security is obvious throughout Korea's history, most notably during the long Cold War period.
One key feature stands out: the integration of South and North
Korea into the two opposing global alliance systems that dominated
the bipolar structure of the Cold War. In contrast to Europe, where
this standoff became institutionalized through the North Atlantic
Treaty Organization (NATO) and the Warsaw Pact, alliance politics in East Asia was mostly based on bilateral arrangements.[7] But
this did not make the situation any less dualistic or dangerous.

The two Korean states became important Asian outposts in the
confrontation between the two ideologically divided camps. Both
the Soviet Union and the United States derived clear strategic privileges by incorporating the rival Koreas into their respective alliance
systems. The degree of alliance incorporation varied somewhat.
North Korea, for instance, retained a relatively high level of flexi-
bility, even though the Soviet Union had a clear strategic interest in
the peninsula.[8] During the early Cold War years North Korea did
indeed receive massive Soviet aid and was correspondingly tied to
Moscow. Some commentators go so far as to speak of a "Soviet satellite."[9] But as a result of China's direct involvement in the Korean
War and the existence of deeply rooted Sino-Korean historical, cultural, and ideological ties, Beijing emerged as Moscow's competi-
tor for gaining influence over Pyongyang. The leverage that North
Korea acquired as a result of this competition provided Kim Il Sung

with a degree of political maneuverability unknown to many other allies of the Soviet Union or, for that matter, to South Korea.

In this chapter I am focusing on U.S. policy toward Korea in an attempt to illustrate the crucial links between identity, threat perception, and the construction of security dilemmas. There is no doubt that the United States has played a key role in Korea's postwar history. According to Moon Chung-in, the United States is "the most important actor in the drama" of Korean security.[10] But Washington's involvement in Korea reaches further back. In chapter 1, I mentioned the U.S. role in opening up Korea during the nineteenth century. In a secret deal to retain influence over the Philippines, Washington then approved Japan's colonial occupation of Korea in 1905. Half a century later the United States played an instrumental role in dividing the peninsula and pulling it into a sustained Cold War confrontation.

To understand the intricate U.S. entanglement in Korea it is necessary to examine South Korea's integration into the American regional order. U.S. military support to Seoul began in the early Cold War period, and since the end of the Korean War the two countries have been bound by a security treaty. For much of the postwar period South Korea's armed forces were in fact partly controlled by Washington. Two key elements of South Korea's defense system, the Combined Forces Command and the United Nations Command, were headed by an American four-star general. Most central functions within them were carried out by American generals, assisted by Korean officers in a deputy position.[11] A significant U.S. military contingent was moved to Korea, and about thirty-seven thousand American soldiers remain stationed there even today. The official reason for this strong U.S. military presence was to dissuade any North Korean aggression.[12] But the wider objective behind this long term-security arrangement was linked to the regional confrontation of the two global alliance systems. A principal objective of U.S. policy in Asia, particularly after the fall of the Kuomintang regime in China, was to contain communism. South Korea thus became one of Washington's strategic outposts in the region and, particularly after the Korean War, an indispensable element in its Cold War standoff with the Soviet Union. The result was a division of spheres of influence, with the United States establishing a regional hegemonic order, "a grand era within which nations oriented themselves toward Washington rather than Moscow."[13]

American efforts to build up and defend a strong South Korea had more than mere strategic reasons. Just as important as geopolitical factors were questions of identity. Or, to be precise, geopolitical and identity factors were intrinsically linked. Economic prosperity, elevated living standards, and high growth rates were important indicators for measuring the "success" of the rival regimes in Korea. The prestige that the leading power of each alliance could gain as a result of successful socioeconomic performances within its hegemonic realm of influence accounted for each superpower's motivation to provide substantial economic aid and trade privileges to its respective Korean ally. The resulting benefits were seen as key measurements for judging the success of the rival alliance camps and their value systems. The objective was, in short, to demonstrate the "superiority" of each superpower's ideological and social regime.[14] This was as clear before as after the Korean War. On June 7, 1949, President Harry Truman declared to Congress: "The Korean Republic, by demonstrating the success and tenacity of democracy in resisting communism, will stand as a beacon to the people of northern Asia in resisting the control of the communist forces which have overrun them."[15] Four years later, and after a war had devastated the peninsula, the American commitment to South Korea intensified. Symptomatic here is President Dwight Eisenhower's request for legislation concerning the political and economic restructuring of South Korea. In a message to Congress on July 27, 1953, he stressed, "The need for this action can quickly and accurately be measured in two ways. One is the critical need of Korea at the end of three years of tragic and devastating warfare. The second is the opportunity which this occasion presents the free world to prove its will and capacity to do constructive good in the cause of freedom and peace."[16]

The statements by presidents Truman and Eisenhower reveal that the Cold War was far more than a geopolitical confrontation: it was a clash over different identities, over what it means to be an individual or a nation; over the role of the state in the economy; and mostly over the values that should be central to social and political life. Expressed in other words, the U.S. engagement in East Asia had as much to do with American identity politics as with the objective strategic constellation in the region.

U.S. economic support to South Korea became an essential element in this struggle about competing forms of identification. Ideological considerations clearly stood behind U.S. economic aid and trade privileges granted to South Korea. The success of this policy was remarkable by any standard. Foreign aid was instrumental in enabling South Korea to reconstruct its industry after the war, increase employment, and suppress high inflation. In short, aid was crucial in the creation of the high growth rates during the thirty years of South Korea's modernization.[17] The assistance was massive, indeed. During the three decades following World War II, South Korea, Israel, and South Vietnam were the world's principal recipients of American aid. The $6 billion that Washington offered to South Korea from 1946 to 1967 nearly equaled the total assistance granted to the entire African continent.[18] Until the mid-1960s most of this aid was provided in the form of grants, rather than loans, which made Korea unique among developing countries.[19] When we look at the military aid figures, Korea's privileged position becomes even more obvious. The $9.05 billion spent between 1955 and 1978 is more than double the $4.2 billion that the United States spent for all of Latin America and Africa together during the same period.[20] Another key political feature that these statistical data reveal involves South Korea's extreme dependency on the United States. Consider how in the critical years before 1965 well over 90 percent of all foreign assistance was provided by Washington alone.[21]

The strong patron-client relationship between Washington and Seoul started to change in the 1970s, partly as a result of successful economic development in South Korea, partly as a result of changes in the global political economy.[22] With the dissolution of the Bretton Woods system, some of Washington's monetary leadership weakened. And so did its willingness to subordinate immediate domestic interest for a continuation of alliance politics in East Asia. Specific national goals related to the U.S. economy, for instance, became more important, while broader geopolitical objectives started to play a less dominant role in U.S. foreign policy.[23] Take 1987, when the United States took 40 percent of South Korea's exports but faced a $10 billion current accounts surplus.[24] Under these circumstances Washington no longer tolerated protectionist Korean trade policies while keeping American markets open. The United States now refused to accept Seoul's contention that its infant industries needed further protection until they could successfully compete in an open world trading system. American pressure to lift trade barriers and to appreciate the Korean currency, the won, became a normal feature of trade relations with South Korea.[25]

The tools of U.S. foreign policy in East Asia changed but not the underlying U.S. political motivations or the dualistic and identity-oriented mind-set that sustains those motivations. The persistence of these identity patterns becomes evident when one observes how the dissolution of global Cold War power struggles influenced politics on the Korean peninsula. With the collapse of the Soviet-led alliance system, the external reasons for Korea's conflict—the existence of global ideological cleavages embedded in a bipolar power structure—vanished too. As a result the clear separation of spheres of influence, which characterized Korea until the 1970s, gradually evolved into a situation in which each great power maintained certain contacts with the opponent of its traditional Korean ally. This is particularly true with China and Russia, which established growing political and economic ties with South Korea. But in its most basic dynamic the security situation in Korea remains as tense as ever and so do the ideological battles that are responsible for the conflict in the first place. Not even the principle of cross-recognition, which was first introduced by U.S. Secretary of State Henry Kissinger in 1975, has been achieved. The concept held that the United States and Japan would recognize North Korea, while the Soviet Union and China would enter into diplomatic relations with Seoul.[26] The latter has happened, but the former has not.

PATTERNS OF ACTION AND REACTION: THE FIRST NUCLEAR CRISIS

The two nuclear crises that emerged in Korea in the 1990s illustrate the persistence of Cold War attitudes toward security. I will demonstrate the interactive and constructed nature of these crises and how each of the parties involved has contributed to the threat perceptions that the other used to justify its confrontational stance.

The first nuclear crisis started to emerge in the early 1990s. Although Pyongyang had signed the Nuclear Nonproliferation Treaty in 1985, it retained its ambition to develop a nuclear program. Or so indicated U.S. intelligence reports, which detected a plutonium-processing plant in Yongbyon. Various rounds of negotiation followed. In 1992 North Korea agreed to have its nuclear facility inspected by the International Atomic Energy Agency. But only a few months later disagreements about the inspections increased, and in March 1993 North Korea declared its intention to withdraw from the nonproliferation treaty. Although Pyongyang agreed a few weeks later to suspend its withdrawal, an intense crisis soon emerged on the peninsula. The chief U.S. negotiator, Robert Gallucci, believed that the crisis "had an escalatory quality that could deteriorate not only into a war but into a big war."[27] As a result of various interventions, such as a semiprivate visit to Pyongyang by former U.S. president Jimmy Carter, a deal was reached. In an agreement signed in October 1994 Pyongyang consented to freeze its nuclear program. In return, the United States promised a number of compensations, including the delivery of aid, heating oil, and the eventual construction of two light-water nuclear reactors that would provide North Korea with energy sources.

One of the most revealing interpretations of the dynamics that led to the crisis and its resolution was made by Leon Sigal. In a counter-reading of U.S. nuclear diplomacy toward North Korea in the years leading up to the crisis, Sigal documents how coercive diplomacy brought Korea to the brink of war. He writes of a U.S. foreign policy pattern that discouraged cooperation and instead promoted a "crime-and-punishment approach" that constituted North Korea as, above all, a threatening rogue state. While acknowledging the numerous instances that would, indeed, give rise to such an image, Sigal also deals with the interactive nature of the conflict. In a crucial passage he asks why, if North Korea was so keen on developing nuclear weapons and had numerous opportunities to do so, did it not simply go ahead and build bombs? Sigal's answers highlight Washington's inability to recognize that North Korea was playing "tit-for-tat in nuclear diplomacy."[28] Some of Sigal's arguments have become controversial. He has, for instance, been accused of downplaying North Korea's failure to uphold its obligations. That may well be the case, but at a more fundamental level Sigal is nevertheless able to reveal a striking empirical pattern: each time the United States used an aggressive policy to pressure North Korea into concessions, the latter became more recalcitrant. By contrast, when Washington adopted a more cooperative attitude, Pyongyang usually responded with concessions. Thus tension on the Korean peninsula decreased only when the United States adopted a "give-and-take" diplomacy that recognized how Pyongyang's recalcitrance can, and should, be read as a bargaining tactic to get something in return for giving up the nuclear option.[29]

FROM DÉTENTE TO THE SECOND NUCLEAR CRISIS

Once the nuclear crisis of 1994 was mitigated, all parties concerned embarked on a more cooperative route. The inauguration of Kim Dae-jung as South Korea's president in early 1998 signaled the advent of a policy that was more conciliatory or at least more willing to engage the archenemy across the dividing line. The Clinton administration was strongly supportive of this approach. Of particular significance here is an official policy review, conducted by William Perry, then the U.S. secretary of defense. In some respects the report offered little new, for it advocated a continuation of Washington's "strong deterrent posture towards the Korean Peninsula." Not surprisingly, the Perry report located the main threat in North Korea's ambition to acquire nuclear weapons and to develop, test, and deploy long-range missiles. "The United States must, therefore, have as its objective ending these activities."[30] At the same time, though, the Perry report called for a fundamental review of U.S. policy toward Pyongyang, advocating a position that rests not only on military deterrence but also on a "new, comprehensive and integrated approach" to negotiations with North Korea.[31] The U.S. ambassador to Korea then reiterated at various points that "deterrence by itself is no longer an adequate strategy."[32] In some sense this new approach sought to implement the very tit-for-tat approach that Sigal found missing during the early days of the Clinton administration. The new policy still revolved around a strong defensive posture and an inherent distrust of North Korea, but it also envisaged the possibility of rewarding Pyongyang for concessions. In this sense the Perry report signified a remarkable departure from the U.S. position of viewing rogue states as inherently evil, irrational, and incapable of compromising.

The more nuanced policy attitudes in Washington and Seoul soon led to several breakthroughs, including the lifting of restrictions on trade with, investment in, and travel to North Korea. Pyongyang responded in turn with a variety of gestures, such as a gradual (although still very timid) opening of its borders, agreements on family exchanges with the South, and a toning down of its hostile rhetoric.

The process of détente culminated in June 2000 with a historic summit meeting between the two Korean heads of state, Kim Jong Il and Kim Dae-jung. The symbolic significance of this meeting cannot be overestimated. Bruce Cumings goes so far as to argue that "Bill Clinton and the two Korean leaders did more to lessen tensions in Korea than all the heads of state going back to the country's division in 1945."[33] Others would undoubtedly disagree, interpreting Clinton's approach to North Korea as a dangerous policy of appeasement that needed to be rectified with a return to a more principled form of realpolitik.

Be that as it may, détente in Korea did not last long. It was soon replaced with a return to familiar Cold War thinking patterns and conflict-prone behavior. According to conventional media and policy accounts, the second nuclear crisis suddenly emerged in the autumn of 2002. The official and largely accepted story line is perfectly captured by a passage in one of Europe's leading newsmagazines. Writing in February 2003 the *Der Spiegel* reporter presented the crisis as follows: "The dispute over Pyongyang's nuclear program began in October last year. North Korea admitted that it had secretly pursued plans for enriching uranium. Then the government threw international inspectors out of the country and withdrew from the nuclear nonproliferation treaty."[34] North Korea's admission had come as a shock to the international community. It was described as "the mother of all confessions."[35] Fears increased dramatically in February 2003, when Pyongyang officially announced that it would restart its nuclear reactor at Yongbyon. The U.S. intelligence assessment concluded that North Korea could turn out enough plutonium to produce five nuclear weapons by the summer.[36]

The situation was now particularly volatile, some observers stress. The first crisis took eighteen months to unfold, but the events in 2002 "occurred in a matter of weeks."[37] Add to this a renewed intensification of North Korea's hostile rhetoric, including threats to turn Seoul into a "sea of fire," and you have a full-blown crisis on the peninsula. The overall verdict thus seemed clear: "Pyongyang is responsible for the crisis that has ensued because it broke the earlier agreement to scrap its nuclear program in return for energy assistance."[38]

Or so goes the prevalent interpretation of events. But one could, and indeed should, stress exactly what Sigal has with respect to the first nuclear crisis: "the standard account is wrong."[39] This is not to say that these events did not occur or that North Korea's nuclear weapons program does not pose a serious threat to regional and world peace. Rather, the point is that the official account is, at minimum, a one-sided and highly inadequate portrayal of events. The crisis neither emerged "out of the blue" in October 2002, nor can it be attributed solely to North Korea's actions, highly problematic as they undoubtedly are. Like any crisis, this one resulted from a sustained interaction of threat perceptions, actions, and reactions to them. It was rooted in entrenched antagonisms and established conflict patterns, involving a variety of different actors, each playing a role in constituting the crisis.

Before I continue, I must stress that my objective here is not to engage the role of these perceptions in detail. The literature on the subject already is extensive.[40] Applying this body of knowledge to the Korean peninsula would go far beyond what is possible in a chapter-length discussion. I will thus examine threat perceptions only as far as it is necessary to demonstrate that the identity-driven rhetoric of rogue states obstructs an adequate understanding of the security situation in Korea.

THE ROLE OF AMERICAN NUCLEAR THREATS

Lets us, for the sake of understanding the interactive dimensions of the crisis, contemplate for a moment how the crisis must have appeared from the vantage point of North Korea's decision makers. The first and undoubtedly most striking feature to notice from Pyongyang would be the long and unbroken period of American nuclear hegemony in Asia. Equally obvious and understandable is that this hegemonic practice must have been—and indeed was—interpreted as a clear threat to North Korea's security.

The United States remains the only nation ever to have used nuclear weapons in a combat situation and this in proximity to Korea, in Hiroshima and Nagasaki. During the Korean War the United States entertained the use of nuclear weapons against North Korea and China as part of its "massive retaliation" doctrine. General Douglas MacArthur specifically requested permission to use twenty-six nuclear bombs to attack specific targets. His successor, General Matthew Ridgeway, renewed the request. In the end no nuclear weapons were used, although the newly inaugurated president, Dwight Eisenhower, hinted in 1953 that the United States would use them if the armistice negotiations failed to make progress.[41] Soon after the Korean War, in January 1958, the United States introduced ground-based nuclear weapons to South Korea, a move that constituted a direct violation of the Armistice Agreement.[42] This move did not occur in response to a specific North Korean threat but was part of a more general worldwide reorganization of American military strategy.[43] The weapons were kept close to the border with the North. Don Oberdorfer reports that "nuclear warheads had been flown by helicopter almost routinely to the edge of the DMZ in training exercises."[44] The very nature of these exercises was a public threat to North Korea. Consider, for instance, how the yearly joint maneuvers between the United States and South Korea, termed "Team Spirit," revolved around an unnecessarily aggressive northbound scenario. They stressed, as Moon Chung-in puts it, "bold and vigorous strikes into the enemy's rear" as part of an overall "offensive military strategy."[45]

The deployment of American nuclear weapons in South Korea was an important element of what Peter Hayes calls "American nuclear hegemony" in the Pacific. It was one of the central military components around which regional security alliances were formed. Hayes also stresses that this nuclear strategy remained a "completely unilateral American activity."[46] Neither South Korea nor any other U.S. ally was given a say in operational decisions, which always remained under the full control of Washington. Moreover, North Korea has never consented to the deployment of nuclear weapons on its soil, either by the Soviet Union or by China. It has not even accommodated foreign military personnel, at least not since the last Chinese troops left in 1958.[47] This contrasts quite sharply to the almost forty thousand U.S. soldiers who remain stationed in South Korea (imagine, just for a moment, how the United States would have perceived forty thousand Soviet troops stationed in North Korea).

The United States withdrew nuclear weapons from South Korea in the early 1990s. Analyses differ on the exact reasons for this withdrawal. Donald Gregg, then the U.S. ambassador to South Korea, suggests that it was a gesture of goodwill designed to facilitate negotiations with North Korea.[48] Other U.S. officials say that it was a more tactical move, linked to experiences in the first Gulf War that suggested that high-yield conventional weapons may actually be more useful than nuclear ones in the context of a controllable regional battlefield.[49] Be that as it may, the withdrawal of U.S. nuclear war-heads from Korean soil hardly removed the nuclear threat from the peninsula. Long-range U.S. nuclear missiles could still easily reach North Korea, a fact that Pyongyang was frequently reminded of, in implicit and not-so-implicit manners.

THE INTERACTIVE DYNAMIC OF THE NUCLEAR CRISIS

U.S. nuclear threats toward Pyongyang intensified again when Washington's Korea policy became more hawkish with the inauguration of President George W. Bush. In his State of the Union Address of February 2002, Bush singled out North Korea as one of three nations belonging to an "axis of evil," citing as evidence Pyongyang's export of ballistic missile technology and its lingering ambition to become a nuclear power.[50] This sudden turnaround in U.S. foreign policy, which sharply reversed the more conciliatory approach pursued during the Clinton administration, can just as easily be seen as the origin of the present nuclear crisis in Korea. In June 2002 details of a "Nuclear Posture Review" became public, according to which the new U.S. strategic doctrine relied on the possibility of preemptive nuclear strikes against terrorists and rogue states. The review explicitly cited North Korea with regard to two scenarios: countering an attack on the South, and halting the proliferation of weapons of mass destruction. It mentioned, for instance, "using tactical nuclear weapons to neutralize hardened artillery positions aimed at Seoul, the South Korean capital."[51] A few months later Washington made its threats official. The new "National Security Strategy," released in September 2002, outlined in detail when preemptive strikes are legitimate and would be used as a way to "stop rogue states and their terrorist clients before they are able to threaten or use weapons of mass destruction against the United States."[52]

Faced with a sudden intensification of U.S. nuclear threats, it is hardly surprising that Pyongyang reacted angrily and called Washington officials "nuclear lunatics."[53] Nor is it surprising that Pyongyang is reluctant to give up its nuclear option, for it could serve as a credible deterrent against a U.S. attack. Indeed, the desire for such a deterrent only mirrors the attitude and behavior of the United States. Some even go so far as to suggest that "when the U.S. insists that nuclear weapons are vital to its own security but harmful to the security of others, it becomes hopelessly lacking in credibility."[54] Be that as it may, declassified intelligence documents, which became available after the collapse of Communist regimes in eastern Europe, do indeed reveal that from the 1980s on North Korea perceived itself as increasingly weak and vulnerable to external attacks.[55] While the first nuclear crisis unfolded, Kim Il Sung talked about this dilemma to Cambodia's head of state, Norodom Sihanouk. Kim stressed that "they want to take off our shirt, our coat and now our trousers, and after that we will be nude, absolutely naked."[56] As a result of this increasing vulnerability, the prime objective of the government in Pyongyang has moved, as many commentators now recognize, from forcefully unifying the peninsula to the simple task of regime survival.[57] But very few Western decision makers have the sensitivity to recognize these factors and take them into account when formulating their policies. Donald Gregg is one of the rare senior American diplomats who acknowledges that "the U.S. scares North Korea."[58] But even he could make such an admission in public only after he had retired from the State Department.

In view of the reinterpretation of events that I have presented here, the question of responsibility for the recurring nuclear crises in Korea becomes a very blurred affair. One could point out, as several commentators have, that before October 2002 North Korea had by and large complied with the terms of the 1994 agreement. This was confirmed not only by the Korean Peninsula Energy Development Organization but also by CIA Director George J. Tenet, who testified on this matter to Congress on March 19, 2002.[59] The "mother of all confessions" does, of course, put this interpretation in perspective. But the United States also did not live up to the Agreed Framework. Construction of the two light-water reactors promised to North Korea was five years behind schedule. Long before the most recent crisis unfolded, the promised annual fuel deliveries became increasingly threatened because of high oil prices and opposition from influential conservative elements within Congress.[60] Perhaps most important, the very existence of long-standing American nuclear threats against North Korea is not only contrary to the 1994 agreement but also a direct violation of the international nonproliferation regime, which foresees that "countries without nuclear weapons must not be threatened by those who possess them."[61]

The point is not to attribute responsibility for the reemergence of a nuclear crisis on the peninsula. Both the United States and North

Korea have contributed a great deal to fuel each other's fears. But decision makers in Washington have clearly not been sufficiently aware of their own role in generating fears and counterreactions. Nor have they learned much from the lesson of the first nuclear crisis. Consider, for instance, how the United States has quickly forgotten, or ignored, a number of rather striking concessions that Pyongyang made in the period leading up to the second crisis. North Korea started to open up its borders: it accommodated several hundred representatives of foreign aid organizations, increased cooperation with (capitalist) Russia, sought to normalize talks with Japan, and entered into diplomatic relations with a dozen Western countries. There were steps toward domestic reform, such as the introduction of quasi–market principles and the opening of special economic zones. There was also progress toward a rapprochement with the South, most notably in domains such as family exchanges, business contacts, and cultural exchanges. Pyongyang started to clear mines in the DMZ and worked toward establishing road and railway links with the South. North Korea's leader, Kim Jong Il, even publicly acknowledged the importance of a continuous deployment of U.S. troops in South Korea. He stressed that their presence is a threat only so long as the relationship between North Korea and the United States remains hostile.[62] This in itself could be seen as the "mother of all concessions," for the removal of U.S. troops had been one of North Korea's key demands for decades.[63]

Instead of appreciating and building on these concessions, U.S. foreign policy toward North Korea focused on Pyongyang's lingering nuclear ambition. But not everyone believed Pyongyang when it declared in October 2002 that it had never ceased its nuclear program. The Russian foreign minister, for instance, called it a North Korean tactical maneuver.[64] Neither claim could at this stage be empirically verified, but that is not the main point anyway. More important is that the United States failed to pay attention to a series of rather obvious North Korean gestures long before the crisis came to be seen as a crisis in October. North Korea's worry began to grow with Bush's "axis of evil" speech earlier that year, in February. At that time an unofficial North Korean representative, Kim Myong Chol, told a *New York Times* journalist, Nicholas Kristof, that he foresaw "a crisis beginning in the latter half of this year." North Korea, Kim mentioned, "will respond to the breakdown of the nuclear deal . . . by starting its nuclear program and resuming its missiles tests."[65] That is, of course, precisely what happened eight months later.

It is striking how North Korea's approach in 2002–2003 paralleled its behavior during the crisis of 1993–1994. Pyongyang most likely assumed, as it did a decade earlier, that a hard-line U.S. administration would not engage in serious dialogue until North Korea threatened to withdraw from the Nuclear Nonproliferation Treaty. Scott Snyder, in an extensive study of Pyongyang's approach during the first crisis, speaks of a "crisis-oriented negotiation style" that is rooted in North Korea's particular historical experience, most notably its partisan guerrilla legacy. Snyder writes of a remarkably rational and entirely consistent approach, one that relies on "threats, bluff, and forms of blackmail to extract maximal concession from a negotiating counterpart."[66] Even the dramatic language that shocked the world media in early 2003 was entirely predictable. The apocalyptic threat of turning Seoul into a "sea of fire," for instance, was literally a rehearsed metaphor from the first crisis.[67] It is part of an all-too-predictable emotional vocabulary that has prevailed in North Korea's press for decades. Once translated into standard English, it is not much different from the more rationally expressed U.S. threat of preemptive nuclear strikes.

One can agree or disagree with North Korea's dramatic brinkmanship tactic, but one cannot ignore its deeply entrenched existence. Doing so may lead to dangerous miscalculations. At minimum, it prevents us from recognizing how Pyongyang may be using its last bargaining chip, its nuclear potential, as a way of entering into dialogue with the United States. In case this was not clear from North Korea's behavior during the first crisis, Kim Myong Chol stressed the same point again in the interview with Nicholas Kristof. In February 2002, several months before the crisis escalated, Kim pointed out that "North Korea cannot kill the heavyweight champion, the U.S. But it can maim one of his limbs, and so the heavyweight champion will not want to fight. That is the North Korean logic."[68] The logic may be flawed, as Kristof notes, but it is entirely consistent with Pyongyang's attitude during the first crisis. It demonstrates that Pyongyang had no interest in a military confrontation with the United States. Indeed, North Korea's press repeatedly stressed that the first nuclear crisis "was settled through negotiations" and that this proves that the more recent issue can be solved in this manner as well.[69] Pyongyang wanted guarantees and concessions. And its demands were not even particularly outrageous. For years Pyongyang has requested a nonaggression pact as well as one-on-one negotiations with the United States, leading to a normalization of the relationship between the two countries or at least to a recognition of each other's sovereignty. The United States, by contrast, has always preferred multilateral negotiations and demanded North Korean disarmament before a normalization of relations.

Despite numerous and obvious signs, and despite detailed and insightful studies of North Korea's previous negotiation behavior, U.S. decision makers repeated exactly the same mistakes that they committed during the first crisis: they believed that by demonizing North Korea as an evil rogue state, they could force Pyongyang into concessions. Whether this policy resulted from ignorance or specific design remains open to debate. The bottom line is that the U.S. position was firm: "America and the world will not be blackmailed," Bush stressed in his 2003 State of the Union address.[70] The result was predictable: Pyongyang became more recalcitrant. A new nuclear crisis started to take hold of the Korean peninsula.

MUTUAL CRISIS DIPLOMACY, OR
THE CONTRADICTIONS OF HAWK ENGAGEMENT

The conflict pattern had been set long before the latest crisis unfolded. Several scholars, most notably Bruce Cumings and Hazel Smith, have for years drawn attention to Washington's inability to see North Korea as anything but a dangerous and unpredictable rogue state.[71] A look at the deeply embedded nature of this policy attitude is thus in order, even if it entails a brief detour from the immediate issue of Korean security. Central here is the transition from the Cold War to a new world order. While the global Cold War power structures collapsed like a house of cards, the mind-sets that these structures produced turned out to be far more resilient. Cold War thinking patterns remain deeply entrenched in U.S. foreign policy, not least because virtually all its influential architects rose to power or passed their formative political years during the Cold War. As a result security has in essence remained a dualistic affair: an effort to protect a safe inside from a threatening outside. Once the danger of communism had vanished, security had to be articulated with reference to a new *Feindbild,* a new threatening other that could provide a sense of identity, order, and safety at home. "I'm running out of demons. I'm running out of villains," said U.S. General Colin Powell in 1991. "I'm down to Castro and Kim Il Sung."[72]

Rogue states were among the new threat perceptions that rose to prominence when Cold War ideological schism gave way to a more blurred picture of global politics.[73] And North Korea became the rogue par excellence: the totalitarian state that disrespects human rights and aspires to possess weapons of mass destruction; the one that lies outside the sphere of good and is to be watched, contained, and controlled. But there is far more to this practice of "othering" than meets the eye. For one, the construction of a rogue threat is to a large extent a post–Cold War phenomenon. During the 1970s and 1980s, for instance, American perceptions of Korea were perhaps more influenced by the television comedy *M*A*S*H* than by Pyongyang's political escapades, provocative as they undoubtedly were at times.[74] Equally revealing are the reasons why some of the key rogue states, such as North Korea, Iraq, and Iran, have recently been constituted as rogue by the United States. It cannot be their authoritarian nature and their human rights violations alone, Robert Dujarric stresses, for many other states, including Saudi Arabia and Egypt, have an equally appalling record. Neither can it be that they possess or aspire to possess weapons of mass destruction. Otherwise, states like India, Pakistan, or Israel would be constituted as rogues too. Dujarric stresses that rogue states share one common characteristic above all: "they are small or medium nations that have achieved some success in thwarting American policy."[75]

The tendency to demonize rogue states considerably intensified following the terrorist attacks on New York and Washington of September 11, 2001. For some policy makers and political commentators the American reaction to these events signified a fundamentally new approach to foreign policy. U.S. Secretary of Defense Donald Rumsfeld heralded the arrival of "new ways of thinking and new ways of fighting."[76] Stephen Walt, likewise, spoke of "the most rapid and dramatic change in the history of U.S. foreign policy."[77] Significant changes did, indeed, take place. The inclusion of a preventive first-strike option, for instance, is a radical departure from previous approaches to deterrence, which revolved around a more defense-oriented military policy. But at a more fundamental, conceptual level the U.S. position represents far more continuity than change. Indeed, one can clearly detect a strong desire to return to the reassuring familiarity of the dualistic and militaristic thinking patterns that dominated foreign policy during the Cold War. The new U.S. foreign policy reestablished the sense of order and certitude that had existed during the Cold War: an inside/outside world in which, in Bush's words, "you are either with us or against us."[78] The first step in such a move back was a massive increase in U.S. military expenditures. Bush's budget for 2002 included, as he said, "the largest increase in defense spending in two decades."[79]

Once again, the world is divided into good and evil, and once again military means occupy a key, if not the only, role in protecting the former against the latter. What must be stressed, though, is that evil here means more than merely "doing harm or inflicting pain on innocents."[80] Rogue states are evil because they attack, as did the Soviet empire, the very foundations of Western civilization: a form of life based on the principles of liberal democracy and market-oriented capitalism.

The new good-versus-evil rhetoric poses various obstacles to security policy on the Korean peninsula. "The opposition between good and evil is not negotiable," Allan Bloom noted during Ronald Reagan's presidency. It is a question of principles and thus "a cause of war."[81] Expressed in other words, the rhetoric of evil moves the phenomena of rogue states into the realm of irrationality. *Evil* is in essence a term of condemnation for a phenomenon that can neither be fully comprehended nor addressed, except through militaristic forms of dissuasion and retaliation. This is why various commentators believe that the rhetoric of evil is an "analytical cul de sac" that prevents, rather than encourages, understanding. Some go so far as to argue that a rhetoric of evil entails an "evasion of accountability," for the normative connotations of the term inevitably lead to policy positions that "deny negotiations and compromise."[82] Indeed, how is it possible to negotiate with evil without being implicated in it, without getting sucked into its problematic vortex?

The contradictions between the rhetoric of evil and the requirements for dialogue have become particularly evident during the most recent nuclear crisis in Korea. All top U.S. officials publicly stressed one common theme: that "there is no reason why discussion about confidence-building measures cannot take place with Pyongyang."[83] At the very same time, though, the projection of threats toward North Korea was carefully maintained, even intensified. "All options are on the table," including military action, Bush stressed.[84] The assumption behind this approach is that including North Korea in an "axis of evil" does not necessarily preclude the possibility of engaging it in dialogue. Indeed, the assumption is that threats will induce dialogue. William Safire expresses this strategy in blunt but entirely appropriate words: "We make clear to weapons traders in the North that their illicit nuclear production is vulnerable to air attack from a nation soon to show its disarmament bona fides in Baghdad. . . . That readiness will bring about what diplomats call 'fruitful, regional, multilateral negotiation.'"[85]

Hawk engagement has emerged as a term to describe the new and much tougher U.S. stance.[86] It is striking how much this policy position resembles North Korea's vilified nuclear brinkmanship tactic. Just as Pyongyang does, Washington explicitly threatens the opponent that it allegedly wants to engage in dialogue. It advances policies that intentionally create a crisis in order to win concessions from its archenemy. As a result it is not surprising that the few contacts that took place between the United States and North Korea could hardly be called negotiations, let alone fruitful ones. Consider the famous encounter that took place in Pyongyang in October 2002, during which North Korean officials made the "mother of all confessions." Led by U.S. Envoy James Kelly, this was the most senior team of U.S. officials to visit North Korea since Bush's inauguration and his adoption of a more confrontational policy. Pyongyang was clearly hoping for a resumption of dialogue but instead encountered a U.S. team that was acting in what the Koreans perceived as a highly "arrogant manner." Even Western diplomats who observed the events agreed. "These were not negotiations," stressed one. "Kelly immediately started with accusations."[87] The next day North Korean officials predictably returned to their own well-practiced crisis diplomacy. They upped the ante and admitted to a nuclear weapons program, fictitious or not.

THE CONCEALING POWER OF SECURITY EXPERTISE

Why is it so difficult to deal with, or even recognize, the interactive dynamics of security dilemmas? Why is it still possible to present as rational and credible the view that North Korea alone is responsible for yet another nuclear crisis on the peninsula? And why have militaristic approaches to security come to be seen, particularly by decision makers, as the only realistic way of warding off the respective threat, even though they are quite obviously implicated in the very dynamic that has led to its emergence in the first place?

Answers to these complex questions are, of course, not easy to find. I certainly do not pretend to offer them here. But at least some aspects can be understood by observing the central role that defense analysis plays in the articulation of security policy. Such analyses have in essence been reduced to discussions about military issues that, in turn, are presented in a highly technical manner. Consider a random example from one of many recent "expert" treatises on North Korea's missile program: "If North Korea launches a ballistic missile attack on South Korean airfields and harbors, it could seriously impede Flexible Deterrence Options (FDO) operations by U.S. forces. The argument has been made that even if the North uses ballistic missiles, the accuracy or circular error probable (CEP) of the Rodong-1 (about 1 km) is such that it would not be able to undertake airstrike missions."[88] A fundamental paradox emerges: on the one hand an array of abstract acronyms and metaphors has moved our understanding of security issues further and further away from the realities of conflict and war. On the other hand we have become used to these distorting metaphors to the point that the language of defense analysis has become the most accepted—and by definition most credible and rational—way of assessing issues of security. The ensuing construction of common sense provides experts (those fluent in the technostrategic language of abstraction) not only with the knowledge but also with the moral authority to comment on issues of defense.[89]

Experts on military technologies have been essential in constructing North Korea as a threat and in reducing or eliminating from our purview the threat that emanates from the United States and South Korea toward the North. The political debate about each side's weapons potential, for instance, is articulated in highly technical terms.

Even if nonexperts manage to decipher the jargon-packed language with which defense issues are presented, they often lack the technical expertise to verify the claims advanced, even though the claims are used to legitimize important political decisions. As a result the technostrategic language of defense analysis has managed to place many important security issues beyond the point of political and moral discussion. Consider how, for decades, the United States and South Korea have argued that the military balance on the peninsula represents one of the most severe imbalances in military power anywhere in the world.[90] During the late 1980s, for instance, North Korean troops were said to outnumber South Koreans by 840,000 to 650,000, with the North enjoying an even greater advantage in tanks, aircraft, and naval forces.[91] The South Korean *Defense White Paper* at the time argued that its military power is only 65 percent of North Korea's and that a military balance would not be reached until after 2000.[92] But in 2000 the refrain remained exactly the same. The *Defense White Paper* still insisted that "North Korea has the quantitative upper hand in troops and weaponry, and it possesses strong capabilities of conducting mobile warfare designed to succeed in a short-term blitzkrieg."[93] Virtually all official defense statistics present a seemingly alarming North Korean presence. They juxtapose, for instance, North Korea's 1.17 million standing forces against the 690,000 of the South, the North's 78 brigades against the South's 19, the North's 23,001 armored vehicles against the South's 2,400, its 50 submarines against 6, and so on and so forth.[94]

Articulated from the privileged vantage point of the state, the strategic studies discourse acquires a degree of political and moral authority that goes far beyond its empirically sustainable claims. For years scholars have questioned the accuracy of the calculations and the political conclusions derived from them. In the 1980s critics were already pointing out that the official statistics compare quantity, not quality, and that in terms of the latter the South enjoys a clear strategic advantage over the North, even without including U.S. nuclear and other weapons stationed in or (possibly) directed toward the Korean peninsula.[95] These critiques have intensified in recent years. In a detailed study of the subject Moon Chung-in argues that even without U.S. nuclear support, "South Korea is far superior to the North in military capacity" and cites major quality differences in such realms as communications, intelligence, electronic warfare, and cutting-edge offensive weapons systems.[96] Sigal, likewise, points out that the much-feared million-man North Korean army is largely a fiction. About half, he estimates, are either untrained or soldier-workers engaged in civil construction. Many of North Korea's tanks and aircraft are obsolete, leaving its "ground forces and lines of supply vulnerable to attack from the air."[97] Humanitarian workers, who have gained access to much of North Korea's territory in the last few years, paint a similar picture. They stress, for instance, that "the few tanks seen on the road cannot get from one village to the next without breaking down or running out of fuel."[98]

The political manipulation of statistics for defense expenditures perfectly illustrates how technical data are used to project threats in a particular manner. Policy makers and security experts keep drawing attention to North Korea's excessive military expenditures. And excessive they are, indeed, averaging an estimated 27.5 percent of the gross domestic product (GDP) over the last few years, even reaching a staggering 37.9 percent in 1998, at a time when the country was being devastated by a famine.[99] Seoul's defensive needs seem much more modest in comparison, located at a mere 3.5 percent of the GDP. But when one compares the expenditures of the two Koreas in absolute terms, which is hardly ever done in official statistics, the picture suddenly looks very different. Given its superior economy, the 3.5 percent that Seoul spends on its military amounts to more than twice as much as the North Koreans spend, no matter how excessive the North's expenditures appear to be in terms of percentage of the GDP.[100] One does not need to be fluent in the technostrategic language of security analysis to realize that over the years this unequal pattern of defense spending has created a qualitative imbalance of military capacities on the peninsula. And yet the myth of the strong North Korean army, of "the world's third largest military capability," is as prevalent and as hyped as ever.[101]

Security policy is about facing threats. And threats are, by definition, a matter of perception. They have as much to do with questions of identity as with objective military realities. I have revealed these linkages of identity and the production of danger by examining the geopolitical dimensions of the Korean security situation. Although all great powers have direct strategic interests in the peninsula, I focused here primarily on the role of the United States, which is undoubtedly the key external influence on Korean security. Nothing can be understood without at least a rudimentary appreciation of how America's political, ideological, and strategic interests are intertwined with the division of the peninsula. The United States played a significant role in the opening of Korea, national division, and the subsequent evolution of the Cold War.

I also examined the underlying patterns that shaped the two nuclear crises that haunted the peninsula during the last decade. In each case, in 1993–1994 and in 2002–2003, the crisis was said to have emerged suddenly. It was largely attributed to North Korea's problematic behavior, most notably to its tactic of nuclear brinkmanship: the effort to generate a crisis in order to win concessions from the West. But a more thorough analysis of the events reveals a far more complex picture. Given the deeply entrenched antagonistic Cold War atmosphere on the peninsula, the most recent crisis comes hardly as a surprise. Indeed, a crisis is always already present: the question is simply when and how it is being perceived and represented as such.

Responsibility for the nuclear crisis is an equally blurred affair. North Korea undoubtedly must bear a big part of it. Pyongyang has demonstrated clearly and repeatedly that it does not shy away from generating tension or embarking on acts of aggression to promote its own interests, particularly when its survival is at stake. Even a primitive North Korean nuclear program poses a grave threat to the region, not least because it could unleash a new nuclear arms race. But Pyongyang's actions have not taken place in a vacuum: they occurred in response to both internal as well as external circumstances. Central here is that North Korea has been subject to more than half a century of clear and repeated U.S. nuclear threats. Few decision makers and defense analysts realize the extent to which these threats have shaped the security dilemmas on the peninsula.

If one steps back from the immediate and highly emotional ideological context that dominates security interactions on the peninsula, the attitude and behavior of North Korea and the United States bear striking similarities. Both have contributed a great deal to intensifying each other's fears. Both have also drawn upon their fears to justify aggressive military postures. And both rely on a strikingly similar form of crisis diplomacy. America's Korea policy, particularly under the administration of George W. Bush, bears stunning resemblance to Pyongyang's much-vilified nuclear brinkmanship tactic, for Washington too relies on the projection of threats in order to win concessions from its opponent, in this case the disarmament of North Korea. Drawing attention to these patterns is not to deny that major debates have taken place in Washington's policy circles. As a result there are periods when a more conciliatory Korea policy has prevailed. Moreover, diplomatic overtures have been advanced even at times when a more confrontational attitude held sway. This was the case during the second nuclear crisis of 2002–2003, when Washington sought to reinforce its negotiating stance with the projection of nuclear and other threats toward North Korea. Such a policy of hawk engagement is highly problematic and not only because North Korea predictably reacted to it in a recalcitrant manner, thereby escalating the situation even further. Hawk engagement fundamentally misunderstands the nature and effect of threats, the interactive dimensions of security dilemmas, and the dangers of miscalculation that issue from them.

The interactive dimensions of security dilemmas in Korea are often hidden behind a realist policy facade that presents threats only in a one-dimensional manner. The image of North Korea as an evil and unpredictable "rogue state" is so deeply entrenched that any crisis can easily be attributed to Pyongyang's problematic actions. Maintaining this image of North Korea, and the threat projections that are associated with it, requires constant work. The specialized discourse on security and national defense contributes its share to the task. It presents threats in a highly technical manner and through a jargon-ridden language that is incomprehensible to all but a few military experts. As a result a very subjective and largely one-sided interpretation of security dilemmas has come to be accepted as real, even commonsensical. Challenging this construction of common sense, and the conflicts that issue from it, is my main task in the pages that follow.

Alternative Security Arrangements for Korea

In this second half of the book, I advance my suggestions about how to promote a more peaceful political environment. Central here is the challenge of figuring out how to deal with the vilified other and the corresponding antagonistic identity constructs. The most promising route out of existing security dilemmas is located in approaches that not only break with realist and militaristic security policies but also with the state-based thinking patterns that underlie them. In chapter 4, I draw attention to the importance of dialogue, particularly those forms that facilitate face-to-face encounters among average citizens across the dividing line. The promotion of such nonstate contacts, although largely seen as desirable, is hampered by a variety of problems, which I discuss in chapter 5. In chapter 6, I then advance arguments for an additional ethics of difference: a willingness to accept that a half-century of antagonistic identity practices has created differences that cannot simply be subsumed into one worldview, no matter how desirable this compulsion appears. Accepting these differences at all levels, from the political to the purely personal, is the most promising way to promote a culture of reconciliation.

4

Toward an Ethics of Dialogue

The challenge is to bring conflicts to the level of discourse and not let them degenerate into violence.
— PAUL RICOEUR, "IMAGINATION, TESTIMONY, AND TRUST"

Few would question that dialogue is an essential aspect of dealing with security dilemmas. Michel Wieviorka is one of many commentators who draw attention to the linkages between conflict and the breakdown or absence of dialogue. Violence, he argues, emerges in a context in which relationships between different societal groups are either strongly reduced or altogether absent.[1]

Although the DMZ remains the world's most tightly sealed border, all parties entangled in the Korean conflict largely acknowledge the desirability of dialogue. Look at the most recent crisis, the nuclear confrontation that started in the autumn of 2002. There were differences about who was to participate in negotiations to solve the dispute—North Korea preferred bilateral talks with the United States and the latter insisted on a multilateral forum. But all countries involved, including China, Japan, and Russia, advocated the need for dialogue. South Korea's then newly elected president, Roh Moo-hyun, stressed that "first, I will try to resolve all pending issues through dialogue."[2] Most previous presidents did, in fact, make similar statements during their inauguration. In 1988, for instance,

Roh Tae Woo announced an "era of dialogue and cooperation between South and North Korea."[3]

Some form of dialogue has always taken place in Korea, from unofficial Red Cross talks, ministerial meetings, and diplomatic gatherings to the spectacular summit between the North and South Korean heads of state in June 2000.[4] But none of the joint declarations and agreements that emerged from these numerous encounters ever managed to solve the issues at stake and establish a lasting atmosphere of peace. Sooner or later each agreement broke down. State-based dialogues may be able to deal with some of the immediate and overt challenges, such as finding ways to limit nuclear proliferation on the peninsula. But diplomatic encounters rarely, if ever, remove the underlying causes and patterns of conflict. None of the various state negotiations and summits have been able to engage the fundamental problem of Korea's culture of insecurity: the antagonistic identity constructs that continuously fuel conflict and undermine agreements, no matter how promising they seem at first sight. The Pyongyang summit of June 2000 is the most graphic case. Although spectacular and symbolically important, it hardly constituted a dialogical breakthrough. Each party came to it driven by interests that were specific to its own state apparatus: the North hoped to get some international recognition and badly needed funds. The South was willing to provide the latter, as it turned out later, through a secret payment of $100 million in return for securing the summit and, as some critics of the South Korean president's engagement policy suggest, helping him to win a Nobel Prize.[5]

Promoting a culture of reconciliation in Korea requires more than state-based dialogue. The recently proliferating literature on human security offers some important help here, for its proponents urge policy makers to view security beyond the conventional defense of the state and its territory. Advocates of human security stress the need to take into account the welfare of average people. Thus I begin this chapter by examining the usefulness of human security for the Korean peninsula. Doing so is central because human security has found little resonance in Korea. And yet Korea offers one of the rare opportunities to open up alternative security arrangements. Just as important, human security perspectives allow us to appreciate new insights into the political, for they recognize how actors other than states can shape the security environment. Indeed, far more important than academic debates about human security, which rarely reach beyond a small circle of intellectual elites, are a variety of largely inaudible grassroots activities that are transforming Korean politics. Among these phenomena are those engendered through the introduction of the so-called Sunshine Policy by South Korea's president Kim Dae-jung, who started to loosen state control of security by promoting more interaction between the two divided parts of the peninsula. Add to this numerous important changes that have occurred in North Korea in the last few years, ranging from increased trade, investment, and tourism to an opening up of the country (albeit very minimal) as a result of the presence of international humanitarian workers.

I pay particular attention to those nonstate interactions between North and South that promote direct communication, information exchange, or face-to-face encounters among ordinary people. Such encounters have so far been very limited. And they are not without risk. But they are of crucial importance, for they offer one of the few opportunities to break down the stereotypical threat perceptions that constitute the main obstacle to a culture of reconciliation on the peninsula. My assessment of these nonstate interactions is not exhaustive. The phenomena in question are far too diverse, complex, and ongoing to allow for an even remotely comprehensive appraisal, especially in the context of a brief examination. I am merely drawing attention to the political implications that emerge from these underestimated low-key events.

FROM STATE TO HUMAN SECURITY

Given the prevalence of state-based ideologies, it is not easy to visualize security arrangements that fundamentally break with this deeply entrenched political practice. And even if one manages to do so, how can one assess the significance of these insights in light of the prevailing state-based construction of security issues? Answers to such difficult questions do not, of course, come easily. But they can be found at both the conceptual and practical levels.

At a conceptual level the idea of human security has gained significant credibility in recent years. Its advocates urge policy makers to view security beyond the conventional military-based defense of the state and its territory. They stress the need to take into account the welfare of ordinary people. Issues such as development, poverty, health, or human rights should thus become part of the security agenda. Although conceptual discussions reach back to the Cold War period, the 1994 *Human Development Report* of the United Nations Development Program is usually credited with having generated broad discussions about human security. The report laments the narrow and deeply entrenched tradition of defining security as "security of territory from external aggression." Instead, it draws attention to much-neglected "legitimate concerns of ordinary people who sought security in their daily lives."[6] Human security gained increased international credibility when, in 1998, the governments of Canada and Norway officially promoted the concept.[7] A rapidly increasing body of scholarship has meanwhile generated intensive debates about the potential and limits of human security.[8] Although some Asian countries are strong advocates of human security,[9] the debate has not yet entered Korea in a significant way.

Can human security find a way out of the problematic political dilemmas on the Korean peninsula? To appreciate the potential of human security it is useful to differentiate between security as a policy domain and security as a field of study that seeks to understand how people, groups, and states affect and are affected by conflict. In the field of policy the concept of human security faces several formidable challenges. Critics of human security see problems with its broad and imprecise definition. Roland Paris stresses that "virtually any kind of unexpected or irregular discomfort could conceivably constitute a threat to one's human security."[10] This poses problems for policy makers. "Securitizing" a domain, such as the well-being of people, means setting priorities in policy making and funding. But given the broad scope of human security, an unlimited range of issues could become security concerns. The result, Yuen Foong Khong fears, is an inability to prioritize at all.[11]

Fears of policy paralysis resulting from a broadening of the term *security* are justified. In Korea these fears are reinforced by a variety of other factors. "Securitizing" the well-being of Korean people may well amount to no more than extending the already problematic role of the state.[12] President George W. Bush, for instance, used the lack of human rights in North Korea as a reason to reinforce a more aggressive military posture toward the government in Pyongyang. Security issues have also frequently been used by both Korean states not to support but to undermine the rights and well-being of people.

Stephen Noerper, for instance, argues that the production of military tension has been an essential component of the North Korean state's effort to sustain itself externally and internally—which, of course, entailed the violent suppression of virtually all dissent.[13] In the South too various military rulers, from Park Chung Hee to Chun Doo-hwan, have used the perception of a hostile North as a strategy to control opposing forces and to consolidate domestic power structures. The situation has improved with South Korea's gradual transition to democracy, but the government still uses the notorious National Security Law to crack down on dissidents who show sympathy for the archenemy in the North.

In addition to providing guidelines for policy making, human security can be seen as a way of broadening our understanding of the factors that affect the security of people. As opposed to conventional approaches, which focus solely on strategic issues, the human security literature does, for instance, pay attention to a wide range of problems, from poverty to environmental degradation. Critics lament that this broad scope prevents the concept of human security from providing useful guidelines for research. In the absence of a precise definition, they fear, human security "means almost anything" and thus "seems capable of supporting virtually any hypothesis—along with its opposite."[14] But imposing rigid academic definitions and guidelines would not necessarily bring us new insight into security. Instead, it would simply enforce the role of academic disciplines, which are already powerful mechanisms that control both the production of knowledge and its application in practice. Innovative solutions to existing problems cannot be found if our efforts at understanding security issues remain confined to a set of rigid and well-entrenched disciplinary rules. The key, rather, lies in understanding connections between a variety of issues that shape the security of people.

The main problem with human security, as it is articulated today, is not the lack of definition but something more substantial: for all their efforts to see beyond the state, human security advocates are unable to escape the state's omnipresent conceptual grip. Consider how Lloyd Axworthy, former foreign minister of Canada and a key advocate of human security, stresses that security policy ought, above all, to be measured by its "success or failure . . . to improve the protection of civilians from state-sponsored aggression and civil, especially ethnic, conflict."[15] People are thus still presented as mere "referents" of security: as passive objects to be protected by the state apparatus. The state clearly remains, as Edward Newman points out, "the central provider of security."[16] Commendable as such a position may be from the vantage point of progressive state policy making, it fails to provide conceptual tools with which the increasingly complex world of security politics can be understood. Because people are mere objects, rather than subjects of security, the ensuing conceptual framework remains statecentric. It fails to recognize many significant instances where people transgress, and at times challenge and transform, the very security environment that regulates (or disrupts) their lives.[17]

VISUALIZING NONSTATE TRANSFORMATIONS OF SECURITY

It is not necessarily surprising that even alternative political projects, such as those associated with human security, tend to fall back into the same statecentric mode of thinking from which they sought to liberate themselves. The state is so omnipresent in modern life that we often do not even recognize its centrality anymore. Open at random any treatise on East Asian security affairs and you are likely to find that states, acting according to the dicta of realist power politics, dominate not only the story line but also the language in which it is couched. Consider, for instance, the following representative reaction to the summit meeting of June 2000. Kent Calder, in a *Foreign Affairs* article, argues that "for the first time since World War II, Seoul and Pyongyang—rather than Washington, Moscow, or Beijing—were driving events."[18] One could take issue with the substance of Calder's argument and point out, for instance, that the United States is perhaps more influential than either Korean state in shaping the security environment on the peninsula. But this is beside the point, or at least beside what I intend to pursue in this chapter. Just as important as issues of substance is the language that Calder and most other security analysts employ. Metaphorically represented through their capital cities, states have become unproblematic and unproblematized entities. These abstracted entities are presented as if they were the only agents that are "driving events." Meetings between state representatives, as in Pyongyang, "catalyze change."[19] By contrast, if progress fails to materialize, then the culprit is usually an individual state, such as the "rogue" regime in Pyongyang or inadequate security arrangements among states, such as the lack of a regional Asian security framework analogous to NATO or the Organization for Security and Co-operation in Europe (OSCE).[20]

States do, of course, play a central role in East Asian security affairs. In that sense the strong statist language is not surprising. It is, perhaps, inevitable. We all slip into it, whether we want it or not. It is often the only way to address the key security dilemmas. But states are not monolithic entities. The policy formations within them are often hotly disputed and under constant transformation. Neither are states the only actors driving events. But statecentric metaphors of security relations make it very difficult to appreciate, or even recognize, the multitude of additional factors that shape security environments. Seen through a strategic studies lens, actors other than states—from international organizations to nongovernmental organizations (NGOs), business representatives, or average citizens—simply have no bearing on the political realm or at least not on its security dimensions. And yet these nonstate interactions offer perhaps one of the best opportunities to overcome the antagonistic identity practices that sustain the Korean conflict.

An excellent model for bringing people into the realm of the political can be found in feminist critiques of international relations scholarship, which, much like its subdiscipline of security studies, remains wedded to a strong statecentric paradigm. In its prevailing neorealist and neoliberal form, international relations scholarship revolves around understanding the influence of structures and norms of state behavior. The only individuals who matter are those imbued with the power of a "decision maker": presidents, diplomats, generals, and the occasional CEO of a multinational company. Cynthia Enloe is among a group of innovative scholars who have challenged this narrow vision of the international. She interprets the dynamics of world politics from the vantage point of the margins, by heeding, for instance, the voices of women migrant workers in Mexico or sex workers in brothels outside U.S. military bases in Asia. By theorizing the international from the margins, Enloe reveals what otherwise would remain unnoticed: that "relations between governments depend not only on capital and weaponry, but also on the control of women as symbols, consumers, workers and emotional comforters."[21]

A similar visualization of nonstate transformations of security environments is needed in Korea. In this sense I now want to examine how a variety of factors, from the gradual opening of North Korea to the introduction of an engagement policy in the South, have engendered cross-border contacts that contain far more transformative potential than security experts acknowledge.

CHANGE AND CONTINUITY IN NORTH KOREA

North Korea is no longer what it used to be, despite its image as a rogue state that always stays the same. Various commentators stress that "North Korea has begun to show signs of genuine change."[22] During the last few years Pyongyang has entered into diplomatic relations with more than a dozen countries that belong to the Organisation for Economic Co-operation and Development (OECD). North-South contacts now take place on a regular basis, and the summit meeting of June 2000 was only the most spectacular event of this series. At the domestic level too one can detect significant change. The government of North Korea has introduced elements of an incentive-oriented agriculture that allows farmers to use surplus production at their own discretion.[23] Then North Korea abandoned its state-directed distribution system in favor of more market-oriented principles. This includes not just new farmers' markets, which have emerged in many parts of the country, but also a radical devaluation of the national currency, large increases in wages (up to twentyfold), and even greater hikes in prices for food, commodities, and housing.[24] Commentators are speaking of "the most significant liberalization measures since the start of communist rule."[25]

But how significant are these changes? What are their security implications? And do they indicate that decision makers in Pyongyang have embraced a genuine desire for systemic change? The last is unlikely to be the case. The transformations were not an expression of newly found neoliberal ideals but a last-minute effort to avoid a collapse of the country's economic and political system. North Korea has been in economic decline since the late 1980s, a tendency that intensified with the disintegration of the Soviet Union and the resulting loss of aid and trading partners.[26] Unprecedented floods in 1995 and 1996 and a drought in 1997 dramatically worsened the situation, leading to major famines that killed anywhere (depending on the estimate) from 200,000 to five million people.[27]

Facing a worst-case scenario, the government in Pyongyang had no choice but to introduce at least some reforms.

Even if they do not reflect a desire for change, the transformations that have taken place in North Korea since the late 1990s are significant. And so are their political consequences, not least because they have increased contacts between North Korean citizens and the outside world. For instance, food shortages led to a large-scale movement of people away from their authorized residence, which produced an otherwise-impossible flow of information about the seriousness of the situation.[28] This migration included a great number of North Koreans who crossed into China in an attempt to forage for food. Although an estimated 100,000 to 200,000 have stayed on as illegal immigrants, most have returned to North Korea. The consequences are important, stresses Shim Jae Hoon, for "the migrants are carrying back new ideas about the world, cracking the hermetic seal that has enabled North Korea's Stalinist regime to survive the end of the Cold War."[29]

The political consequences of such seemingly inaudible transformations may take years to unfold, but that does not make them any less significant. The same can be said about the effects that set in when, faced with the famine of 1995, North Korea made an unprecedented appeal to the international community for assistance. A large number of organizations responded by providing food and other emergency aid as well as more general development cooperation. At various stages more than one hundred foreign aid workers were living in the North, representing organizations as diverse as the United Nations Development Programme, World Health Organization, UNICEF and the World Food Program, Caritas, World Vision, and the Swiss Development Agency. The World Food Program alone had forty-six foreign resident staff members. Many of these organizations remain in the country, and so do various smaller NGOs, which support projects that range from long-term agricultural assistance to the exploration of alternative energy sources.[30] Representatives of foreign humanitarian organizations eventually gained access to about two-thirds of the North Korean territory, or about 80 percent of the population.[31] This is highly significant for a country that until recently was extremely reclusive and secretive. Hazel Smith, one of the most authoritative commentators on the humanitarian crisis in North Korea, speaks of a "de facto opening up of the country to the outside world."[32] To be more precise, the opening occurs in several ways. The outside world has gained not only increasingly detailed information about the once unknowable hermit kingdom[33] but also the recognition that it is possible to do business with North Korea.[34] Just as important is that more and more North Koreans are interacting with the outside world, which can help contextualize and perhaps reduce some of the negative images that have prevailed on both sides of the DMZ for decades. In either case, an increasing number of collaborative projects, even if they are only of a small-scale nature, have the potential to contribute to the eventual establishment of trust among people who for decades had been divided by fear and political indoctrination.[35]

THE IMPORTANCE OF FACE-TO-FACE ENCOUNTERS

Many transformations in North Korea would not have been possible without certain changes in the South. Nicholas Eberstadt believes that South Korea's economic difficulties in the wake of the 1997 financial crisis reduced Pyongyang's resistance to inter-Korean dialogue and economic cooperation. The South now appeared as a less fearsome adversary or at least as somewhat less keen (and able) to absorb the North.[36] But there are more intentional dimensions too.

Starting with his inaugural speech in February 1998, South Korea's president Kim Dae-jung called for a new approach toward the North. Kim's initiative, the Sunshine Policy, revolved around moving from a deeply entrenched politics of containment toward a more active engagement that promotes cooperation and reconciliation. This new and more tolerant policy generated various forms of cross-border exchanges, from tourist visits and cultural and sports engagements to family reunions. Although still of very limited scope, these exchanges are nevertheless important. To highlight their significance I now focus, by way of illustration, on the role of cross-border economic activities, which were all but nonexistent until recently. This changed with the introduction of the Sunshine Policy, which was based on the assumption that increased economic cooperation would eventually engender common interests and understanding. As a result a key policy leitmotif became "economy first, politics later."[37] But that is perhaps not quite the right way of conceptualizing it. Economic cross-border contacts, be they related to trade or

aid, are hardly apolitical in nature. Indeed, they are highly politi-
cized. A better way of understanding the issues at stake is to see the
challenge as one that consists of broadening the political to include
the economic and to question the long-held insistence that the state
should be the only actor allowed to deal with the archenemy.

Despite obstacles of various kinds, not least the highly unpredictable investment climate in the North, there has been a series
of bold business ventures since Kim Dae-jung's inauguration. A
breakthrough occurred in June and November 1998, when Chung
Ju-yung, founder of the Hyundai conglomerate, crossed into North
Korea via Panmunjom with several hundred head of cattle to be
donated to the North. The visit of the South Korean business ty-
coon signaled the arrival of a new era of inter-Korean economic
relations. While many of the bigger South Korean conglomerates,
such as Samsung and LG, took a more cautious approach, Hyundai
aggressively pursued a wide range of investments in the North.[38]
The flagship project was the opening of Mount Kumgang for tourists arriving by boat. So far, more than half a million South Koreans
have been on these tours; Hyundai agreed to pay roughly $1 billion
over a six-year period ($12 million per month) for the right to oper-
ate these tours.[39] The company plans to add a large-scale Western
leisure complex (including golf and skiing facilities) and hopes that
the number of tourists will crease dramatically with the opening of
the first direct land link in 2003, but it is as yet too early to gauge
its success. Other projects include the establishment of an industrial
site in Kaesong, where Hyundai foresees investing almost $200 mil-
lion to develop a site for manufacturing textiles, clothing, and electronic goods.[40]

Trying to promote reconciliation through economic interactions
is not unproblematic. For one, economic activities lack democratic
accountability. They are driven by the search for profit rather than
by ethical or political leitmotifs. But profit has so far been elusive.
The example of Hyundai perfectly illustrates the economic and political difficulties involved in promoting cross-border interactions.
The Hyundai boat tours to Mount Kumgang soon ran into financial
difficulties. They had to be rescued in 2002 through substantial government subsidies. None of the other Hyundai projects has managed
to engender profit or shows any signs of doing so in the foreseeable
future. The problems at stake became particularly public with the

suicide of Chung Mong-hun, head of Hyundai-Asan, a subsidiary of Hyundai that runs the company's business ventures in North Korea.[41] Experts stress that investments in North Korea will continue to be hampered by a great many obstacles, from a lack of infrastructure, property rights, and generally accepted dispute settlement procedures to attitudinal differences regarding business interactions.[42] Add to that the intricacies of the general political climate, and long-term economic engagement with North Korea becomes a rather unpredictable affair.

While eluding profitability and facing various obstacles, cross-border business activities have nevertheless been remarkable. In the early 1990s inter-Korean trade was virtually nonexistent. In 1998, the year the Sunshine Policy was introduced, it already amounted to $222 million and reached $642 million in 2002.[43] In addition to humanitarian assistance and other forms of aid, which is still the largest component, northbound shipments included textiles and chemical goods. Imports from the North include agricultural, fishery, and metal products, although Pyongyang's most lucrative export item probably remains remains ballistic technology and income from a range of unconventional activities, such as the narcotics trade.[44] In any case, in 2001 more than a hundred South Korean companies were engaged in business activities in the North.[45] During the same year more than eight thousand South Korean businesspeople visited the North.

By international standards these economic activities may be insignificant. But they are spectacular in the context of the hermetically sealed Korean peninsula. Historians of tomorrow may well identify the turning point in northeast Asian politics with these and other low-key interactions, rather than the diplomatic summits that attract global media attention. Some go so far as to portray the Hyundai Group as the "leading inter-Korean mediator."[46] It is not so much, as some commentators suggest, that these nonstate actors are able to "speak with one or both parties to the dispute without prejudice to either."[47] The Korean situation is far too emotionally and politically charged to allow for assessments free of prejudice. But nonstate actors are nevertheless important. They are bound by fewer restrictions than states and can thus pursue agendas that governments cannot.

The traditional liberal assumption is that cross-border economic activities engender levels of interdependence that contribute to the promotion of a peaceful environment. In a context where commercial activities are at stake, the key actors have a strong interest in reducing the likelihood of conflict because it would jeopardize profit and investment.[48] But there is more to cross-border economic activities than mere interdependence. The ensuing contacts may also help to "update the world's psychological map of North Korea" by replacing stereotypes with a more differentiated understanding of people who had been divided for decades.[49] This is the case because face-to-face encounters offer perhaps the best opportunity to create dialogical spaces and to dismantle threat perceptions. Compromise needs confidence, and the building of confidence requires personal encounters that can build trust over time.

Promoting face-to-face encounters among Koreans, through economic or any other means, is clearly not a straightforward political task. And it has become significantly more difficult with the advent of a more confrontational U.S. policy. During the Clinton administration Washington was highly supportive of the Sunshine Policy, taking a number of additional steps, such as lifting restrictions on investment in and trade with North Korea. The inauguration of George W. Bush in 2001 marked a dramatic shift toward a more confrontational Korea policy. In chapter 3, I drew attention to the consequences of ostracizing North Korea as an evil rogue state. Suffice it at this point to stress that the more hawkish U.S. position also posed serious difficulties for Kim Dae-jung's Sunshine Policy. The policy had already been criticized within South Korea, but the presidential election of 2002 produced a winner, Roh Moo-hyun, who strongly believed in the need to continue his predecessor's engagement policy. A significant policy rift thus emerged between Washington and Seoul, not least because Roh won the election in the context of a nationwide wave of anti-Americanism.[50]

The recurrence of tension among the various parties entangled in the Korean conflict is hardly astonishing. It is, in fact, inevitable so long as antagonistic identities and realist security thinking dominates politics on the peninsula. Far more surprising is that nonstate interactions across the DMZ continued to take place even at the height of the nuclear crisis of 2002–2003. Security experts have failed to pay sufficient attention to the significance of these persistent low-key contacts. If defense experts take nonstate actors into account at all, they do so only in the context of so-called track two diplomacy:

interventions by private citizens into the machinery of high politics. Such interventions can indeed play a crucial role in defusing tensions, for they allow for levels of informal interactions that are not possible in official state-to-state negotiations. For instance, various prominent individuals, such as former U.S. president Jimmy Carter, the Reverend Billy Graham, and the scholar Selig Harrison played a significant role in defusing the 1993–1994 nuclear crisis.[51] But important as they are, track two activities remain elite-level interactions. They may well attenuate or at times even resolve political dilemmas, but they do not directly engender face-to-face interactions among ordinary Korean citizens. And without such contacts it is virtually impossible to dismantle or even attenuate the antagonistic identities that lie at the heart of the Korean conflict.

Despite their limited nature thus far, and the obstacles they face, nonstate interactions across the DMZ have unleashed a dynamic that cannot be reversed. They offer important alternatives to more established practices of security and conflict resolution. Such alternatives are particularly important in Korea, where state control of security has been unusually strong and where conventional diplomatic negotiations have failed to attenuate the antagonistic identity practices that continuously fuel the culture of insecurity.

In this chapter I have drawn attention to the significance of nonstate contacts between North and South, particularly those that promote direct contacts between ordinary Korean citizens. Face-to-face encounters between people are essential for removing entrenched stereotypes and threat perceptions. They contribute to the creation of a culture of reconciliation, which is an essential—and so far absent—precondition for a significant diplomatic breakthrough on the Korean peninsula. To understand the ensuing dynamics is to pay attention to relatively mundane daily interactions, which have not usually been considered relevant by a security studies community that is preoccupied with the heroic dimensions of high politics. But informal interactions offer promising possibilities to achieve something that resembles true dialogue and sustainable peace. The promotion of nonstate contacts does not, of course, supersede the need for conventional security and diplomatic initiatives.[52] But such contacts contribute to an eventual establishment of a public sphere that could generate open cross-border discussions on the meaning and form of unification.[53] Such public discussions are hardly conceivable in the current political environment, but nonstate interactions across the DMZ already have political content and direct relevance today, for they demonstrate what R. B. J. Walker identified as a key component of creative security arrangements: "a certain skepticism about the claim that the modern state and state system offer the only plausible way of responding to questions about the political."[54]

My purpose in this chapter was not to offer a comprehensive analysis of nonstate interactions in Korea. Doing so would have exceeded by far what is possible in the context of a short discussion. Rather, my purpose was merely to draw attention to the potential and political significance of these low-key and seemingly apolitical features. I have done so by illustrating the respective dynamics through economic activities that have taken place between the two parts of the peninsula. But economic interactions are, of course, not the only cross-border activities. A whole range of other contacts have taken place, including humanitarian engagements, tourist visits, family reunions, and exchanges in the domain of culture and sport. Symbolic gestures here include the use of a common flag during the 2000 Olympic Games, North Korea's limited broadcast of World Cup Soccer matches played in South Korea in 2002, and North Korea's participation in the Asian Games, held in Pusan the same year. The latest breakthrough occurred in mid-2003 and included a symbolic reconnection of cross-border railroads and the first direct tourist crossings of the DMZ.[55] Data on the exact number of visitors vary somewhat. But they are certainly in the tens of thousands, and all sources, including the "official" website of South Korea's Ministry of Unification, indicate a steady increase over the last few years. South-North visits numbered 3,317 in 1998, 5,599 in 1999, 7,280 in 2000, 8,551 in 2001, and 12,825 in 2002.[56] Marcus Noland goes so far as to speak of a "dramatic increase in the number of North and South Koreans coming into contact with each other."[57]

The concept of human security offers some help in identifying and promoting nonstate interactions. But caution is required. A broadening of the security agenda, as advocates of human security call for, is not unproblematic. It could lead to paralysis or confusion at the level of policy making. Perhaps even more fatefully, broadening the security agenda would run the risk of extending the already problematic role of the state and of the militaristic mind-set that pervades defense-oriented thinking. A more promising route is to simply let defense experts do what they have always done: advise the state on how to organize its military-based defense. At the same time this process of state protection must be submitted to regular and critical scrutiny. It must also be supplemented with a more broadly defined approach to security and North-South relations. The latter should be able to explore possibilities for economic, cultural, personal, and other interactions without being restrained by the narrow dictates of realist defense thinking. Needed, in other words, is a politicization of security, rather than a securitization of politics. That this process is already underway, although largely unacknowledged, is perhaps one of the most reassuring aspects of a peninsula that is still plagued by the constant specter of violence.

5

Dilemmas of Engagement

The use of force on the Korean peninsula retains high probability that it will escalate into an all-out, full scale war. . . . Sunshine Policy's strategy is to win without fighting.

— LIM DONG-WON, SPECIAL ADVISER
TO THE SOUTH KOREAN PRESIDENT

Although underestimated by defense experts, the promotion of dialogue and face-to-face encounters is by no means a radical idea. Most state actors entangled in the Korean security situation display a preference for the so-called soft landing scenario, which foresees an incremental rapprochement between North and South. All but the most radical critics of engagement advocate policies that are geared toward avoiding either a direct military conflict with or a sudden collapse of North Korea. Since the late 1990s the South Korean government has been particularly active in promoting such a step-by-step approach toward normalizing political interactions on the peninsula. While the engagement policy offers much potential, as I outlined in chapter 4, the concrete results of this policy have so far been limited. Nonstate interactions have increased, perhaps dramatically when compared with the past, but they are far from reaching the scale where they can influence the population at large. Moreover, engagement has not prevented the recurrence of yet another nuclear crisis on the peninsula.

Rapprochement does, of course, take time. And so does the task of dismantling the hostile identities that drive the Korean conflict. But there are also more direct obstacles to a viable policy of dialogue and engagement. In this chapter I identify some of these fundamental but often ignored obstacles. I do so as a preliminary step before embarking on the last task of this book: an attempt to outline what promoting a culture of reconciliation in Korea entails.

True engagement and dialogue require what Jürgen Habermas called an "ideal speech situation," a context in which people can express their opinions freely and without fear of intimidation. In Korea this would entail a political forum in which each party to the conflict "is able to speak, with equal opportunity, what it wants to say from its own perspective."[1] Habermas, of course, refers to an ideal scenario. No political forum, no matter how open and free, is devoid of power and domination. But to be successful, dialogue and engagement require a minimum amount of tolerance, perhaps even an acceptance of difference. They presuppose a political willingness to listen to the other, even if one knows from the beginning that one may never be able to accept or even fully understand the other's position. Such an acceptance of difference is clearly missing on the Korean peninsula, despite occasional rhetorical flourishes that seemingly suggest the opposite.

North Korea continues to hold on, at least formally, to its constitutionally entrenched objective of "communizing" the peninsula. The South has softened some of its positions, but it still retains the National Security Law, which defines North Korea as the "main enemy." This means, in essence, that any act of supporting or even sympathizing with the North is "tantamount to committing treason."[2] These are more than simply minor legal residues from the height of the Cold War. They are powerful and highly symbolic reminders that neither side in Korea is ready to accept the other.

I will begin by demonstrating how North Korea is unwilling to tolerate difference within its own system. That is, of course, a well-recognized feature of its totalitarian regime. It is also a key obstacle to the promotion of large-scale nonstate interactions on the peninsula. Pyongyang's policies are geared toward attracting economic benefits through aid and international trade while doing everything possible to minimize contact with the outside world and thus with difference. Then I examine how this fear is linked to South Korea's approach to engagement, which is seemingly far more tolerant than North Korea's but in the end still rests upon a refusal to embrace difference. Kim Dae-jung may have reiterated at various points that Seoul has no intention of absorbing the North. But at the same time the Sunshine Policy assumes that an improvement in North-South relations "would require an incremental exposure of North Korea's society to the outside world."[3]

Politicians and commentators in South Korea speak of the need to "integrate" North Korea and to "normalize" relations on the peninsula. *Integration* and *normalization* are terms that suggest processes of adjustment to one standard norm, a desire to erase difference in favor of a single identity practice. The immediate objective of engagement as articulated today may well be to avoid an open conflict or a sudden collapse of North Korea, but the underlying rationale remains a desire to prevail over the other side. The purpose is "to win without fighting," as expressed by Lim Dong-won, a key architect of the Sunshine Policy. These policies revolve around the assumption that peace emerges when North Korea eventually embraces the virtues of democracy and market economics and therefore the values and identity practices of the South. Of course, few commentators— including me—would opt for a North Korean style of governance. But this is beside the point, for an adequate security policy must start with existing realities, with acknowledging that North Korea does exist and will continue to exist for the foreseeable future. And so will the diverging identity practices that have been created through half a century of national division. Dealing with such differences is precisely what a democratic ethos ought to be all about: an attempt to recognize that people have diverging perspectives and that political institutions and decision-making procedures must find a way of redeeming these differences or at least of taking them into account when formulating policies.

NORTH KOREA'S FEAR OF THE OUTSIDE WORLD

North Korea's engagement with the South is hampered by a variety of factors other than the obvious: Pyongyang's repeated reliance on nuclear brinkmanship to gain concessions from the international community. Underlying these highly problematic policy moves are a number of fundamental contradictions that characterize North Korea's seeming willingness to open up and participate in dialogue with the outside world. Look at some of the dynamics that took place at the height of détente on the peninsula, during the summit meeting of June 2000. North Korea heralded the meeting as "an important occasion," foreseeing a "bright prospect of removing distrust and confrontation between the North and the South, promoting trust and reconciliation between them."[4] In the period that followed, Pyongyang even toned down its traditionally harsh rhetoric. Only weeks before it had characterized the South and its U.S. ally as "warhawks" and "warmongers" that "crack a smile of reconciliation at negotiating table and sharpen knife against the dialogue partner behind it."[5] While now showing more tolerance toward the South, the North at the same time underlined its full commitment to the existing system and its ruler. The official press organ, *Rodong Shinmun*, stressed that the Korean people continue to "cherish absolute worship of the leader," that, in fact, their faith in Kim Jong Il and the revolution is "growing stronger as days go by."[6] The preamble to the constitution of the North Korean Workers' Party continued to state, as it had for decades, that "the ultimate objective is to turn the entire society into that of *juche* ideology and construct a Communist society."[7] At various moments Kim Il Sung also stated explicitly that "we must drive out the U.S. imperialists and liberate parents and brothers in south Korea."[8] Of course, these statements are part of a deeply entrenched rhetorical practice and should therefore not be taken literally. At least since the early 1990s North Korea has been far too much concerned with its own survival to retain a realistic ambition of communizing the entire peninsula. But these rhetorical residues nevertheless reflect important features, most notably Pyongyang's unwavering commitment to a political system that does not tolerate diversity or even critique.

A fundamental contradiction thus emerges: North Korea must open up its borders in order to attract badly needed aid and generate economic interaction with the outside world. At the same time, though, the survival not only of Kim Jong Il but also of the political order in general may well be contingent on the regime's ability to shield the population from subversive outside influences. It is highly unlikely that a popular consensus emerging from the interaction between two strong, open, and free civil societies in the North and the South will work to the benefit of Pyongyang's present ideological worldview. The leadership in Pyongyang is certainly aware of the dangers that a free flow of information would entail for its regime. Already in the early 1990s North Korean officials privately emphasized that they were wary of the "decadent capitalist culture" that carries the potential of undermining North Korean socialism.[9] This fear has been intensified through the precedent of German unification and not only because the Communist East was absorbed by the capitalist West. Just as significant is that West German radio and television were readily available in the East for decades, thus perpetually undermining the regime's attempt to spread its official ideological discourse. The final blow to the regime came when the Iron Curtain crumbled and hundreds of thousands of East German citizens escaped to the West. German unification, in that sense, was precipitated, as one commentator puts it, "by a large-scale movement of people and, even more, by the fear of even greater movement."[10]

Fear of such movements, and of the outside world in general, is something that Kim Jong Il expressed on various occasions. "Opening up," he stressed in a secretly recorded conversation, "is no different from the withdrawal of a country's troops." It would be "tantamount to disarmament."[11] Fear of subversion intensified again as the United States turned to a more confrontational policy in 2002. An official government statement, for instance, justified Pyongyang's desire for a nuclear deterrence capability as a necessary response to what it perceived as a key strategic change in Washington's approach to security on the peninsula: a move away from simply awaiting the disintegration of North Korea and toward a policy that "forcefully seeks to cause a collapse."[12]

Pyongyang's fear of subversion has clearly constrained attempts to promote face-to-face interactions on the Korean peninsula. Virtually all domains of nonstate interaction are shaped by Pyongyang's compulsion to retain control of the flow of information and the movement of people. A key example here is North Korea's promotion of a tourist industry. It is geared toward generating revenues, but its tourism activities are planned and controlled in a manner that either avoids or minimizes all contact with the local populace. Consider the highly revealing statistical data provided by South Korea's Ministry of Unification. The total number of South Korean visitors to the North during the last few years usually was a few hundred per month, sometimes just more than one thousand. Compare this figure to the number of participants in the Mount Kumgang tours, which are counted separately. The greatest number arrived in October 2000, when a total of 27,950 people visited the North Korean mountain area. Since then the number has fluctuated between 1,500 and 11,000 per month.[13] But participants in the Kumgang tour still outnumber by far the sum of all other visitors to North Korea. By 2003 more than half a million tourists had taken the Kumgang trip. This statistical fact is both striking and highly relevant politically. Visitors to Pyongyang and other cities have various opportunities to encounter the local populace. The Kumgang tour, by contrast, can be contained and is highly lucrative at the same time. Although Hyundai's monthly payment of $12 million was subsequently reduced because of the company's financial difficulties, the money still constitutes a big part of North Korea's foreign revenues. And it appears to be channeled directly to an organization controlled by Kim Jong Il.[14] Perhaps most important, participants on the Kumgang tour can easily be controlled, to the point that they have virtually no contact with ordinary North Koreans. During the initial stage passengers were forced to return for the night to the cruise ship, which had to stay five miles from the coastline.[15] But even when overnight accommodation became possible, the tour activities were carefully organized to minimize face-to-face contact with North Korean citizens.

The same principle holds true for most aspects of North Korea's "engagement" with the outside world. Ideally, investment and trade activities are channeled to sealed-off and easily controllable "special economic zones," most notably at Rajin-Seonbong.[16] A new site is under discussion for Shinuiju, at the China–North Korea border. Plans call for this capitalist enclave to be sealed off by a major wall from the rest of North Korea.[17] Comparable containment measures also apply to the reunion of families that had been separated during the war. Several thousand North and South Koreans met in half a dozen rounds of reunions in the three years following the Pyongyang summit of 2000. In all instances the North Korean participants were carefully chosen. Contact took place in a well-controlled environment and was limited to the short period of the official reunion. South Korea's suggestion of a permanent reunion center was rejected. Other domains of engagement are more difficult to control and contain. This is the case, for instance, with regard to the international humanitarian organizations that have been active in North

Korea since the famine of the mid- and late 1990s. Their representatives have gained access to a considerable part of the country. They regularly interact with ordinary citizens. But obstacles of various types exist, not least because there are no nongovernmental organizations (NGOs) in a North Korean context where the state has virtually annihilated civil society. The engagement is thus of a very asymmetrical nature, and even at this level the extent of interaction is minimized wherever possible. Members of UNICEF, for instance, were severely restricted when conducting a nutrition and health survey. The North Korean authorities insisted that the "actual physical contact with the surveyed population would remain restricted to Korean personnel."[18] In the years that followed, North Korea grew less suspicious and increased its cooperation with foreign humanitarian workers,[19] but the fundamental dynamic has hardly changed. The North Korean government remains torn between, on the one hand, having to open up to attract badly needed economic assistance and, on the other hand, trying to stay in power by retaining as much control as possible over the flow of information.

PROMOTING A SOFT OR HARD LANDING?

While North Korea's challenges primarily revolve around the question of regime survival, the South and its allies face dilemmas of a different nature. These have to do with the question of how to approach a North Korean regime that clearly violates the human rights of its citizens and poses a threat to regional and even global peace. Should one engage in a dialogue with North Korea? Should one try to reach a compromise in order to avoid a dangerous escalation of tension or even a war on the peninsula? Or is such an approach merely a policy of appeasement that prolongs the suffering of people and renders the situation more dangerous in the long run?

The political and ethical dilemmas of how to engage North Korea are as difficult as they are open ended. These debates are, in essence, dominated by two opposing approaches. The first advocates a hard-line policy toward North Korea that is aimed at undermining the authoritarian regime as fast as possible, leading to a quick collapse and subsequent unification. "If the North Korean regime is irredeemable," Marcus Noland asks, "should not the rest of the world act to hasten its demise?"[20] Withdrawing support would undoubtedly worsen the economic situation in the North and precipitate yet another famine. But is this not the price to pay for the promotion of a more just political order? Providing Pyongyang with trade possibilities and humanitarian aid would, according to this logic, not only sustain a dictatorial and dangerous regime but also prolong the suffering of the North Korean people. The longer the peninsula is divided, Nicholas Eberstadt stresses, the bigger the economic chasm between North and South will grow. This, in turn, will render eventual unification more expensive and more difficult.[21] Consider some of the immediate practical dilemmas. Several NGOs that provided humanitarian aid, such as Oxfam, left North Korea because they were prevented from adequately monitoring and evaluating the effect of their aid, which they feared did not reach the most vulnerable part of the population. Most explicit in its critique was Médecins sans Frontières, which also protested the existence of alleged concentration camps that hold people who were caught foraging for food across the border in China.[22] If humanitarian assistance is channeled directly through the repressive regime, a representative of the doctors' organization argued, then it "has become part of the system of oppression."[23]

The second and opposing approach advocates a gradual rapprochement between the two sides despite the dilemma that this policy entails. This so-called soft landing strategy assumes that engagement is the best opportunity to prevent both a military escalation and a sudden collapse of the North Korean regime. Proponents of rapprochement stress that collapse alone could create a major crisis, including large-scale refugee movements or a civil war.[24] Most humanitarian organizations, for instance, stayed behind in North Korea, believing that humanitarian assistance and development cooperation are essential, even if the conditions of engagement are far from ideal.[25] Withdrawing aid, they fear, would only heighten the danger of a confrontation and worsen the situation of the populace but not necessarily bring about change for the better. Underlining the logic of this position is that there are "few if any examples of authoritarian governments being brought down by famine conditions."[26]

Politicians, diplomats, humanitarian workers, and academics continue to debate the merits and demerits of the soft versus the hard landing scenario. These approaches are correspondingly diverse. The United States, for instance, clearly supported engagement during the Clinton administration but then switched to a more hawkish position with the election of George W. Bush in 2000. South Korea has consistently favored engagement since the election of President Kim Dae-jung in 1998. His successor, Roh Moo-hyun, was elected in 2002 on a platform that revolved around the continuation of the Sunshine Policy. Kim pursued his engagement policy often against considerable domestic opposition, and Roh won the presidential election only by a narrow margin over Lee Hoi-chang, who strongly believed in the need to return to a more confrontational approach to North Korea.

While the debate continues, the soft landing scenario has become influential enough to be adopted in one way or another as the preferred policy option of all great powers concerned with Korea. Moscow, Beijing, and Tokyo all assume, either explicitly or implicitly, that a step-by-step approach would, for both financial and geopolitical reasons, be a far more stable way of achieving Korean unity.[27] To avoid the highly volatile situation that would emerge from a sudden collapse of North Korea, their policies are now directed toward assisting Pyongyang enough to ensure some sort of controlled transition. Even the more confrontational U.S. policy under President Bush accepts the logic of engagement to some extent. Washington has not only become the biggest provider of food aid to North Korea[28] but also pursued negotiations with Pyongyang, even at the height of the nuclear crisis in 2003. This seemingly contradictory stance may be the result of power struggles between hawks and doves in Washington, or it may simply be a reflection of policy restraints and a lack of alternative scenarios: North Korea does exist and needs to be dealt with, no matter how much Bush professes to "loathe Kim Jong-il."[29]

FROM ABSORPTION TO RAPPROCHEMENT?

The prevalence of the soft landing approach suggests a certain discourse of tolerance: a commitment to "normalize" political interactions on the peninsula and to "integrate" North Korea into the world community. But are the interests that underlie these approaches and the policies that they engender as tolerant of diversity as their labeling suggests?

A closer look reveals nearly as many contradictions in South Korea's approach to engagement as one finds in the North: a strong desire to suppress the other's sense of identity is hidden beneath a seeming willingness to engage in dialogue and embrace difference.

This does not mean, of course, that Seoul's position on the issue of unification has remained static. In the immediate postwar period an absorption of the North was accepted as a normal objective. It was only with Syngman Rhee's fall from power in 1960 that violence was explicitly renounced as a means of "restoring the northern area."[30] During Park Chung Hee's long period of rule from 1961 to 1979, South Korea viewed North Korea as being occupied by an illegal regime that was so alien in its ideology that it could not even be counted as part of the Korean nation.[31] Even during the subsequent presidential reigns of Chun Doo-hwan, Roh Tae-woo, and Kim Young-sam, unification by absorption was never explicitly ruled out. South Korean school textbooks, for instance, continued to call, either implicitly or explicitly, for unification by "having the South drive out the Communists and transform the North in a way that confirmed the South's superiority."[32] The first South Korean leader to explicitly revoke this model was Kim Dae-jung, who declared in his inaugural speech in 1998 that "we do not have any intention to undermine or absorb North Korea."[33] He consistently repeated this promise.[34] The United States eventually endorsed this position, even under the more confrontational Bush administration. Secretary of State Colin Powell declared in November 2002 that "we have no intention to impose our sovereignty upon their sovereignty."[35]

The South Korean and American positions of the last few years suggest a certain willingness to accept difference. At least the corresponding positions seem to recognize, as a semiofficial South Korean statement puts it, "that the national society has been divided into two."[36] But there is a clear gap between political rhetoric and political reality. In chapter 3, I outlined how, beneath a discourse of dialogue, the United States, particularly under the Bush administration, pursed a highly problematic form of crisis diplomacy that revolved around repeated nuclear threats toward Pyongyang. Washington continuously refuses to sign a nonaggression pact, which has been one of North Korea's key—and seemingly reasonable—demands for decades.[37] South Korea's Sunshine Policy is more nuanced and tolerant in its methods but perhaps not altogether different when it comes to fundamental objectives. While there is no more direct talk of "capitalizing" the North, contradictions are omnipresent. Consider two examples among many. President Kim announced on September 15, 1999, that he was "ready to hold dialogue and co-operate with the North" by adopting a policy of engagement that called for a "give and take approach."[38] On the very same day, however, government authorities indicted three South Korean political activists for violating the National Security Law. Their crime consisted of nothing but the act of traveling to Beijing in order to talk to North Koreans during a seminar.[39] The same tension between engagement and confrontation is visible in many other government policies and documents. The official website of the South Korean Army warns that "there are still spies who reject the liberal democratic system . . . and leftists who plot to weaken our military power by infiltrating the nation and the army." The site then offers tips about how to identify "spies, leftists and criminals." Among the potential suspects are "people who visit North Korea–related websites, . . . who praise the North when comparing the two Koreas, . . . who sympathize with the North's unification policies, . . . who reject the liberal democratic system, . . . who arouse class consciousness."[40]

That current South Korean and American rhetoric eschews immediate absorption is more a reflection of pragmatism than a desire to accept the North on its own terms. Engagement and the related soft landing scenario are seen as essential not only to avoid a dangerous military escalation but also to retain economic and political stability.

The German precedent can offer some revealing insights here. For one, it demonstrated amply that South Korea would never have the means to absorb the North as West Germany did the East. Most Korean decision makers and commentators thus concluded, as one prominent report did, that "Korea should avoid rushing or getting pressurized into unification."[41] But Germany is nevertheless seen as a key role model for the soft landing approach. Essential here is not the actual process of unification that took place between November 1989 and October 1990 but the long period of détente that preceded the collapse of East Germany. *Ostpolitik,* which was initiated by West Germany's chancellor Willy Brandt in the late 1960s, started a period of normalization between East and West. Egon Bahr, one of Brandt's key advisers, perhaps best expressed this policy through the key term *Wandel durch Annäherung* (transformation through rapprochement). *Ostpolitik* postponed the question of national unification in favor of reaching a modus vivendi with the vilified other half of the divided nation. After the *Grundlagenvertrag* (basic treaty) between the two German states was signed in 1972, cross-border communication and travel became increasingly frequent. By 1987 the number of cross-border visits reached three million per year.[42]

Ostpolitik required Brandt to recognize the Communist political system in East Germany. The latter, in turn, hoped to gain economic benefits and international legitimization, which it did.[43] But recognition abroad, Werner Pfennig stresses, "was not paralleled by legitimization and acceptance at home."[44] Contact with the West and the presence of alternative information sources increasingly undermined the East German regime and its attempt to win popular support. In the end *Ostpolitik* was a key factor behind the collapse of East Germany. Brandt prepared for unification, as Günter Grass stressed, although Brandt almost never spoke of it. But he did so by doing the obvious: easing travel restrictions, building transit routes, and encouraging family reunions, communication, and the like.[45]

The German model of normalization first, unification later is clearly appealing. It has permitted a reduction of enemy images and threat perceptions before the actual lifting of political boundaries, which is one of the reasons why German reunification occurred in a largely nonviolent manner. *Ostpolitik* can thus serve as a viable model for the soft landing approach in Korea. And in many ways it has. In an almost perfect rehearsal of *Ostpolitik* principles, Kim Dae-jung stressed that "reconciliation and cooperation between South and North is more important than the issue of unification."[46] Lim Dong-won, who is perhaps South Korea's equivalent to Egon Bahr, stressed likewise that unification is a "process" and that it "can be achieved in a gradual step-by-step manner rather than something that has to be realized overnight."[47] But caution is warranted. German unification occurred after more than two decades of engagement policy. Thus Korea has a long way to go in its attempt to dismantle hostile identity practices before unification. This is all the more the case because levels of hostility in Korea are far higher than they ever were in Germany.

NORMALIZATION AND THE POLITICS OF IDENTITY

Normalization carries certain risks, for it is, at least in the currently practiced version, still based on a model that ultimately rejects the notion of coexisting identity practices. Beneath a mantle of tolerance and engagement, processes of normalization also reflect the desire to impose one common norm, to erase difference in favor of a standard identity practice. All eight South Korean governments since 1948 were driven by this "strategic goal of hegemonic unification," stresses Koh Byung Chul. They all advocated, either through the hard or the soft landing scenario, an approach to unification "in which either the South Korean system, or a system embodying democratic values, prevails over the North Korean system."[48] Evidence in support of this argument is easy to find. Various versions of the South Korean *Defense White Paper,* for instance, foresee unification based on principles that "uphold basic values such as liberty, justice and human dignity."[49] They call for a peaceful construction of a unified nation but one that is carried out on South Korean terms. The Communist identity that has permeated the North for more than half a century is to be eradicated, for "an environment should be created in which the North can transform into an open society with a free market economy."[50] Desirable as this objective may appear to many people to be, it does not rest upon a willingness to accept a different model of social, political, and economic interactions.

The soft landing approach is still driven by the fundamental assumption that unification can occur only by reforming the North and bringing it, sooner or later, to the level where it can be integrated without difficulties into the value system and institutional structure that prevails in the South and in much of international society. Opening up North Korea is central to this process of normalization. In highly representative testimony to a committee of the U.S. House of Representatives, Scott Snyder emphasized that all assistance to Pyongyang should be judged on a "single criterion," namely, whether it can "facilitate North Korea's integration with the international community."[51] A similar argument is advanced by Moon Chung-in, one of South Korea's most influential political commentators and advocates of the Sunshine Policy. He too argues that the North "should be more actively brought into the world society so that it can turn into a normal state."[52] Normalization, Moon adds, entails acquiring a market economy and a democratic system. Other observers are more direct. Heiner Meulemann simply believes that Korean unification, like the German precedent, "will result from the demise of the communist political regime and will be asymmetric."[53] This assumption even is shared by many commentators who promote tolerance for difference. Min Kyung-Hwan, for instance, believes that unification will mean that "the South Koreans with capitalistic characteristics and the North Koreans with socialistic ones will have to live together in a capitalistic society."[54]

Aside from the merits of democracy and market economics, the present policy of rapprochement has not addressed—let alone overcome—the antagonistic identity constructs that have given rise to the conflict in the first place. The tactical elements of engagement may seem more tolerant than those of hard-line approaches. The ideal model may have shifted from an immediate and military-based absorption of the North to a more contained and controllable collapse scenario, but the fundamental strategic goal remains strikingly similar: to annihilate the archenemy and strip away its sense of identity. It is still a "long-term absorption theory," as one commentator put it.[55] The U.S. position under the Bush administration goes one step further. Dialogue and engagement are simply seen, in Victor Cha's words, "as the best practical way to build a coalition for punishment tomorrow."[56] In both the hard and soft version, engagement as articulated today remains problematic, for the underlying objective remains "winning the war," that is, a way of conquering the North by means other than weapons.[57]

In this chapter I examined a number of problems that have so far hampered the promotion of dialogue and face-to-face contacts. North Korea's fear of the outside world must be seen as the key obstacle. Pyongyang has embarked on a tightrope dance, attracting desperately needed foreign aid and capitalist trade partners while trying to resist pressures to open up its borders, which would increase the likelihood that a popular challenge could threaten Kim Jong Il's totalitarian regime. This double imperative dominates virtually all forms of engagement with the outside world. The concession to let South Korea's Hyundai Corporation bring foreign tourists to Mount Kumgang is one of many examples of this policy. It is designed to attract a maximum amount of foreign currency while minimizing tourists' contact with the local populace. It is difficult to anticipate how successful the regime will be in performing this balancing act. But one can at least try to understand the factors that fuel or mitigate it.

South Korea's approach to the promotion of engagement is not

without contradictions, either. Driven by a seemingly newfound tolerance for its archenemy across the dividing line, the Sunshine Policy
officially eschews an absorption of the North. Instead it advocates
a gradual rapprochement and eventual normalization of political
relations on the peninsula. This approach strongly resembles West
Germany's *Ostpolitik*, which successfully managed to prepare for
unification by promoting communication and face-to-face encounters across the dividing line. But *Ostpolitik* not only took decades
to unfold, it was also based on a process of normalization that foresaw, explicitly or implicitly, that a capitalist form of identity would
eventually prevail over a Communist one. The soft landing scenario
in Korea operates on a similar premise: that peace and unification
would emerge only when North Korea opens up and embraces the
values and virtues of democracy and market economics. The outcome remains a gradual and controllable collapse and absorption of
North Korea. It is thus not surprising that Pyongyang has opposed
from early on not only an application of *Ostpolitik* but also the very
term *normalization*.[58] Pyongyang's fears grew substantially when it
became clear that *Ostpolitik* contributed to the downfall of the East
German regime and its subsequent absorption by West Germany.
Mistrust of the Sunshine Policy has thus been manifested at various
levels, formal and informal. For instance, North Korean participants at one of the joint North-South conferences that took place
in the wake of the summit meeting of June 2000 stressed that they
mistrust the Sunshine Policy despite its advocacy of "cooperation,
peace and coexistence." The "real implication" behind this "super-
ficial message," so the argument goes, is a "policy aimed at long-
term systemic change, . . . bringing about unification by absorption."[59] Whether this perception is justified remains open to debate,
but that does not change its deep-seated existence and the political
challenges that emerge from it. As a result one needs to deal with
Pyongyang's fear of absorption and of the outside world in general.
And one needs to anticipate and minimize the specter of violence
that inevitably accompanies this fear.

Toward an Ethics of Difference

North and South need to view each other as "the other within oneself."
—SONG DU-YUL, *DONGA ILBO*

To redefine its relations to others, a constituency must also modify the shape of its own identity.
—WILLIAM E. CONNOLLY, *THE ETHOS OF PLURALIZATION*

Drawing attention to the contradictions and problems of normalization, as I did in chapters 4 and 5, is not to oppose engagement or to eschew democratic values. Quite the contrary. An active engagement policy is badly needed on the peninsula, but in order to overcome some of the most difficult existing security dilemmas, the policy must integrate an understanding and appreciation of difference. Democracy is crucial to this endeavor too, for in its essence a democratic ethos is all about finding ways of appreciating and redeeming difference. In this chapter I will outline the contours of an ethics of difference.

An ethics of difference demonstrates why and how an alternative to present insecurity politics would have to be based on a concept of justice that subsumes, at its core, a fundamentally different conception of the relationship between self and other. An articulation of an adequate security policy must combine the ongoing and encouraging search for dialogue with a new and more radical willingness to accept that the other's sense of identity and politics may be inherently incommensurable with one's own. Expressed in other words, a peaceful rapprochement can occur only if a multitude of identity practices are recognized as legitimate and, indeed, as essential to laying the foundation for what one day may be a truly unified, or at least peaceful, peninsula.

In this chapter I will illustrate the requirements for and potential of such an approach through a variety of examples, most notably the relationship between the remembrance of things past and the possibilities for reconciliation. The trauma of the Korean War continues to haunt the peninsula, not least because North and South Korean historical interpretations are closely intertwined with the antagonistic identity practices that have shaped the present climate of confrontation and fear. I argue that a more tolerant and peaceful future can be constructed only once the notion of a single historical narrative gives way to multiple visions of the past and the future. The ethical challenge, then, consists of finding dialogical agreements on certain historical "truth" claims, without necessarily embedding them in a single interpretative modality.

THE SPECTER OF WAR AND THE SPECTER OF COLLAPSE

Before outlining what an ethics of difference entails, I will demonstrate that such an approach is essential for two reasons: to deal with the specter of war and the specter of a North Korean collapse. Earlier in the book, most notably in chapter 3, I dealt in detail with the danger of a military escalation. Taking the rhetoric of evil of the Bush administration as an example, I have shown how a refusal to accept difference, or an attempt to erase it, only perpetuates existing security dilemmas. By contrast, the dangers of a military confrontation can be substantially reduced if decision makers and defense analysts make an attempt to understand how threats are perceived from the other side and how these perceptions are part of an interactive security dynamic in which all actors are implicated, including the United States and South Korea.

A second major source of instability and violence on the peninsula is the possibility of a North Korean collapse. Most political commentators, but also most key decision makers, acknowledge that an uncontrolled collapse of North Korea could be highly problematic, precipitating anything from a civil war to a major refugee crisis. The soft landing scenario, which is accepted in one way or another by all great powers involved in the Korean peninsula, is geared precisely toward avoiding an uncontrolled collapse of the North.

Whether the soft landing approach can actually prevent a sudden disintegration of the North Korean system is an entirely different question. So far, predictions of an imminent collapse have been proved wrong, although some scholars and politicians regularly warn that the system "shows explicit signs of impending implosion,"[1] that "we may now be approaching the end game in the Korean peninsula's division."[2] But most observers portray North Korea as relatively stable, despite famine conditions and a highly anachronistic political and economic ideology. The same opinion is shared by many defectors, even former elites who had insight into the decision-making procedures. They tend to believe that the lack of oppositional space makes a popular uprising rather unlikely.[3]

Although the North Korean political system displays a remarkable degree of stability, its collapse cannot be excluded. Indeed, the likelihood of a North Korean collapse increases in direct proportion to the promotion of dialogue and face-to-face encounters. The German precedent is a key reminder that change can come very suddenly and against the plans and wishes of political elites. This is why it would be unwise to put all trust and hope in the soft landing scenario, desirable as it undoubtedly is. Some schools have already drawn attention to the dangers. "The North," Nicholas Eberstadt believes, "is more likely to implode than to be integrated gradually." The feasibility of gradualism hinges on a number of unlikely scenarios, he stresses, such as the assumption that "the North Korean government will someday embrace a program of economic liberalization and somehow survive to complete the decade of transformation the program would entail."[4] Although Paik Nak-Chung represents a different political position, he is doubtful of such a scenario as well. He does not anticipate unification in the near future but believes that when it comes, it will be a swift "German type."[5] Likewise, Martin Hart-Landsberg stresses that a key lesson of the German precedent is that a "gradual unification by absorption" is not possible.[6] We do indeed know that once the Iron Curtain was gone, retaining two politically and economically distinct national entities became virtually impossible. The push west was simply too strong to hold back what Jürgen Habermas called "D-Mark Nationalismus."[7] As soon as the border was open, hundreds of thousands of east German citizens left for the west, hoping for better working and living conditions. But mass migration was not the only factor pressing for a quick unification. There are ethical considerations too, and they are highly relevant for Korea. How would it be possible to justify keeping an ideologically united nation divided into two political parts, one rich, the other poor? Even the best-case scenario, one that revolves around an optimal economic approach to unification, suggests that "after a decade of adjustment the level of North Korea's per capita income would still be less than 40% that of the South's."[8] Keeping Northerners, particularly young ones, from migrating south in search of opportunities will be difficult, if not impossible, under such conditions.

The exact scenario of North Korea's demise cannot be determined. A sudden collapse seems more likely than a gradual integration. The timing of the demise is open as well. North Korea may collapse tomorrow. Or it may survive for another decade or more. But the disintegration of the present system seems merely a matter of time. In an age of globalization and neoliberal economics, an authoritarian regime based on a self-reliant Communist ideology is unlikely to survive in the long run.

Aside from avoiding a military confrontation, thinking ahead to what life will be like after the demise of North Korea should be a central concern of an adequate security framework for the peninsula. Major problems will undoubtedly emerge, particularly if policies of engagement and normalization put all hope in the soft landing scenario, and even more so if that scenario continues to be dominated by a long-term absorption model that fails to accommodate different identity practices.

An ethics of difference ought to be an essential element of a long-term security strategy, for the antagonistic identity constructs that emerged with the division of the peninsula will undoubtedly survive and pose problems long after the demise of North Korea. Here too the German precedent is highly revealing. In chapter 2, I outlined in detail the major identity differences that exist between east and west, even more than a dozen years after unification. These differences, which had been formed during the period of national division and have to do with people's understanding of themselves, cannot easily be overcome, even in the context of a politically unified and ethnically homogeneous society. And these differences continued to pose a variety of psychological, social, political, and economic difficulties. But the problems that Germany experienced are likely to pale in comparison to what awaits Korea. The two German states never fought a war against each other, and the hostilities that nevertheless existed could be substantially reduced during two decades of *Ostpolitik*. Both mitigating factors are absent in Korea, where a three-year war devastated the peninsula. The memory of this traumatic event continues to shape virtually all aspects of politics on the peninsula. Given these highly problematic residues, and the almost total lack of interaction between the two parts, identity constructs in Korea are far more entrenched, hostile, and volatile than they ever were in Germany.

OUTLINE OF AN ETHICS OF DIFFERENCE

The success of future efforts toward Korean rapprochement hinges largely on how successful the leaders and their respective societies are in dealing with the legacy of half a century of division, hostility, and grief. Dialogue alone cannot pave the way to reconciliation. No matter how successful dialogical interactions between the opposing sides are, they will always have to deal with the remainder, with positions that cannot be subsumed into compromise or perhaps cannot even be apprehended from the vantage point of those who do not live and represent them. If current efforts at engagement with the North are not followed up by a more tolerant approach to the fundamental values espoused by the other side, progress will either stall or be accompanied by the constant specter of a relapse into violence.

Another form of ethics is necessary to deal with this problematic remainder—not an ethics of dialogue but an ethics of accepting the other as other, of not subsuming her/him/it into one's own viewpoint. The task ahead thus consists of articulating identity in less antagonistic ways and in rendering these articulations politically acceptable. The work of Emmanuel Levinas offers some guidelines here, for it revolves around an attempt to develop an ethics of responsibility that refuses to hammer difference into sameness. Ethics then becomes a question of developing a relationship to alterity that displays understanding of and respect for the other's different identity performances.[9] In an ideal scenario such respect would go beyond tolerance, for tolerance assumes a basic standard against which anything else is to be judged. Accepting alterity, by contrast, requires abandoning this privileged standpoint, perhaps even at those moments when one is deeply convinced of the superiority of one's own moral position. Some even argue that an engagement with alterity is most crucial precisely at those moments when the other's position poses a fundamental danger to one's own values.[10]

The antagonistic identity constructs that have emerged and evolved during the five decades of Korea's division cannot simply be erased by a redrawing of political boundaries. Differences between the two Koreas are too deeply rooted to be merged into one common form of identity, at least in the near future. In the context of such a well-entrenched and well-protected separation of diametrically opposed identity performances, it is imperative that an ethical position on national division and unification be based on an approach that does not subsume the other into the self. As a result the security situation on the Korean peninsula will remain volatile as long as current identity constructs continue to guide policy formation. A soft landing approach may well be the most reasonable and desirable scenario, but it can unfold and develop to its fullest potential only once it incorporates, in a central manner, issues of identity and difference.

The key is not to deny difference but to make it part of a new, more pluralistically defined vision of identity and unity that may one day replace the present, violence-prone demarcation of self and other. A few isolated Korean scholars occasionally draw attention to the need for such an approach. Kwon Hyeok-beom, for instance, argues for a "politics of difference" or a "discourse of difference." Although this would require both Korean states to renounce "the assumption that they have the superior system," he stresses that it would not require that the South accept everything about the North and its current governing style.[11] Perhaps the most sustained, book-length defense of an ethics of difference, at least in English, has been advanced by the anthropologist Roy Richard Grinker. He calls upon Koreans to abandon the myth of homogeneity and embark on a process of mourning—that is, accept that Korea has been divided for half a century and that different identity practices have emerged during this period. Grinker therefore argues for a vision of heterogeneity and a "plural society in which north and south Koreans can one day live."[12]

Practical examples of an ethics of difference are more difficult to find. Most existing unifications of divided nations were carried out according to the absorption model. This is the case for Germany, Yemen, and Vietnam. The latter, though, is a prime example of a Communist society that successfully opened up and embraced economic reforms without collapsing. The same is, of course, the case with China, whose arrangement with Hong Kong and Macao also offers a potentially relevant example of a country's tolerating different systems within it. North Korea suggested a similar arrangement, termed the "Democratic Confederal Republic of Koryo." First advanced by Kim Il Sung in 1960 and reiterated several times since, this proposal was designed to promote a unified peninsula that nevertheless tolerates two different political systems. This solution, so the argument went, would give the two Korean states the chance to maintain their respective ideologies and institutions but at the same time establish a nationally unified government, the so-called Supreme National Confederal Assembly.[13] Despite its seemingly visionary and tolerant nature, Pyongyang's proposal was doomed to fail, not least because North Korea itself is the example par excellence of a political system that denies difference.

REMEMBERING AND FORGETTING THE KOREAN WAR

To examine the potential and limits of an ethics of difference in Korea, I now return to a theme that I introduced in chapter 1: the use and abuse of history. Both Korean states have gone to great lengths to promote historical narratives that legitimize their own regime while discrediting that of the rival across the DMZ. I drew upon a series of existing studies of school textbooks, most notably by Denis Hart, to demonstrate how the incorporation of a "national other" has become an integral part of identity politics on each side.[14] Central here are understandings of the origin and nature of the Korean War. No other event on the peninsula has shaped the past and present as profoundly. Each side sponsors an entirely different narrative, one that remains dominated by the memory of pain and death, as well as by the desire to overcome this trauma through an annihilation of the other side.

South Korean school textbooks hold that during the late 1940s the North Korean Communists tried to topple the Southern government by promoting various demonstrations and labor strikes. When these efforts failed, the North wanted peace talks but in fact secretly planned an invasion of the South. Once Kim Il Sung had received Russian and Chinese support for an invasion, he ordered his armies to cross the DMZ on the morning of June 25, 1950, thus starting the war.[15] North Korean school textbooks, by contrast, present the war as a criminal aggression for which the U.S. government and its South Korean "puppet regime" are responsible. This text stresses that Pyongyang initiated peace talks and tried everything possible to prevent a conflict but that the South rejected the peace offer and, on the morning of June 25, 1950, crossed the thirty-eighth parallel and marched north.[16] There are similarly incompatible narratives with regard to other aspects of the war, such as its evolution and the reason for the cessation of direct hostilities.

For half a century now both sides have rehearsed their ideologically tainted memories of the war. They have done so ad infinitum while making every effort to shield their populations from the diametrically opposed narrative promoted by the other side. One of the most explicit confirmations of how much these two versions of the past diverge, and how they influence societal consciousness, is that most North Korean defectors are "simply stunned" when they are first confronted with South Korean representations of the Korean War.[17]

While the North usually uses the term *Choseon Haebang Jeonjaeng* (national liberation war), South Korean history textbooks tend to present the conflict by referring to what is considered its starting date, June 25, 1950. Thus the 1979 version of textbooks calls the war the "6.25 incident"; in 1982 it is the "6.25 intrusion" and in 1990 the "6.25 war."[18] This way of labeling the conflict puts emphasis on its beginning and thus on questions of causality and responsibility. Several revisionist historians, most notably Bruce Cumings, have pointed out that questions of responsibility are far too complex to be attributed to a single side. He also believes that historians and politicians must look beyond issues of origin and causality. People are no longer interested in who started the American Civil War or the Vietnam War, Cumings points out. And he thinks that Koreans will one day "reconcile, as Americans eventually did, with the wisdom that civil wars have no single authors."[19] There already are a variety of revisionist South Korean historians, such as Choi Jang-jip, Chong Hae-gu, and Kim Nam-sik, who have advanced representations that defy the entrenched black-and-white logic that constitutes North Korea as the evil other and only cause of the war.[20]

The trauma of the Korean War is undoubtedly still too fresh to stop debating and disagreeing about questions of origin and responsibility. But the arguments advanced by Cumings and revisionist South Korean historians get to the heart of what the war is today: a past event, a contentious memory, a site for political struggles.

To move from trauma to reconciliation some aspects of the war have to be "forgotten." Nietzsche stresses that the past suffocates the present unless we forget it. He calls upon people to have the courage to "break with the past in order to live."[21] Forgetting, in this sense, does not mean ignoring what happened. Forgetting, it must be remembered, is a natural process, an inevitable aspect of remembering. We all do it, whether we want it or not. We cannot possibly remember everything. We cannot give every event the same weight. Our memory of the past is the result of a process through which certain events and interpretations are remembered and prioritized, while others are relegated to secondary importance or forgotten altogether. This is particularly the case with a major event like the Korean War, which is far too complex to be remembered in its totality.

The task of historians is to select the few facts, perspectives, and interpretations that ought to be remembered. The combination of forgetting and remembering is as inevitable as it is political. History is, in fact, as much about the present and the future as it is about the past. At the time an event takes place there is no memory. Historical awareness emerges later and by necessity includes values and interests that have nothing to do with the original occurrence. History, in this sense, is one of the prime sites of politics. Nietzsche is particularly critical of periods during which historical understandings lack critical awareness of this process—situations, say, when powerful rulers fail to gain legitimacy on their own and thus rely on the misappropriation of historical figures and events to justify their form of dominance.[22] Such is undoubtedly the case in contemporary Korea, where history has been geared far more toward supporting particular regimes than toward actually representing what happened in the past.

But South Korea also displays signs of what Nietzsche calls "critical histories": attempts to challenge the notion of a single historical reality and create the political space in which diverging narratives of the past can compete with each other, perhaps even respect each other, despite the differences that divide them. A recent example of a breakthrough in this direction, timid as it may well be, can be found in revisions of history textbooks. Several generations of history texts that are used in South Korea's schools have studiously avoided even mentioning the role that Northern Communist guerillas played in the fight against the Japanese colonial occupiers. Textbooks released in early 2003 for the first time deal with a 1937 clash between Japanese colonial forces and resistance fighters allegedly led by Kim Il Sung, the future leader of North Korea. The passage reads as follows:

> In June, 1937, the Northeast Anti-Japanese United Army crossed the Yalu river and seized Bocheonbo, south of Hamgyong province. . . . The Japanese were shocked by the attack and began to aggressively crack down on the Korean national movement. After Korea was liberated from Japan, Kim Il Sung was revered by North Koreans as a leader of Korean independence. . . . Some academics in South Korea have been critical of North Korea for exaggerating the battle.[23]

This account is undoubtedly far more balanced and less hostile than the overtly ideological representations that had prevailed for decades. A representative of the Ministry of Education called it an attempt to present "strictly the facts."[24] That is hardly possible, of course, but even so, the more balanced representation still created protest from conservative segments of South Korea's society. Park Sung Soo, head of the Institute of Documenting Accurate History, warned of succumbing to North Korea's propaganda. He argued that "the reference to the battle needs to be removed or it may taint the pure minds of youth."[25]

Other attempts to present a more accurate account of Korea's past met similar and similarly strong opposition. Grinker presents a highly insightful analysis of a South Korean television feature on the Korean War. The program, broadcast in 1996, was aimed at elementary-school children. In contrast to "normal" historical representations, the program did not portray North Koreans as evil, nor did it clearly blame them for causing the war.[26] It simply sought to present the war as a human and national tragedy. Here too opposition emerged immediately. Journalists argued that the program was "too neutral and objective," that it failed to clearly identify the North as the side that caused the war. There was also opposition to the relatively detached terms *Northern soldiers* and *Southern soldiers,* which were used instead of the usual concepts, such as *Northern Communists* and *invasion of the South.*[27]

The struggle over historical consciousness in South Korea partly reflects generational tensions. The television program about the war was produced by a young Korean who was eager to move beyond the memory of hatred and fear. Opposition to such revisionist history tends to come from the older generation of Koreans, from people who experienced the war and are thus directly marked by the trauma it caused.[28] Duncan Bell's distinction between memory and myth is helpful in conceptualizing the generational tensions and disagreements in Korea. He argues that the concept of memory is usually used in an imprecise manner, as a way simply of referring to collective representations of history.[29] However, such representations can assume multiple, conflicting forms. Consequently, Bell proposes that we limit the concept of memory to the experiences of people who directly witnessed and shared the events under consideration. Memory, he argues, is always anchored in common experience, as is the case, for instance, with the older generation of Koreans who lived through the war. Such memories, he continues, should be distinguished from myths, from the more general processes of generating national (or other) identities by representing the past through media- and state-sanctioned discourses, school curricula, art, music, and so forth. The latter mode of understanding history is the only way in which many of the younger Koreans have come to "know" the Korean War. That a certain tension emerges from these different genres of historical representation is thus inevitable.

EXCHANGING NARRATIVE MEMORIES

Acknowledging the political and inherently contestable dimension of history is one of the most important ways of overcoming the cycle of violence that has dominated Korea for half a century. The memory of pain and death is far too strong for a single historical narrative to emerge in the foreseeable future. Given the deeply entrenched antagonisms on the peninsula, there will necessarily be different interpretations of how to understand and represent the war.

Recognizing the existence of historical differences is a crucial element in the effort to promote a culture of reconciliation. Paul Ricoeur stresses that by "acknowledging that the history of an event involves a conflict of several interpretations and memories, we in turn open up the future."[30] Linking an ethics of difference and a promotion of a tolerant historical consciousness entails a variety of different dimensions. For one, it necessitates what Richard Kearney calls an "exchange of narrative memories." Although writing in the context of Northern Ireland, Kearney's recommendation is just as relevant for Korea, for such exchanges would allow the opposing sides to "see each other through alternative eyes."[31]

North and South need to open up political spaces in which it becomes possible to contemplate the other's memory of the past, even if this memory appears distorted and inherently wrong. Such a level of tolerance is possible only once each side accepts within its own political culture the possibility of multiple pasts, presents, and futures. Dipesh Chakrabarty uses the term *minority histories* and refers to the need to protect various versions of the past, even if they contradict each other and cannot be subsumed into prevailing narratives of the nation.[32] This is precisely why the work of revisionist historians is important. Their interpretations and conclusions may well be contentious, but far more important is that they defy the prevailing black-and-white logic and thus open up spaces for multiple narratives of the past. Promoting and protecting such an ethics of difference is an ongoing and inevitably incomplete process. Consider some of the contradictions that became evident in the work of revisionist South Korean historians, such as Choi Jang-jip and Chong Hae-gu. They may well have overcome the prevailing tendency to abuse history and to discredit the North at any cost, but they have done so through a new nationalist narrative that entails its own problems and contradictions. Or so Henry Em believes. He argues that these revisionist narratives, although critical in a variety of ways, are still based on the assumption of a "preexisting subject." As a result they too run the risk of oppressing and suppressing other identities, for instance, those of marginalized segments of society, such as women and ethnic Chinese residents in Korea.[33]

The greatest impetus toward a historical awareness that respects difference may not come from historians, and certainly not from politicians, generals, and diplomats, but from the realm of the everyday. One highly positive development is that a select number of North

Korean films are now screened in the South, as, for instance, at the Pusan International Film Festival.[34] And an increasing number of South Korean films defy the tendency to vilify the North. Recent releases include *Heuk Su Seon* (Last Witness, 2001), *Swiri* (1999), and *Joint Security Area* (2000). The domestic and international success of the last is particularly important, for it is one of the rare feature films that clearly resists perpetuating the entrenched stereotypical image of cold and evil North Koreans. Instead, *Joint Security Area* tells the story of how a small group of soldiers from both sides develops a friendship, secretly and against all odds. In the end conflict becomes inevitable, and the soldiers must choose country over friendship. But the film is nevertheless a milestone, for it portrays soldiers on both sides as normal Koreans, with a variety of similar emotions, concerns, and interests. This contrasts quite sharply not only with the realist security discourses that still dominate high politics but also with more general outside perceptions of Korea. A recent James Bond film, *Die Another Day* (2002), portrays North Koreans in the stereotypical role of evil madmen bent on destroying the world. Not surprisingly, there was considerable public protest against the Cold War antics of 007, not only in the North but also in the South.[35] While Her Majesty's secret agent, judging the world from neoimperial London, was clearly out of sync with the need for reconciliation on the peninsula, *Joint Security Area* has demonstrated, as one commentator puts it, that there is a "surging demand for films and literary works that can be shared by the two sides to promote understanding and accommodation."[36] While such works offer possibilities for healing, there is also a certain skepticism regarding them. Consider, for instance, that *Joint Security Area* received a restrictive "R" rating in South Korea, rather than an "M," for it was judged that young people would not have the maturity necessary to watch a film that presents North Korea in a favorable light.

The role of humor, literature, and theater is equally important. William Callahan, for example, draws attention to the often-neglected significance of laughter.[37] Likewise, Choi Chungmoo examines how folk theater, such as the *madang guk,* may overcome stereotypical images of the other. A mixture of ritual and carnivalesque communal festival, folk theater is able to challenge the notion of a single narrative of the nation. *Madang guk* can thus be seen as a cultural practice that tolerates a variety of different, overlapping, or often even contradictory beliefs and narratives. The promotion of such diversity is all the more significant because folk theater is actually able to reach and politicize a significant part of the population.[38] Mikhail Bakhtin's examination of the sixteenth-century French author François Rabelais is perhaps the best-known study that demonstrates the power of such carnivalesque interventions in the public sphere. Rabelais's grotesque and satirical stories were part of a popular culture of laughter—a subculture, so to speak—that was deeply subversive, for it opposed, even ridiculed, the seriousness and hypocrisy of the official feudal culture. It mocked the clergy and its rigid Christian rituals. In this sense, Bakhtin stresses, laughter was freedom because it "celebrated temporary liberation from the prevailing truth and from the established order; it marked the suspension of all hierarchical rank, privileges, norms, and prohibitions."[39] This suspension and, in a more general sense, the language of the marketplace and of carnival created possibilities for uninhibited speech. Laughter opened up, at least for a short moment, a glimpse of utopian freedom, a life beyond the Christian mythology of death and eternal punishment. Laughter, Bakhtin argues, creates distance from dogmatism and pedantry, from fear and intimidation. It shatters the belief that life has a single meaning.[40]

Perhaps even more revealing are some of the dynamics that take place in the everyday context of teaching history in South Korea's schools. History instruction illustrates the constant oscillation between, on the one hand, the deeply entrenched practice of imposing and disseminating a single and highly ideological narrative of the past and, on the other hand, the newly emerging desire to advance a more balanced historical consciousness. At some levels teachers have few options when it comes to selecting historical sources. The publication of history texts is, as I discussed in chapter 1, strictly controlled and censored by the Ministry of Education. Each school may well be able to choose among different publicly and privately published texts, but all need the approval of the ministry.

In the course of a joint project that we were working on, my colleague Hoang Young-ju conducted a series of interviews with administrators, teachers, and students of various secondary schools in South Korea in 2002 and 2003. They revealed a significant grassroots willingness to open up spaces for the promotion of alternative understandings of the past. An official at the Busan Metropolitan Office of Education, for instance, suggested that narrative memories could be exchanged between North and South by making available, on both sides, a range of commonly agreed-upon historical documents and teaching methods, which could then be used in addition to the official textbooks that each side uses.[41] A similar readiness to innovate was present among the teaching staff of several schools. Younger teachers in particular tended to be increasingly keen to supplement the prescribed textbooks with alternative methods, such as historical simulation, television documentaries, cartoons, and newspapers.[42]

But these efforts are hampered by a variety of obstacles. One of the main problems is the nature of South Korea's education system, especially the emphasis that it places on standard entrance exams for universities. Success or failure in these exams determines to a large extent a student's educational opportunities, even his or her entire professional and personal future. The exams are set and administered in an unusually strict and standardized manner. Although the most important disciplines are mathematics, Korean, and English, knowing the content of the state-sponsored history textbook, even memorizing it in parts, is still essential for succeeding on the exam.[43] This institutionalized practice is all the more fateful because it comes on top of a long cultural tradition that emphasizes memorization as part of the learning process.[44] As a result teachers have only limited possibilities of diverging from the standard texts, even though no official rules prevent them from doing so. One interviewee pointed out that he tried to use a variety of auxiliary means, such as newspapers, to teach the Korean War and modern history in general. But he was pressured to abandon this practice, not only by school authorities but also, and mostly, by parents, for they feared that students "would not study enough for the university entrance exam."[45] Other interviewees related similar experiences, noting that "usually students want to memorize the content of textbooks for preparing the exam."[46]

AGAINST RELATIVISM AND ESSENTIALIZING DIFFERENCE

The experience of teaching history in South Korea shows that tolerance simply takes time to emerge, that entrenched identity practices cannot be transformed overnight. Reconciliation is a long and ongoing process. But there are also more direct, or at least more directly recognizable, challenges to an ethics of difference. They involve the pitfalls of relativism and the dangers of essentializing difference. The first could presumably lead to a situation in which one can no longer advance and defend moral and political judgments. The second could eventually engender an apartheid society in which differences are not tolerated but are used to confirm and assert a single notion of identity. First, to the latter point.

If history is to be placed in the service of reconciliation, it has to go beyond merely acknowledging that the two sides have different notions of the past. Leaving it at that would only entrench prevailing antagonisms and thus legitimize or even intensify the existing conflict. An ethics of difference must seek to create the conditions under which different identities can coexist and explore common ground. Here too the role of the Korean War is essential, for a process of reconciliation would need to seek out the lowest common denominator that could unite the diverging historical narratives on the peninsula. Susan Dwyer identifies three stages in the process of reconciliation. The first, she says, consists of an effort to find agreement on "the barest of facts." The second stage involves identifying a range of different interpretations of the events. And the third stage would entail narrowing things down to a limited set of interpretations that the two sides can tolerate.[47] While such a goal of agreeing to disagree seems modest, the path to achieving it is littered with seemingly insurmountable obstacles. The first hurdle alone is gargantuan, for Dwyer defines agreeing on "the barest of facts" as finding a clear view of "who did what to whom and when."[48] In Korea these "bare facts" are, of course, precisely the major point of contention—and the source of trauma and hatred. And even if there were agreement on certain truth claims, promoting them may not necessarily bring more justice. Kwon Hyeok-beom, for instance, warns of searching for common roots between North and South and using them as a basis for reconciliation. The strong masculinism that still dominates both parts of the peninsula promotes identity practices that constitute women as "kind, gentle, and subservient." Thus grounding reconciliation in common Confucian values may only strengthen the patriarchal social order and lead to further discrimination against women.[49]

While finding and developing commonalties between North and South is a major challenge, developing tolerance for the differences that remain may be even more difficult. Such tolerance requires an ethics of difference that is often dismissed, for it tends to be associated with relativism. Many international relations scholars are concerned that a postmodern embrace of difference would lead to a situation where anything goes and "any narrative is as valid as another."[50] As a result, these scholars fear, we would no longer be able to defend certain values and political projects, such as democracy or human rights. But there are no reasons why an appreciation of difference would prevent us from judging and choosing between opposing values or political options. To the contrary, understanding and engaging questions of difference is essential for understanding political challenges and taking informed decisions. For instance, historians who open up alternative interpretations of the past actually reduce the danger of relativism, for they increase the sources available for judging whether our understanding of history is appropriate. In so doing, historians may oppose "the manipulation of narratives by . . . providing a space for confrontation between opposing testimonies."[51]

Making choices, drawing lines, and defending them are inevitable, particularly in a context like Korea, where interests and perspectives clash. An unconditional acceptance of otherness cannot—and indeed should not—always work in practice. There are moments when the reassertion and imposition of one perspective or value system over another becomes desirable, perhaps even a political imperative. But successful and fair solutions to political challenges are more likely to emerge if positions are not dogmatically asserted but carefully justified through a critical and self-reflective understanding of the tensions between identity and difference.

Advancing an ethics of difference does not entail abandoning the ability to judge, particularly when it comes to questions of responsibility for war and conflict on the Korean peninsula. Gerrit Gong stresses that addressing such questions will be one of the main challenges in a unified Korea.[52] Claus Offe, writing about the task of coming to terms with Germany's divided past, argues likewise that a general amnesty is out of the question.[53] But one must recall at the same time that the institution of amnesty is not to be equated with amnesia. Paul Ricoeur, for instance, stresses that there is a duty to forget as much as there is a duty to remember, for "the duty to remember is a duty to teach, whereas the duty to forget is a duty to

go beyond anger and hatred."[54] Richard Kearney adds that "genuine amnesty" is a way of remembering that goes beyond a form of
memory dominated by "the deterministic stranglehold of violent
obsession and revenge."[55] Korea needs such a willingness to forgive
in the service of healing and reconciliation: it needs a way out of the
cycle of violence and hatred that has dominated interactions on the
peninsula for half a century now.

The role of history is illustrative, not least because it forces us to
confront questions of evidence and truth. Not any version of the past
can be sustained. Although the content of a historical account is inevitably intertwined with the values espoused by the narrator, a his-
torian cannot simply make up events and interpretations. Ricoeur
seeks to avoid an abuse of memory by grounding it in "what really
happened."[56] This is, of course, an aspiration that inevitably remains
unfulfilled, for history is a form of representation, and a representation is always incomplete and, at least to some extent, distorted.
It cannot capture the object that it represents as it is, void of perception and perspective.[57] Ricoeur stresses the need to supplement
historical memory with documentary and archival evidence.[58] Even
so-called postmodern historians stress the need for rules of scholarship and verification. Hayden White, for instance, admits that
every historical narrative contains a "desire to moralize" the event
that it seeks to capture. But to count as "proper history," White
emphasizes, the narrative "must manifest a proper concern for the
judicious handling of evidence, and it must honor the chronological
order of the original occurrence of events."[59] Chakrabarty, likewise,
defends the notion of "minority histories" while rejecting relativist
positions that may dismiss such accounts as purely personal or arbitrary. He stresses that an alternative memory of the past can only
enrich, or be absorbed into, the mainstream historical discourse if
the following questions can be answered in the affirmative: "Can
the story be told/crafted? And does it allow for a rationally defen-
sible point of view or position from which to tell the story?"[60]

Some of the highly ideological and hagiographical narratives that
make up North Korea's national mythology are unlikely to with-
stand a confrontation with rigorous historical testing principles.
But the same can be said about aspects of South Korea's historical
consciousness as well. A recent example of the need to revise the
official memory of the Korean War can be found with regard to the

No Gun Ri massacre. For decades citizens of the small village of No Gun Ri had insisted that on a summer day in July 1950, American soldiers had machine-gunned hundreds of civilians under a railroad bridge near the village. But U.S. military officials, as well as the South Korean government, consistently denied that such events ever occurred, arguing that they could find no basis for the allegations. No history text mentioned the event. Public discussion of the issue emerged only in the late 1990s, when a dozen former U.S. soldiers gave evidence to an investigative team from the Associated Press that largely confirmed the claims that No Gun Ri's inhabitants had advanced for decades. After a yearlong review the U.S. Army had to admit officially that "U.S. ground forces fired toward refugees in the vicinity of No Gun Ri during this period. . . . As a result, an unknown number of refugees were killed or injured."[61]

Histories are never finished. They are written and rewritten constantly, reflecting the emergence of new evidence as well as the evolution of political doctrines and knowledge conventions. This constant reassessment of the past is both a source of tension and a chance to find pathways toward a more peaceful political environment. In few parts of the world is this process of remembering and forgetting more controversial and volatile than in divided Korea, where the memory of war and death continues to dominate virtually all aspects of politics and society.

I have argued in this chapter that a route from trauma to reconciliation can open up if an ethics of dialogue is supplemented with an ethics of difference: a willingness to recognize and deal with the different and incompatible identities that developed in the divided parts of Korea during the last half-century. I have sought to outline the contours of an ethics of difference by supplementing a variety of theoretical sources with an effort to identify attempts to translate these ideas into practice. The latter undoubtedly remain isolated efforts, but the democratizing South Korean society shows increasing signs of developing a more tolerant attitude. Among the examples are efforts by historians and teachers to promote tolerance for multiple narratives of the past. Although neglected by security experts, such low-key efforts are crucial for developing a culture of reconciliation.

Advancing and developing an ethics of difference is important for several reasons: to avoid an escalation of military tensions on the peninsula, to lay the foundations for a sustainable policy of engagement, and to prepare for some of the conflicts that would emerge in the eventuality of a North Korean collapse.

I have focused here on the few signs of hope that exist on the Korean peninsula at the moment: efforts within South Korea to promote aspects of an ethics of difference. These efforts remain timid and isolated, and they have so far not been reciprocated by the North. But this in itself is not discouraging. Promoting an ethics of difference as part of a reconciliation process inevitably takes time. Entrenched identities cannot be uprooted overnight nor can the antagonistic political attitudes and practices that are intertwined with these identities. But there are more immediate challenges too, most notably the danger that an ethics of difference may either promote more conflict or generate a form of relativism that prevents us from judging and defending particular political projects. Neither fear is justified, at least not if an ethics of difference is articulated and applied in a consistent manner. Indeed, if there is a source of tension and conflict on the peninsula, it is located precisely in the attempt to erase difference and impose one memory of the past and one vision for the future. This is why the most serious cause of violence today stems not from interactions with difference, but, as William Connolly convincingly argues, from doctrines and movements that suppress difference by trying to reinstate a unified faith in one form of identification.[62] Tolerating different coexisting narratives does not prevent making judgments about their content or desirability. Quite to the contrary, reasonable decisions about key political and ethical challenges can be made only after taking into account a variety of perspectives, interests, and arguments. Repressing the difference will neither lead to better decisions nor avoid the fact that they are based on certain political and moral values.

Conclusion

Occasionally I hear talk from the dead
of the Korea of centuries past.
They usually leave out a few things, I think.
After all, how could they say everything
in one brief resurrection?

—KO UN, "DISCIPLINE AND AFTER"

Korea is an open book whose story line has yet to be written to the end. Whether peace or conflict will prevail is to a great extent dependent on the mind-sets that will guide not only future decision makers but also the societies at large in both Koreas. I have sought to advance a number of suggestions about how to understand and engage this ongoing political struggle. Two components have been essential in this endeavor.

The first task consisted of presenting the conflict on the peninsula not only in conventional ideological and geopolitical terms but also, and primarily, as a confrontation between competing identities. Thus I examined in Part I how antagonistic identity practices have emerged historically and how they continue to shape the current conflict. Of central importance here is understanding how the division of the peninsula and especially the legacy of the Korean War have dominated subsequent political dynamics. An unusually high degree of state control of security policy led to a situation in which each side sought to legitimize itself by demonizing its arch-enemy across the dividing line. The result was two sets of diametri-cally opposed identity patterns—one shaped by Communist and the other by capitalist ideologies—that continuously fuel hatred and fear. A political crisis is thus always already underway on the penin-sula. The question is simply when and under what circumstances it reemerges. The latest standoff became apparent in 2002 when U.S. foreign policy suddenly became more aggressive and a controversy erupted in regard to North Korea's nuclear ambition.

An inquiry into the emergence of hostile identity patterns in Korea does more than merely widen our understanding of current security dilemmas, for the key to a more peaceful future lies in recognizing the *constructed* nature of identities and the conflicts that issue from them. Expressed in other words, difference does not necessarily lead to violence. The source of conflict is located in the *political manipu-lation* of the tension between identity and difference, in attempts to isolate a few arbitrarily selected elements of the past in order to construct around them a mythological division between inside and outside. "Politicians," one commentator points out, "have no hesita-tion in appealing to the collective memory—in a carefully selective way—in order to justify their present conduct by the past."[1] Once these artificial demarcations of identity have become internalized in language, school curricula, political institutions, moral discourses, and the like, their mythical origin appears more and more real until the ensuing worldview, and the conflicts that they generate, seem inevitable, even natural. This process has been particularly pro-nounced in Korea, where an unusually hermetic dividing line has provided each state with the opportunity to disseminate its ideo-logical worldview without being challenged by the other side.

The second major task, and the content of Part II, consisted of ar-ticulating the contours of an alternative and more peaceful security arrangement. I argued that two components are essential for locating a way out of the current culture of insecurity: the promotion of com-munication and face-to-face contacts among Koreans on both sides of the Demilitarized Zone, and a willingness to accept that after half a century of division, North and South Korean people have de-veloped a different—and perhaps inherently incompatible—sense of identity and politics. Some progress has recently been made in both realms, but much more needs to be done. The state continues to control intra-Korean dynamics in both parts of the divided peninsula, and only very few signs indicate that either side might be willing to accept the other on its own terms.

The purpose of my concluding remarks is not only to recapitulate the main insights and arguments that I have advanced in the preceding pages but also, and primarily, to outline how processes of globalization will intensify the security challenges ahead—and therefore also the need to search for a path to reconciliation.

GLOBALIZATION AND INFORMATION TECHNOLOGY

Cultures of insecurity, and the dualistic and antagonistic thinking patterns that sustain them, are, of course, not unique to Korea. They are part of a much more deeply embedded tendency to define security in militaristic and repressive ways. But the mind-sets and political practices are particularly pronounced in Korea, where they have contributed significantly to the very conflict that they seek to ward off. To deal adequately with present and future security threats in Korea, including a potential collapse of the North, requires a fundamental rethinking of identity and difference. Policies born out of dualistic and statecentric Cold War thinking patterns are no longer adequate for understanding the realities of today and for facing the problems that lie ahead. They should give way to multilayered analyses that recognize the political dimensions of security and take into account how a variety of transnational and nonstate dynamics can contribute—or already shape—aspects of security. Paying heed to such new and unheralded forces would amount to no less than an inaudible revolution in military affairs, less spectacular but in the long run perhaps at least as significant as the much more technically and narrowly framed "revolution in military affairs" that has preoccupied defense intellectuals for the past few years.[2]

Challenging the deeply entrenched inside/outside (il)logic that prevails in realist security thinking is not to question that a military-based defense is necessary for maintaining stability on the Korean peninsula. The key, rather, consists of supplementing conventional security with a broader political engagement. A rethinking of security must explore this more fundamental domain of politics. It must address issues of perception and identity. It must confront the political discourses that have objectivized and legitimized the current culture of violence.

I have identified the promotion of dialogue as the first key aspect of an alternative security framework. Although state-based dialogues have always taken place in Korea, they have never managed to engender a lasting breakthrough. Attempts to reach agreements were usually dominated, and eventually undermined, by a deep sense of distrust for the enemy on the other side of the DMZ. Speaking about the North Korea threat during the 1970s, President Park Chung Hee perfectly captured this suspicion: "Whenever they think we are weak, they will swoop down upon us, using arms and violence; but when they think we are strong, they turn to negotiations and bargaining. This is their strategy, common to all communists in the world."[3] Much has changed since then, of course, although some commentators would interpret Pyongyang's current nuclear brinkmanship tactic along similar lines. Be that as it may, South Korean positions have become more tolerant in recent years. But diplomatic negotiations have still not managed to reach a lasting breakthrough. They have, indeed, not even been able to achieve the minimum goal: replacing the Armistice Agreement with a peace treaty. And as long as the underlying sources of conflict remain intact, chances of such a breakthrough remain slim.

The promotion of nonstate contacts, I have argued, has the potential to dismantle at least some of the hostile identity practices that continuously fuel the conflict on the peninsula. South Korea's Sunshine Policy has taken important steps in this direction, although the level of face-to-face encounters and communication remains both very low and hampered by a variety of contradictions. Rather than rehearsing these challenges to engagement, which I discussed in chapter 5, I draw attention to how processes of globalization may engender more nonstate interactions in Korea, even if state policies seek to contain them.

North Korea may continue its efforts to stay in power by keeping contacts with the outside world to a minimum. South Korea may maintain its ambivalence toward the North, combining openness and engagement with a sense of distrust, even hatred. But time cannot be held back, nor can the thirty-eighth parallel remain as tightly sealed as it has been for the last half-century. The gradual democratization of South Korean society will inevitably penetrate foreign policy decision making, leading to further challenges to the state's monopoly on dealing with the North.[4] The emergence of common challenges, such as those related to environmental problems, may create shared interests and thus opportunity for peaceful cooperation.[5] But most impetus will come from the more general dynamics of globalization, which take place, at least in part, beyond the control and confines of the state.

Globalization is a process of redrawing boundaries, not only the geographical boundaries that determine the outer spatial limits of a particular state but also, and perhaps more important, boundaries of ideology, society, politics, and identity. States no longer play the only role in a world in which financial, productive, cultural, and informational dynamics have come to disobey, transgress, and challenge the deeply entrenched principle of sovereignty. Globalization is gradually eroding the privileged position of the state. It is also challenging the discourses that have come to justify this privileged standpoint. Jürgen Habermas, when analyzing the role of global markets, refers to a legitimacy crisis of the nation-state.[6] Others speak of an increasing "deterritorialization" of the world: of processes that call into question the very spatial organization of the state and interstate system, that is, the key pillars of "state sovereignty, territorial integrity and community identity."[7] States have, of course, never been as sovereign as they appear.[8] Nor have they lost their central position in domestic and global politics.[9] This is particularly the case in Korea, where state control remains unusually prominent, particularly in the North.

Even the hermetically sealed DMZ will not be able to persist in the face of globalization. Even the reclusive state of North Korea will be penetrated by a variety of forces that lie beyond the control of the state. A limited amount of outside information is already reaching the populace. Accounts by North Korean defectors reveal, for instance, that occasional broadcasts from abroad influence certain segments of the populace, although the sale of radio receivers is closely monitored and punishments are imposed for tuning in to anything but the official channel. "Radio programs from the South," one defector claims, "made it possible for us to sharpen our criticism of Kim Il Sung's regime."[10] The exact extent to which such broadcasts actually reach the population is an open question, and so is the reliability of information provided by defectors. But there is little doubt that technological changes will increasingly undermine a state's effort to control the flow of information. It is only a matter of time until fax, radio, satellite televisions, e-mail, and the Internet start reaching greater parts of the North Korean population. Likewise, it is only a matter of time before South Koreans have access to information from (and interactive communication with) the North that is not censored by the state apparatus.

Globalization has become a major public theme in South Korea ever since former president Kim Young-sam made it a policy priority of his government.[11] But the debates have only rarely penetrated the domain of security studies, and when they do, no one talks about the crucial issue of information technology.[12] This is surprising, for the evolution of information technology in the South is rather stunning. South Korea has one of the world's most sophisticated Internet systems. High-speed Internet service is available to about 60 percent of all households, which is the highest rate among all states that participate in the Organisation of Economic Co-operation and Development.[13] The situation in the North is, of course, very different. In the euphoria that followed the 2000 summit meeting, fiber optic cables were laid to connect the two sides. All major South Korean telecommunication companies, from SK Telecom to Hyundai Information Technology, stressed their eagerness to do "groundbreaking work for wired, wireless and other information infrastructure" in the North.[14] But for both financial and political reasons few, if any, of these projects have been realized. North Korea still has one of the world's lowest rates of Internet access, although there is a significant national intranet system, which is administered by the Central Scientific and Technological Information Agency.[15] But access to e-mail and web services is restrained by the lack of computers and networks as well as by strong restrictions about usage, which is limited to government officials, research institutes, and the military. Commentators stress that information technology has three main purposes in the North: information gathering for the government, promotion of external trade, and the dissemination of ideological ideas. With regard to information gathering it is interesting to note that North Korea is one of the most frequent visitors to U.S. military websites.[16] North Korean spies in the South are said to use "Hotmail," rather than conventional means, to send and receive information.[17] The main promotional websites are located outside North Korea. The Korean Central News Agency, or KCNA (www.kcna.co.jp), the state-run wire service, is operated by a pro–North Korean organization (Jochongryeon) in Tokyo. It posts excerpts from the major North Korean newspapers. Choson Infobank (www.dprkorea.com) is run by a North Korean trade promotion body based in Beijing. Although it offers "news services" mostly by subscription, it is part of a broader North Korean effort to promote its political doctrines via the Internet.[18]

Information technology cannot be controlled entirely, not even by a state as dominant as the one in North Korea. The evolution in China is indicative here, for its government too is concerned about the flow of information. But by 2001 about 22 million Chinese already had online access. In 2003 it was 78 million, and by 2005 the number of users is expected to reach 200 million, rendering the current regulation of websites and e-mail usage increasingly difficult. Existing mechanisms of control, such as the imposition of site-blocking software on Internet cafes, are simply not enough to prevent people from accessing a broad range of information that would not pass state censorship rules.[19] Even though North Korea is far from reaching this stage, the Internet already plays a limited political role. Both sides devote specific military resources to electronic warfare. North Korea is said to have an elite "hacking program," and the South Korean military has trained about 200,000 information technicians for a variety of functions.[20] But there are also efforts at promoting understanding. Consider a few random examples: the aforementioned KCNA site has become a key source for South Koreans interested in the North, although it is still illegal for South Koreans to access Northern websites without permission from the government. As early as 1999 a space research institute at the University of California at Berkeley reported that 123 North Korean net surfers had participated in an online joint project related to space exploration.[21] Or look at how several South Korean newspapers have set up online mailboxes to help separated families try to contact their relatives in the North.[22] So far, these and similar efforts to promote communication and understanding have had little effect. But it is only a matter of time until information technology, and processes of globalization in general, open up more and more spaces for interactions that defy state dominance of inter-Korean relations.

IDENTITY, DIFFERENCE, AND THE PROMOTION OF RECONCILIATION

As the exchange of information and communication across the DMZ increases, so will the need to find ways of dealing with the differences that remain between North and South. Otherwise, tensions and conflicts will emerge and reemerge ad infinitum. In many ways the major challenge ahead consists of how to deal with the other and, once national unification has occurred, with the residues of deeply embedded identity constructs that are based on an antagonistic interaction between inside and outside. The ability to meet this challenge determines to a great extent the level of violence that will accompany intranational relations and a possible unification process.

I have sought to show that a sustainable culture of reconciliation has the best chance of emerging if a politics of engagement not only promotes dialogue but also recognizes the inevitable existence of difference and alterity as an essential aspect of preventing violent encounters. A more peaceful future does not emerge from avoiding or even repressing difference but from articulating and realizing a more tolerant relationship between identity and difference—a relationship that consists of finding nonviolent forms of identification and of viewing difference not as a threat to identity but as an inevitable, and perhaps even enriching, aspect of life. Various commentators do indeed stress the central importance of this task. Emanuel Levinas sees peace as "a relation with the other in its logically indiscernible alterity," and David Campbell defines justice as "the relationship to the other."[23] Accepting the otherness of the other is essential if reconciliation is to prevail over conflict. Otherwise, a situation emerges in which one identity practice prevails over another, thereby creating resentment, more antagonisms, and, most likely, overt forms of conflict. Reconciliation, in this sense, is a "point of encounter where concerns about both the past and the future can meet."[24] In Korea this encounter would need to deal with competing memories of national division and war. And it would need to find an appropriate mixture of remembering and forgetting, of forgiveness and of holding people accountable for what happened in the past.

Books on issues of security usually end with a set of concrete policy recommendations. Not so this one. Advancing specific policy recommendations is an entirely different task than identifying underlying conflict patterns and searching for the broad mind-set with which the challenges ahead may be approached more successfully. The ambition of this book was limited to the latter two tasks, which are of a more long-term nature. Advancing concrete and policy-relevant advice would, by contrast, entail analyzing immediate challenges and the unique political constellation within which they emerged. In order to be effective the ensuing decision-making process privileges one interpretation over others, one perspective over others, one solution over others. Even a thorough examination of all the dimensions and factors involved in a dilemma cannot avoid such practices of exclusion. They are as inevitable as they are desirable. Politicians and diplomats, faced with the pressure of finding principled responses to immediate challenges, must avoid ambivalence and defend positions that are clear-cut and definitive. Quite rightly so, for many problems require determined actions.

But equally essential is the existence of a counterforce that balances the imperatives of short-term decision making, for the foundations of an adequate security policy can remain adequate and fair only if its norms and procedures are submitted to periodic scrutiny and adjustment. Advancing such a counterweight was the main task of this book, and it entailed suspicion of political positions that are grounded in universal norms and principles. The foundations for an alternative and nonviolent constitution of identity and difference cannot be based on a set of predetermined guidelines that are then automatically applied to all contexts. William Connolly convincingly argues that "one of the defining characteristics of an *ethical* orientation is cultivation of a critical responsiveness that can never be automatic, deducible, guaranteed, or commanded by some unquestionable authority."[25] Thus I have presented the ethical challenge that prevailing security dilemmas pose as an inherently relational issue, as "an ongoing historical practice" that must be approached and understood in its complexities and ever-changing dimensions.[26]

Such an approach to peace and reconciliation in Korea requires a fundamental rethinking of security. While some aspects of conventional security concerns will (and should) remain central to both academics and security practitioners, one must also recognize that political change can occur only after the underlying issue of identity has become a topic of discussion and scrutiny. This, in turn, entails searching for a mind-set that reaches beyond the parameters of current political maneuverings. Such a search is inevitably a long-term affair, for it revolves around the need to transform notions of security that are deeply entrenched in political practice and societal consciousness, not just in Korea but in international politics in general.

Perhaps security may one day no longer be associated with order and certainty, for it is exactly the search for order and certainty that has generated problematic demarcations between inside and outside. "Total security," one of J. G. Ballard's narrators says, "is a disease of deprivation."[27] The process of drawing a rigid line across the thirty-eighth parallel perfectly illustrates how artificially created political and mental boundaries have generated a violent and highly volatile environment. An alternative understanding of security would, in Costas Constantinou's words, "desynchronize security from safety and certitude." He, alongside a number of other scholars, now seeks to validate a different notion of security, one that points not to an (impossible) escape from danger but to a situation in which one can "feel secure-in-danger . . . and dwell next to one's enemy in security, without surrendering, or dominating, or making the foe friend."[28] Clearly, these and a range of other related security challenges cannot be solved today, nor can they be addressed at the level of the nation-state. But there is reason for optimism nevertheless, and this hope is contained in the ethics of dialogue and the ethics of difference that I have articulated in this book. Some of the ensuing policy positions may be difficult to implement, or they may even be haunted by contradictions, but they constitute the best hope that we have to find a way out of the current and highly dangerous culture of insecurity. Needed, then, are ways of locating, promoting, and expanding tolerance and the cross-territorial bonds that develop between people and the human ideals that they stand for. To think ahead of security in such a broad and postnational way is a first step—necessary and long overdue as it is—toward establishing political interactions in Korea that are no longer defined by the constant specter of violent encounters.

Notes

PREFACE

1. For reasons of accessibility I am using the somewhat colloquial terms *South Korea* and *North Korea,* rather than the official names of the respective states: Republic of Korea and Democratic People's Republic of Korea.

2. Doug Struck, "North Korean Threat Erodes Japan's Pacifism," *Guardian Weekly,* February 20, 2003, 28.

3. The most recent contributions are Victor D. Cha and David C. Kang, *Nuclear North Korea: A Debate on Engagement Strategies* (New York: Columbia University Press, 2003); Selig S. Harrison, *Korean Endgame: A Strategy for Reunification and U.S. Disengagement* (Princeton, N.J.: Princeton University Press, 2003); and Bruce Cumings, *North Korea: The Hermit Kingdom* (New York: New Press, 2003).

4. I am referring, of course, to Gertrude Stein's famous pronouncement: "A rose is a rose is a rose." See Stein, "Sacred Emily," *Geography and Plays* (Lincoln: University of Nebraska Press, 1993), 178.

5. Milan Kundera, *The Book of Laughter and Forgetting,* trans. M. H. Heim (New York: HarperCollins, 1994), 8.

6. Michael C. Williams and Keith Krause, preface to Keith Krause and Michael C. Williams, eds., *Critical Security Studies* (Minneapolis: University of Minnesota Press, 1997), xii.

7. Carol Cohn, "Sex and Death in the Rational World of Defense Intellectuals," in John A. Vasquez, ed., *Classics of International Relations* (Englewood Cliffs, N.J.: Prentice Hall, 1996), 327–37.

8. Cited in Gilles Deleuze, "What Is a Dispositif?" in *Michel Foucault: Philosopher,* ed. T. J. Armstrong (New York: Harvester Wheatsheaf, 1992), 165.

INTRODUCTION

1. William J. Perry, "The United States and the Future of East Asian Security," in Woo Keun-Min, ed., *Building Common Peace and Prosperity in Northeast Asia* (Seoul: Yonsei University Press, 2000), 121.

2. James Dao, "Bush Administration Defends Its Approach to North Korea," *New York Times,* July 7, 2003; Shane Green, "North Korea Warns Final Showdown with U.S. Will Be a Nuclear One," *Sydney Morning Herald,* February 8, 2003.

3. Jang Si Young and Ahn Pyong-Seong, "Direction of Military Build-up and Defense Spending," *Korea Focus,* November–December 2001, 85.

4. Chuck Downs, *Over the Line: North Korea's Negotiating Strategy* (Washington, D.C.: American Enterprise Institute, 1999), 282.

5. Moon Chung-in, *Arms Control on the Korean Peninsula* (Seoul: Yonsei University Press, 1996), 9.

6. Gregory Henderson, *Korea: The Politics of the Vortex* (Cambridge, Mass.: Harvard University Press, 1968).

7. For an excellent analysis of identity and difference, focusing on South Korea, see Roy Richard Grinker, *Korea and Its Futures: Unification and the Unfinished War* (London: Macmillan, 1998).

8. Fred C. Alford, *Think No Evil: Korean Values in the Age of Globalization* (Ithaca, N.Y.: Cornell University Press, 1999), 103–6.

9. Hazel Smith, "Bad, Mad, Sad or Rational Actor? Why the 'Securitization' Paradigm Makes for Poor Policy Analysis of North Korea," *International Affairs* 76, no. 3 (July 2000): 594–96; Bruce Cumings, *Parallax Visions: Making Sense of American–East Asian Relations at the End of the Century* (Raleigh, N.C.: Duke University Press, 1999).

10. Leon V. Sigal, *Disarming Strangers: Nuclear Diplomacy with North Korea* (Princeton, N.J.: Princeton University Press, 1998), 21.

11. Ibid., 207–28.

12. Cumings, *Parallax Visions,* 122.

13. Yuh Ji-Yeon. "Dangerous Communists, Inscrutable Orientals, Starving Masses," *Peace Review* 22, no. 2 (June 1999): 317–24; Smith, "Bad, Mad, Sad or Rational Actor?" 606. Drawing attention to these representational practices is not to deny that mismanagement is chiefly responsible for the deplorable state of North Korea's economy. Stressing the latter point is Marcus Noland, *Avoiding the Apocalypse: The Future of the Two*

Koreas (Washington, D.C.: Institute for International Economics, 2000), 171–94.

14. Douglas Klusmeyer and Astri Suhrke, "Comprehending 'Evil': Challenges for Law and Policy," *Ethics and International Affairs* 16, no. 1 (2002): 37; Roxanne L. Euben, "Killing (for) Politics: Jihad, Martyrdom, and Political Action," *Political Theory* 30, no. 1 (February 2002): 4.

15. Smith, "Bad, Mad, Sad or Rational Actor?" 593–94.

16. Lee Joon-Koo, "Reflections on Korean Unification Cost Studies," in Kang Myoung-kyu and Helmut Wagner, eds., *Germany and Korea: Lessons in Unification* (Seoul: Seoul National University Press, 1995), 119. See also Nicholas Eberstadt, "South Korea's Economic Crisis and the Prospects for North-South Relations," *Korea and World Affairs* 22, no. 4 (Winter 1998): 541; Moon Chung-in and Hideshi Takesada, "North Korea: Institutionalized Military Intervention," in Muthiah Alagappa, ed., *Coercion and Governance* (Stanford, Calif.: Stanford University Press, 2001), 357; Kim Hyung-chan, "North Korea: A Nation of Tragedy," *Korea and World Affairs* 23, no. 4 (Winter 1999): 579–80.

17. Robert F. Derenberger, "The Economies of China, North Korea, and Vietnam: A Comparative Study," in R. A. Scalapino and D. C. Kim, eds., *Asian Communism: Continuity and Transition* (Berkeley, Calif.: Center for Korean Studies, 1988), 243.

18. Donald Macintyre, "A Hermit's Debut," *Time*, September 7, 1998, 14–15; Orville Schell, "In the Land of the Dear Leader," *Harper's*, July 1996, 58–66; Peter Smerdon, "The Road Less Traveled," *Far Eastern Economic Review*, December 27, 2001, 14–20; Urs Schoettli, "Kim Jong Il? Diktator ohne Konturen" [Kim Jong Il—Dictator without Contours], *Neue Zürcher Zeitung*, August 18, 2002, 4; "Eine Hölle, kalt und dunkel" [A Form of Hell: Cold and Dark], *Die Zeit*, February 20, 2003, 3.

19. Most notable is Scott Snyder, *Negotiating on the Edge: North Korean Negotiating Behavior* (Washington, D.C.: U.S. Institute of Peace Press, 1999).

20. Omawale Omawale, "An Exercise in Ambivalence: Negotiating with North Korea," *Harvard Asia Pacific Review* 3, no. 2 (Summer 1999): 60–62.

21. Hazel Smith, "Opening Up by Default: North Korea, the Humanitarian Community and the Crisis," *Pacific Review* 12, no. 3 (1999): 454; and Smith, "Bad, Mad, Sad or Rational Actor?" 603.

22. Bruce Cumings, "The Last Hermit," *New Left Review*, November–December 2000, 152.

23. Suh Byung-Chul and Suh Jae-Jean, eds., *White Paper on Human Rights in North Korea* (Seoul: Korean Institute for National Unification, 2001).

24. William J. Perry, *Review of United States Policy Towards North Korea* (Washington, D.C.: U.S. Department of State, 1999), 5, 12, http://usinfo.state.gov/regional/ea/easec/nkreview.html. For a similar argument see Choi Won-Ki, "Dealing with North Korea 'as It Is,'" *Nautilus Institute Policy Forum Online*, 1999, http://www.nautilus.org/fora/security/9907K _Choi.html.

25. Choi Wan-Kyu. "The Current State and Task of the Study of Change in the North Korean Political System," in Moon Chung-in, ed., *Understanding Regime Dynamics in North Korea* (Seoul: Yonsei University Press, 1998), 26; *Bukhan-eun eodi-ro: Jeonwhanki "Bukhanjeok Jeongchi Hyeonsang-ui jaeinsik"* (Masan, Korea: Kyungnam University Press, 1996), 25–26; Edward W. Wagner, preface to the translation, in Lee Ki-baik, *A New History of Korea* (Seoul: Ilchokak, 1984).

26. Park Gi-sun and Ryeong Jeon-ri, "Hankuk sinmun-e banyeongdoen Bukhan 'image'" [North Korea's "Image" Reflected in South Korean Newspapers], Hanlim Science Institute Report No. 25, Seoul, 73–74, 110.

27. Jutta Weldes, "The Cultural Production of Crises: U.S. Identity and Missiles in Cuba," in Jutta Weldes, Mark Laffey, Hugh Gusterson, and Raymond Duvall, eds., *Cultures of Insecurity: States, Communities, and the Production of Danger* (Minneapolis: University of Minnesota Press, 1999), 36–37.

28. John Pomfret, "Reforms Turn Out Disastrous for North Koreans," *Guardian Weekly*, January 1, 2003; Hamish McDonald, "Kim Ups Ante in Bold Poker Game," *Sydney Morning Herald*, February 14, 2002.

29. Or so goes Pyongyang's official line. See "DPRK to React to Unreasonable 'Countermeasure' with Toughest Stance," *KCNA Bulletin*, January 19, 2003, http://www.kcna.co.jp/, and Elisabeth Rosenthal, "U.S. 'Compelled' Arms Steps, Pyongyang Asserts," *New York Times*, June 1, 2003, 1.

30. David Campbell, *Writing Security: United States Foreign Policy and the Politics of Identity* (Minneapolis: University of Minnesota Press, 1998). See also Weldes, Laffey, Gusterson, and Duvall, *Cultures of Insecurity*, 9–12.

31. The prevalence of realism is acknowledged by policy makers and analysts alike. See, for instance, William T. Tow, *Asia-Pacific Strategic Relations: Seeking Convergent Security* (Cambridge: Cambridge University Press, 2001), 1–6, and Roberto Toscano, "The Ethics of Modern Diplomacy," in Jean-Marc Coicaud and Daniel Warner, eds., *Ethics and International Affairs* (Tokyo: United Nations University, 2001), 42–83.

32. Most notable are K. N. Waltz, *Man, State, and War* (New York: Columbia University Press, 1959), and Waltz, *Theory of International Politics* (Reading, Mass.: Addison-Wesley, 1979). For broader discussions of realism see Michael Joseph Smith, *Realist Thought from Weber to Kissinger*

(Baton Rouge: Louisiana State University, 1986), and Jack Donnelly, *Realism and International Relations* (Cambridge: Cambridge University Press, 2000).

33. See D. A. Baldwin, ed., *Neorealism and Neoliberalism: The Contemporary Debate* (New York: Columbia University Press, 1993); Charles W. Kegley, ed., *Controversies in International Relations Theory: Realism and the Neoliberal Challenge* (New York: St. Martin's Press, 1995).

34. Peter van Ness, "Globalization and Security in East Asia," *Asian Perspective* 23, no. 4 (1999): 315–42; John Ikenberry, "From Containment to Engagement: East Asia and American Liberal Grand Strategy," in Moon Chung-in, Odd Arne Westad, and Gyoo-hyoung Kahng, eds., *Ending the Cold War in Korea: Theoretical and Historical Perspectives* (Seoul: Yonsei University Press, 2001), 279–318.

35. Moon Chung-in and Judy E. Chung, "Reconstructing New Identity and Peace in East Asia," in Kim Dalchoong and Moon Chung-in, eds., *History, Cognition, and Peace in East Asia* (Seoul: Yonsei University Press, 1997), 265.

36. Michael Dillon, *Politics of Security: Towards a Political Philosophy of Continental Thought* (New York: Routledge, 1996), 1.

37. Kihl Young Whan, "Seoul's Engagement Policy and U.S.-DPRK Relations," *Korean Journal of Defense Analysis* 10, no. 1 (1998): 23.

38. Calvin Sims, "Life in South Hard for North Koreans," *New York Times,* April 24, 2000.

39. Kim Dae-jung, "Presidential Inaugural Address, February 1998," in Yong-ho Ch'oe et al., eds., *Sources of Korean Tradition: From the Sixteenth to the Twentieth Centuries* (New York: Columbia University Press, 2000), 2:450.

40. *Defense White Paper* (Seoul: Ministry of National Defense, 1999), 94. A variety of scholars have drawn attention to this dilemma. See, for instance, Kim Se-kyun, "NamBuk jeongsanghoedam ihu-e NamBukHan gwangae mit NamBukHan sahoe" [Postsummit North-South Relations and North-South Society], *Jinbo Pyeong-ron,* no. 5 (Summer 2000), http://prome.snu.a.kr/skkim/presentation/article/files/skkim07.html.

41. Roy Eccleston and Patrick Walters, "North Korean Missile Could Hit U.S.," *Australian,* February 14, 2003.

42. See, for instance, Snyder, *Negotiating on the Edge*; Downs, *Over the Line*; Robert Dujarric, "North Korea: Risks and Rewards of Engagement," *Journal of International Affairs* 54, no. 2 (Spring 2001): 464–87; Han S. Park, "North Korean Perceptions of Self and Others: Implications for Policy Choices," *Pacific Affairs* 73, no. 4 (Winter 2000): 504; Michael J. Mazarr, "Going Just a Little Nuclear: Nonproliferation Lessons from North Korea," *International Security* 20, no. 2 (Fall 1995): 92–122.

43. Don Oberdorfer, *The Two Koreas: A Contemporary History* (London: Warner, 1998), 369–411; Christopher W. Hughes, "Japanese Policy and the North Korean 'Soft Landing,'" *Pacific Review* 11, no. 3 (1998): 395.

44. James Dao, "U.S. Planning Sanctions Against North Korea," *New York Times,* February 17, 2003.

45. Nicolas Eberstadt, "Hastening Korean Unification," *Foreign Affairs,* March–April 1997, 77–92; Helen-Louise Hunter, *Kim Il Sung's North Korea* (Westport, Conn.: Praeger, 1999); Condoleezza Rice, "Promoting the National Interest," *Foreign Affairs,* January–February 2000.

46. Selig S. Harrison, "Promoting a Soft Landing in Korea," *Foreign Policy,* no. 106 (Spring 1997): 57–75; Scott Snyder, "Managing Integration on the Korean Peninsula: The Positive and Normative Case for Gradualism with or without Integration," in Marcus Noland, ed., *Economic Integration of the Korean Peninsula* (Washington, D.C.: Institute for International Economics, 1998).

47. Victor D. Cha, "Korea's Place in the Axis," *Foreign Affairs,* May–June 2002; James Miles, "Waiting Out North Korea," *Survival* 44, no. 2 (Summer 2002): 38–39.

48. Selig Harrison, "Time to Leave Korea?" *Foreign Affairs,* March–April 2001; Dujarric, "North Korea: Risks and Rewards of Engagement"; and Moon Chung-in, "The Kim Dae Jung Government's Peace Policy Towards North Korea," *Asian Perspective* 25, no. 2 (2001): 177–98.

49. Robert Cox, "Social Forces, States, and World Orders: Beyond International Relations Theory," *Millennium* 10, no. 2 (1981): 130.

50. Tow, *Asia-Pacific Strategic Relations,* 3.

51. Quoted in David E. Sanger, "North Korea Crisis Is Different from the One in Iraq, Bush Says," *International Herald Tribune,* January 1, 2003, 5.

52. James Dao, "U.S. to Resume Food Aid to North Korea After 2-Year Halt," *New York Times,* February 25, 2003; "South Korean Leader Is Sworn in as Tensions Grow," *New York Times,* February 25, 2003.

53. Jochen Buchsteiner, "Die Hierarchie des Bösen" [The Hierarchy of Evil], *Frankfurter Allgemeine Zeitung,* October 27, 2002; Wolfgang Koydl, "Moral und Realpolitik" [Morality and Realpolitik], *Süddeutsche Zeitung,* January 11, 2003, 2; Michael R. Gordon, "A Tale of Two Crises," *New York Times,* February 17, 2003.

54. See Alan M. Dershowitz, *Why Terrorism Works* (New Haven, Conn.: Yale University Press, 2002).

55. See Brian Massumi, "Translator's Foreword," in Gilles Deleuze and Félix Guattari, *A Thousand Plateaus: Capitalism and Schizophrenia* (London: Athlone, 1996/1980).

56. For Janice Bially Mattern, discoveries are attempts to find "a new, previously untouched fact," while uncoveries imply "an excavation from

underneath layers of ossified or never problematized knowledge." See Bially Mattern, *Ordering International Politics: Identity, Crisis and Representational Force* (London: Routledge, forthcoming).

57. Andrew Mack, "Civil War: Academic Research and Policy Community," *Journal of Peace Research* 39, no. 5 (2002): 515–25.

58. Martin Heidegger, "Nur noch ein Gott kann uns retten" [Only a God Can Still Save Us], interview conducted in 1966, reprinted in *Der Spiegel*, November 11, 2002, 142.

59. Tow, *Asia-Pacific Strategic Relations*, 4.

60. Friedrich Nietzsche, "Über Warheit und Lüge im aussermoralischen Sinn," *Erkenntnistheoretische Schriften* (Frankfurt: Suhrkamp, 1968), 103. For a good translation see Walter Kaufmann's, "On Truth and Lie in an Extra-Moral Sense," in *The Portable Nietzsche* (New York: Penguin, 1954), 47.

61. Weldes, Laffey, Gusterson, and Duvall, *Cultures of Insecurity*, 20.

62. Michel Foucault, *L'Ordre du Discours* (Paris: Gallimard, 1971), 31–38.

63. On the notion of indirect policy relevance, see Stephen K. White, *Sustaining Affirmation: The Strengths of Weak Ontology in Political Theory* (Princeton, N.J.: Princeton University Press, 2000), 11–12.

64. Paul Celan, "Ansprache anlässlich der Entgegennahme des Literaturpreises der Freien Hansestadt Bremen" and "Der Meridian," both in *Gesammelte Werke* (Frankfurt: Suhrkamp, 1986), 3:186, 198. For good translations see R. Waldrop's, "Speech on the Occasion of Receiving the Literature Prize of the Free Hanseatic City of Bremen," and "The Meridian," both in Paul Celan, *Collected Prose* (Riverdale-on-Hudson, N.Y.: Sheep Meadow Press, 1986), 33–35, 37–55.

1. THE EMERGENCE OF ANTAGONISTIC IDENTITIES

1. "Tae Sung Dong Exercises," mimeograph, April 1988.

2. *Defense White Paper* (Seoul: Ministry of National Defense, 1998), 83.

3. Chung Pai-chi, "The Cultural Other and National Identity in the Taiwanese and South Korean Media," *Gazette* 62, no. 2 (2000): 112. See also Park Gi-sun and Ryeong Jeon-ri, "Hankuk sinmun-e banyeongdoen Bukhan 'image'" [North Korea's "Image" Reflected in South Korean Newspapers], Hanlim Science Institute Report No. 25, Seoul, 1995, 73–74, 110.

4. Quoted in Lee Kyong-hee, "The True Face of Kim Jong-il," *Korea Herald*, May 8, 2000.

5. Gong Ro-Myung, "South-North Reconciliation and Ending the Cold

War on the Korean Peninsula," in Woo Keun-Min, ed., *Building Common Peace and Prosperity in Northeast Asia* (Seoul: Yonsei University Press, 2000), 161. See also Charles K. Armstrong, "The Kim Is Dead! Long Live the Kim!" *Journal of International Affairs* 54, no. 2 (Spring 2001): 509–13.

6. Kim Tack-whan, "Image of North Korea after Inter-Korean Summit," *Korea Focus,* November–December 2000, 121.

7. Several scholars stress the need to see political events in Korea beyond the conventional black-and-white version of Cold War confrontation. See Barry K. Gills, *Korea Versus Korea: A Case of Contested Legitimacy* (London: Routledge, 1996), and Odd Arne Westad, "The Cold War and Korean Parallels," in Moon Chung-in, Odd Arne Westad, and Kahng Gyoohyoung, eds., *Ending the Cold War in Korea: Theoretical and Historical Perspectives* (Seoul: Yonsei University Press, 2001), 24–28.

8. Chun Chae-sung, "The Cold War and Its Transitions for Koreans: Their Meanings from a Constructivist Viewpoint," in Moon, Westad, and Kahng, *Ending the Cold War in Korea,* 115–45. See also Shin Wookhee, "The Political Economy of Security: South Korea in the Cold War System," *Korea Journal* 38, no. 4 (Winter 1998): 147–68.

9. Keith Krause and Michael C. Williams, "From Strategy to Security: Foundations of Critical Security Studies," in Keith Krause and Michael C. Williams, eds., *Critical Security Studies* (Minneapolis: University of Minnesota Press, 1997), 47.

10. Karl A. Wittfogel, *Oriental Despotism, A Comparative Study of Total Power* (New Haven, Conn.: Yale University Press, 1957); Gregory Henderson, *Korea: The Politics of the Vortex* (Cambridge, Mass.: Harvard University Press, 1968). For more recent works see Han Sung Joo, *The Failure of Democracy in South Korea* (Berkeley: University of California Press, 1974), 7; Norman Jacobs, *The Korean Road to Modernization and Development* (Urbana: University of Illinois Press, 1985), 42; Lucian W. Pye, *Asian Power and Politics: The Cultural Dimensions of Authority* (Cambridge, Mass.: Belknap, 1985), 56–61, 101–35. For a more contemporary, and in many ways more nuanced, analysis of Confucian cultural values and Korean identity, see William A. Callahan, "Negotiating Cultural Boundaries: Confucianism and Trans/national Identity in Korea," *Cultural Values* 3, no. 3 (1999): 329–64.

11. Although democratic rights were less prevalent among Asian philosophers than among their Athenian contemporaries, such rights clearly do exist and even date to what Karl Jaspers called the Axial Period, the epoque between 800 and 200 B.C. For example, Mencius talks of popular rights for overthrowing a ruler should his conduct be judged untrustworthy by the people. See *Book of Mencius,* in Chan Wing-Tsit, *A Source Book in Chinese Philosophy* (Princeton, N.J.: Princeton University Press, 1963), 62.

12. Korean Constitution, appendix 4, in Kil Soong Hoom and Moon Chung-in, eds., *Understanding Korean Politics* (Albany: State University of New York Press, 2001), 328. See also Kim Ki-Jung and Park Jae-min, "Paradox of Dismantling the Cold War Structure," in Moon, Westad, and Kahng, *Ending the Cold War in Korea,* 321–22.

13. *Hamel's Journal and a Description of the Kingdom of Korea, 1653–1666,* transcription of Hoetink arranged by Br. Jean-Paul Buys of the Taize Community (Seoul: Royal Asiatic Society Korea, 1994).

14. Quoted in Bruce Cumings, *Korea's Place in the Sun: A Modern History* (New York: W. W. Norton, 1997), 88.

15. Ibid., 96–97.

16. Marlene Mayo, "Attitudes toward Asia and the Beginnings of Japanese Empire," in J. Livingston, J. Moor, and F. Oldfather, eds., *Imperial Japan, 1800–1945* (New York: Random House, 1973), 214–15; Mikiso Hane, *Modern Japan: A Historical Survey* (Boulder, Colo.: Westview, 1986), 157–62.

17. Don Oberdorfer, *The Two Koreas: A Contemporary History* (London: Warner, 1998), 6–7.

18. Yong-ho Ch'oe et al., eds., *Sources of Korean Tradition: From the Sixteenth to the Twentieth Centuries* (New York: Columbia University Press, 2000), 2:369.

19. Park Chung Hee, "Three Basic Principles for Peaceful Unification," in *Towards Peaceful Unification: Selected Speeches and Interviews by Park Chung Hee* (Seoul: Kwongmyong, 1976), 110.

20. Dennis Hart, "Creating the National Other: Opposing Images of Nationalism in South and North Korean Education," *Korean Studies* 23 (1999): 81.

21. Edward W. Wagner, preface to the translation, in Lee Ki-baik, *A New History of Korea* (Seoul: Ilchokak, 1984), vii.

22. Cumings, *Korea's Place in the Sun,* 238. For his detailed treatment of the subject see Bruce Cumings, *The Origins of the Korean War: Liberation and the Emergence of Separate Regimes* (Princeton, N.J.: Princeton University Press, 1981), and his *Origins of the Korean War: The Roaring of the Cataract* (Princeton, N.J.: Princeton University Press, 1990).

23. Challenged in particular is Cumings's claim that an escalation of border clashes along the thirty-eighth parallel led to the war. Released Soviet documents indicate that plans for a Northern invasion of the South had existed well before June 1950 and were approved by Stalin. See Kim Younghoo, "International Dimensions of the Korean War," *Korea Journal* 38, no. 4 (Winter 1998): 134; Moon Chung-in, *Arms Control on the Korean Peninsula* (Seoul: Yonsei University Press, 1996), 50.

24. Allan R. Millett, "The Korean War: A 50-Year Critical Historiography," *Journal of Strategic Studies* 24, no. 1 (March 2001): 190.

25. Jun Sang-in, "A Pro-North Korean and Anti-American Interpretation of Modern Korean History," *Korea and World Affairs* 23, no. 2 (Summer 1999): 262–67.

26. Kim, "International Dimensions of the Korean War," 143–44.

27. The generally accepted estimates of wounded and dead are 900,000 Chinese, 520,000 North Koreans, and 400,000 U.N. command troops of which approximately two-thirds were South Koreans. The United States counted 54,000 dead and 103,000 wounded. See Oberdorfer, *The Two Koreas,* 9–10. For slightly different figures see Oh Kongdan and Ralph C. Hassig, *North Korea through the Looking Glass* (Washington, D.C.: Brookings Institution Press, 2000), 7.

28. Choi Jang Jip, "Political Cleavages in South Korea," in Hagen Koo, ed., *State and Society in Contemporary Korea* (Ithaca, N.Y.: Cornell University Press, 1993), 21–22.

29. Park Myung-Lim, "Beyond Dichotomy, Beyond Parallel: On How to Study the Korean War," in Moon, Westad, and Kahng, *Ending the Cold War in Korea,* 225.

30. Cumings, *Korea's Place in the Sun,* 298.

31. Donald Stone Macdonald, *The Koreans, Contemporary Politics and Society* (Boulder, Colo.: Westview, 1988), 265.

32. Leon V. Sigal, *Disarming Strangers: Nuclear Diplomacy with North Korea* (Princeton, N.J.: Princeton University Press, 1998), 19.

33. Park Chung Hee, "Open the Dark, Closed North Korean Society," in *Towards Peaceful Unification,* 129.

34. Feminist theory has advanced particularly insightful analyses of the role that multiple identities plays in private and political domains. See, for instance, Kathy Ferguson, *The Man Question: Visions of Subjectivity in Feminist Theory* (Berkeley: University of California Press, 1993); Jane Flax, *Thinking Fragments: Psychoanalysis, Feminism, and Postmodernism in the Contemporary West* (Berkeley: University of California Press, 1990); Trinh Minh-ha, *Woman, Native, Other* (Bloomington: Indiana University Press, 1989).

35. Chun, "The Cold War and Its Transitions for Koreans," 132.

36. Hart, "Creating the National Other," 67–69.

37. Laura Hein and Mark Selden, "The Lessons of War, Global Power, and Social Change," in Laura Hein and Mark Selden, eds., *Censoring History: Citizenship and Memory in Japan, Germany, and the United States* (Armonk, N.Y.: M. E. Sharpe, 2000), 3. See also Sirkka Ahonen, "Politics of Identity through History Curriculum," *Journal of Curriculum Studies* 33, no. 2 (2001): 179–94.

38. See Lee Yoonmi, *Modern Education, Textbooks, and the Image of the Nation: Politics of Modernization and Nationalism in Korean Educa-*

tion (New York: Garland, 2000); Georgie D. M. Hyde, *South Korea: Education, Culture, and Economy* (New York: St. Martin's, 1988).

39. See Nikolas Rose, *Inventing Our Selves: Psychology, Power, and Personhood* (Cambridge: Cambridge University Press, 1996); Nikolas Rose, *Governing the Soul: The Shaping of the Private Self* (London: Free Association Books, 1999); Mitchell Dean, *Governmentality: Power and Rule in Modern Society* (London: Sage, 1999); Graham Burchell, Colin Gordon, and Peter Miller, *The Foucault Effect: Studies in Governmentality* (Chicago: University of Chicago Press, 1991).

40. See Yung Yong-young, "Gugsa Gyogwaseo Balhaeng Jedo-e Kwanhan Gochal" [A Study of Korean History Textbook Publications], *MunmyongYonJi* 1, no. 2 (2000): 17–82.

41. Denis Hart, "Remembering the Nation and Self: Construction of the March First Movement in North and South Korean History Textbooks," paper presented at the Annual Convention of the International Studies Association, Los Angeles, March 18, 2000, 2.

42. Ibid., 4.

43. Quoted in Cho Myung Chul and Zang Hyoungsoo, "North Korea's Education Policy and System, and External Cooperation with International Organizations," *Journal of Asia Pacific Affairs* 3, no. 2 (2002): 75.

44. Kim Il Sung, "Über die Durchsetzung der Prinzipien des sozialistischen Pädagogik" [Regarding the Implementation of the Principles of Socialist Pedagogy], *Werke, January–December 1971* (Pyongyang: Verlag für fremdsprachige Literatur, 1986), 26:517.

45. Kim Il Sung, "For the Successful Introduction of Universal Compulsory Eleven–Year Education," *Works, January–December 1975* (Pyongyang: Foreign Languages Publishing House, 1987), 30:207.

46. See Kil Soong Hoom and Moon Chung-in, introduction to Kil and Moon, *Understanding Korean Politics,* 2.

47. Shin Gi-Wook, "Nation, History, and Politics: South Korea," in Hyung Il Pai and Timothy R. Tangherlini, eds., *Nationalism and the Construction of Korean Identity* (Berkeley, Calif.: Institute of East Asian Studies, 1998), 152.

48. Choi, "Political Cleavages in South Korea," 23.

49. Choi Chungmoo, "The Discourse of Decolonization and Popular Memory: South Korea," *Positions* 1, no. 1 (1993): 81.

50. Hart, "Creating the National Other," 75–78.

51. Hart, "Remembering the Nation and Self," 14.

52. Roy Richard Grinker, *Korea and Its Futures: Unification and the Unfinished War* (London: Macmillan, 1998), 148.

53. Han S. Park, "North Korean Perceptions of Self and Others: Implications for Policy Choices," *Pacific Affairs* 73, no. 4 (Winter 2000): 504.

54. Erich Follath, "Stalin's Schattenreich" [Stalin's Shadow Kingdom], *Der Spiegel,* February 24, 2003, 126.

55. These epithets appeared in April and May 2000 in various issues of the *Korean Central News Agency (KCNA) Bulletin,* http://www.kcna.co.jp/.

56. Cumings, *Korea's Place in the Sun,* 404.

57. Suh Dae Sook, *Kim Il Sung, the North Korean Leader* (New York: Columbia University Press, 1998), 302–7.

58. Fumiko Ikawa-Smith, "Construction of National Identity and Origins in East Asia: A Comparative Perspective," *Antiquity,* September 1999, 629.

59. Ross King, "Language, Politics, and Ideology in Postwar Koreas," in David R. McCann, ed., *Korea Briefing: Toward Reunification* (Armonk, N.Y.: M. E. Sharpe, 1997), 109–44.

60. Pai Hyung-il, *Constructing Korean "Origins": A Critical Review of Archaeology, Historiography, and Racial Myth in Korean State-Formation Theories* (Cambridge, Mass.: Harvard East Asian Monographs, 2000); James Huntley Grayson, *Myths and Legends from Korea: An Annotated Compendium of Ancient and Modern Materials* (Richmond, U.K.: Curzon, 2001).

61. Oh and Hassig, *North Korea through the Looking Glass,* 186.

62. Ibid., 107.

63. Moon, *Arms Control on the Korean Peninsula,* 250.

2. THE PERSISTENCE OF COLD WAR ANTAGONISMS

1. Kihl Young Whan, *Politics and Policies in Divided Korea: Regimes in Context* (Boulder, Colo.: Westview, 1984), 5.

2. Moon Chung-in, *Arms Control on the Korean Peninsula* (Seoul: Yonsei University Press, 1996), 72.

3. Roy Richard Grinker, *Korea and Its Futures: Unification and the Unfinished War* (London: Macmillan, 1998), 4.

4. Randall Caroline Forsberg, "South Korea–U.S. Cooperation for Building Peace on the Korean Peninsula," *KNDU Review: Journal of National Security Affairs* 6, no. 2 (December 2001): 6. See also a similar statement from Gregory Henderson, quoted in Kihl, *Politics and Policies in Divided Korea,* 5; Moon, *Arms Control on the Korean Peninsula,* 19, 72.

5. Min Kyung-Hwan, "Psychological Preparations for the Korean Unification," in Kang Myoung-kyu and Helmut Wagner, eds., *Germany and Korea: Lessons in Unification* (Seoul: Seoul National University Press, 1995), 293.

6. Oh Kongdan and Ralph C. Hassig, *North Korea through the Looking Glass* (Washington, D.C.: Brookings Institution Press, 2000), 30, 142–43.

7. Suh Dae Sook, *Kim Il Sung, the North Korean Leader* (New York: Columbia University Press, 1998).

8. Hagen Koo, introduction to Hagen Koo, ed., *State and Society in Contemporary Korea* (Ithaca, N.Y.: Cornell University Press, 1993), 2.

9. Prominent cases include those of the Reverend Moon Ik-hwan, the Roman Catholic priest Moon Kyu Hyon, the author Hwang Sok-yong, and a student, Lim Su-kyong. See Grinker, *Korea and Its Futures,* 211–23.

10. Bruce Cumings, *Korea's Place in the Sun: A Modern History* (New York: W. W. Norton, 1997), 343.

11. Valerie Reitman, "South Koreans on Trial for Warming to Those from North," *Sydney Morning Herald,* October 30, 2001.

12. See Jutta Weldes, Mark Laffey, Hugh Gusterson, and Raymond Duvall, introduction to Weldes, Laffey, Gusterson, and Duvall, eds., *Cultures of Insecurity: States, Communities, and the Production of Danger* (Minneapolis: University of Minnesota Press, 1999), 17–18.

13. Michel Foucault, *Surveiller et Punir: Naissance de la Prison* (Paris: Gallimard: 1975). For a translation by Richard Howard, see *Madness and Civilization: A History of Insanity in the Age of Reason* (London, Routledge, 1992).

14. Cumings, *Korea's Place in the Sun,* 140.

15. Grinker, *Korea and Its Futures,* x.

16. See Benedict Anderson, *Imagined Communities: Reflections on the Origin and Spread of Nationalism* (London: Verso, 1983).

17. See Shin Gi-Wook, "Nation, History, and Politics: South Korea," and Pai Hyung Il, "The Colonial Origins of Korea's Collected Past," both in Pai Hyung Il and Timothy R. Tangherlini, eds., *Nationalism and the Construction of Korean Identity* (Berkeley, Calif.: Institute of East Asian Studies, 1998), 148–65 and 13–32, respectively.

18. Frank Hoffmann, "Monoculture and Its Discontents," *Art in America,* November 2000, 74.

19. Kim Taehyun, "Enemy or Brother? South Korean Mass Public Images of North Korea and Policy Attitudes," paper presented at the Annual Convention of the International Studies Association, Washington, D.C., February 16–20, 1999, 10.

20. See Kwon Hyeok-beom, "Nae-ga NamBuk Jeongsang Hoedam-e keun gidae-reul hajiahnneun Kaddakeun? Naengjeon munhwa-wa Hanbando-ui pyeonghwa" [Why Don't I Have Great Expectations about the North–South Summit? Cold War Culture and Peace on the Korean Peninsula], *Chamyeo-wa Jachi,* June 2000, http://dragon.taejon.ac.kr/kwonhb/papers/buddalec.htm; and Paek Sang-Chan, "On the Significance of Psychoanalytic Approaches to the Reunification of Divided Korea," in Werner Pfennig, ed., *United We Stand? Divided We Are: Comparative Views on Germany and Korea in the 1990s* (Hamburg: Abera Verlag, 1997), 195.

21. *Korea Herald*, June 20, 2000.

22. Kim Tack-whan, "Image of North Korea after Inter-Korean Summit," *Korea Focus*, November–December 2000, 117.

23. Choi Won-Ki, "Dealing with North Korea 'as It Is,'" *Nautilus Institute Policy Forum Online*, 1999, http://www.nautilus.org/fora/security/9907K_Choi.html.

24. Yoon In-Jin, "North Korean Diaspora: North Korean Defectors Abroad and in South Korea," *Development and Society* 30, no. 1 (June 2001): 2–3; Grinker, *Korea and Its Futures*, 228–29.

25. Yoon, "North Korean Diaspora," 14; Lee Woo-young, "Northern Defectors in South Korea," *Korea Focus*, May–June 1997, 31–40.

26. Yoon, "North Korean Diaspora," 8.

27. Grinker, *Korea and Its Futures*, 233.

28. Kim Hong Gi, "Kuknae geoju 800yeo Bukhan italjumin salm-ui hyeonjuso" [The Current State of the 800 -plus North Korean Defectors in the South], *Kyeongyang Sinmun*, July 12, 1999, 27.

29. Ross King, "Language, Politics, and Ideology in Postwar Koreas," in David R. McCann, ed., *Korea Briefing: Toward Reunification* (Armonk, N.Y.: M. E. Sharpe, 1997), 142. See also Kim Chin Wu, "Divergence in Language Politics in Korea," in Kim Chin Wu, ed., *Papers in Korean Linguistics* (Columbia, S.C.: Hornbeam Press, 1978), and Lee Min-bok, "Budaecheop sseokeulbbun tal-Bukjadeul" [Defectors Endure Inhospitality], *Donga Ilbo*, February 10, 1997, 27.

30. Calvin Sims, "Life in South Hard for North Koreans," *New York Times*, April 24, 2000.

31. Yoon, "North Korean Diaspora," 12–13; Grinker, *Korea and Its Futures*, 234.

32. Yo Geum-joo, "Namnyeo-ga chingu-rani!" [Boys and Girls Are Friends!], *Donga Ilbo*, March 17, 1997, 27.

33. Jeon Woo Taek and Min Seong Il, "Saram-ui tongil: Jeongsin-uihakjeok jeopkeun" [Unification of People: A Psychological Approach], in Song Ja and Lee Yeongseon, eds., *Tongil sahoe-ro ganeun gil* [On the Road to a Unified Society] (Seoul: Orum, 1996), 93–94.

34. No Yeong-dae. "Manmyeong 8 nyeon cheheom: 'Dangsindeuli keuroke . . .' pyeonaen Chang-si [Yeong-chul's *Why Are You So Arrogant?* Eight Years as a Refugee], *Munwha Ilbo*, September 24, 1997, 35.

35. Jeon and Min, "Saram-ui tongil," 93–94. See also Lee, "Pudaejeop sseokeulbbun tal-Bukjadeul," 27; Choi Jae-bong, "Namjoseonaramdeuleu wae keuri chalnasseoyo?" [Why Are Southern People So Arrogant?], *Hankyorae Sinmun*, September 23, 1997, 11; Chang Yeong-chul, "Yeojeonhi nopeun 'maeumui byeok'" [The Ever-High "Wall of the Heart"], *Donga Ilbo*, May 31, 1997, 27; and Kang Chol-Hwan and Pierre Rigoulot, *Aquari-*

57. Herta Müller, "Das Ticken der Norm" [The Ticking of the Norm], in *Hunger und Seide* (Reinbeck: Rowolt, 1997), 45.

58. Richard I. Hofferbert and Hans-Dieter Klingenmann, "Democracy and Its Discontents in Post-Wall Germany," *International Political Science Review* 22, no. 4 (2001): 366; Heiner Meulemann, "Werte und Wertwandel im vereinten Deutschland" [Old and New Values in United Germany], *Aus Politik und Zeitgeschichte*, September 15, 2002, 13–22; Beate Gilliar, *The Rhetoric of (Re)unification: Constructing Identity through East and West German Newspapers* (New York: Lang, 1996).

59. Kapfer, "Nostalgia in Germany's New Federal States," 273–76.

60. "Rückfall in die Nische" [Relapse into the Niche], *Der Spiegel*, Wahlsonderheft [special election issue], September 24, 2002, 34–35; "Dann ist die Partei tot" [Then the Party Was Dead], *Der Spiegel*, September 30, 2002, 38.

61. Werner van Begger, "Schwindelnde Nostagie: Die Ostdeutschen entfernen sich langsam von der PDS" [Fading Nostalgia: East Germans Are Gradually Distancing Themselves from the PDS], *Frankfurter Allgemeine Zeitung*, September 29, 2002, 38.

62. Meulemann, "Werte und Wertwandel im vereinten Deutschland," 22.

63. Maaz, *Das gestürtzte Volk*.

64. Kim Woon-Tai, "Korean Politics: Setting and Political Culture," in Kil Soong Hoom and Moon Chung-in, eds., *Understanding Korean Politics* (Albany: State University of New York Press, 2001), 19.

65. Han Man-gil, Hyeun Ju, Kim Chang-hwan, and Oh Ki-Seung, eds., *Bukhan ital jumin-ui Namhan gyoyuk jeogeun yeongu* [A Study of the Educational Adaptation for Defecting North Korean Residents] (Seoul: Korean Education Development Institute, 1999), 22–23.

3. THE GEOPOLITICAL PRODUCTION OF DANGER

1. Gregory Henderson, *Korea, the Politics of the Vortex* (Cambridge, Mass.: Harvard University Press, 1968), 7.

2. See Barry Buzan, *People, States, and Fear* (London: Harvester Wheatsheaf, 1991); R. B. J. Walker, "The Subject of Security," in Keith Krause and Michael C. Williams, eds., *Critical Security Studies* (Minneapolis: University of Minnesota Press, 1997), 61–82.

3. Elizabeth Kier, "Culture and French Military Doctrine before World War II," in Peter J. Katzenstein, ed., *The Culture of National Security: Norms and Identity in World Politics* (New York: Columbia University Press, 1996), 200.

4. "Initiativen Chinas im Nordkorea-Konflikt" [China's Initiatives in the North Korean Conflict], *Neue Zürcher Zeitung,* February 25, 2003.

5. Quoted in Howard French, "North Korea Tests Missile," *New York Times,* February 25, 2003.

6. Nicholas Eberstadt, "Korea," in Richard J. Ellings and Aaron L. Friedberg, eds., *Strategic Asia: Power and Purpose 2001–02* (Seattle: National Bureau of Asian Research, 2001), 135.

7. François Godement, "Une paix asiatique est-elle possible sans architecture régionale? [Is Peace in Asia Possible without a Regional Framework?], *Politique Étrangère,* no. 1 (2001): 85–91.

8. Peter Polomka, *The Two Koreas: Catalyst for Conflict in East Asia?* (Letchworth, U.K.: International Institute for Strategic Studies, 1986), 23; Yu Suk Ryul, "Soviet–North Korean Relations and Security on the Korean Peninsula," *Asian Perspective* 2, no. 1 (1987): 75.

9. Michael Yahuda, *The International Politics of the Asia-Pacific, 1945–1995* (London: Routledge, 1996), 167.

10. Moon Chung-in, *Arms Control on the Korean Peninsula* (Seoul: Yonsei University Press, 1996), 280.

11. Stephen Gilbert, "Northeast Asia in American Security Policy," in W. T. Tow and W. R. Feeney, eds., *U.S. Foreign Policy and Asian-Pacific Security* (Boulder, Colo.: Westview, 1982), 84; Clive Hamilton and Richard Tanter, "The Antinomies of Success in South Korea," *Inter-national Affairs* 41, no. 1 (Summer–Fall 1987): 84.

12. Louis C. Menetrey, "Statement by U.S. Army Forces Korea, before the Committee on Armed Service ate," *Korean Journal of Defense Analysis,* no. 1 (1989

13. Bruce Cumings, "Power and Plenty in Northeas *Journal* 5, no. 1 (1987): 80.

14. Stephen M. Walt, "Alliances in Theory an Ahead," *Journal of International Affairs* 43, no. 1 (Ralph N. Clough, *Embattled Korea: The Rivalry for Internationaı* (Boulder, Colo.: Westview, 1987), 67.

15. Truman is quoted in James I. Matray, "Korea: Test Case of Containment in Asia," in Bruce Cumings, ed., *Child of Conflict, The Korean-American Relationship, 1943–1953* (Seattle: University of Washington Press, 1983), 193.

16. Dwight D. Eisenhower, "Message from the President to the Congress Requesting Legislation for the Rehabilitation and Economic Support of the Republic of Korea, July 27, 1953," appendix F, in Gene M. Lyons, *Military Policy and Economic Aid, The Korean Case, 1950–1953* (Columbus: Ohio State University Press, 1961), 259–60.

17. Chung Young Iob, "U.S. Economic Aid to South Korea after World War II," in A. C. Nahm, ed., *The United States and Korea, American–Korean*

Relations, 1866–1976 (Kalamazoo: Western Michigan University Press, 1979), 212; Anne O. Krueger, *The Developmental Role of the Foreign Sector and Aid* (Cambridge, Mass.: Harvard University Press, 1979), 224.

18. Bruce Cumings, "The Origins and Development of the Northeast Asian Political Economy: Industrial Sectors, Product Cycles, and Political Consequences," in F. C. Deyo, ed., *The Political Economy of the New Asian Industrialism* (Ithaca, N.Y.: Cornell University Press, 1987), 67.

19. Krueger, *The Developmental Role of the Foreign Sector and Aid*, 152.

20. Cumings, "Origins and Development," 67.

21. Edward S. Mason et al., *The Economic and Social Modernization of the Republic of Korea* (Cambridge, Mass.: Harvard University Press, 1980), 166.

22. See Robert Gilpin, *The Political Economy of International Relations* (Princeton, N.J.: Princeton University Press, 1987), 140–42.

23. Stephen D. Krasner, "American Policy and Global Economic Stability," in W. Avery and D. Rapkin, eds., *America in a Changing World Political Economy* (New York: Longman, 1982), 43.

24. *Asia Yearbook* (Hong Kong: Far Eastern Economic Review, 1988), 168.

25. See, for example, "U.S. Embassy Replies to Korean Farmers," in *Backgrounder,* press release issued by the Press Office of the U.S. Embassy in Seoul, January 25, 1988, 1.

26. Kim Hong U, "Japan's Two Korea Policy and Its Implications for Inter-Korean Relations," *Korea Observer,* Autumn 1986, 307.

27. Quoted in Don Oberdorfer, *The Two Koreas: A Contemporary History* (London: Warner, 1998), 306.

28. Leon V. Sigal, *Disarming Strangers: Nuclear Diplomacy with North Korea* (Princeton, N.J.: Princeton University Press, 1998), 13, 125.

29. Ibid., 21.

30. William J. Perry, *Review of United States Policy towards North Korea* (Washington, D.C.: U.S. Department of State, 1999), 5, 6, 10, 12, http://usinfo.state.gov/regional/ea/easec/nkreview.html. See also Moon Chung-in, Maso Okonogi, and Mitchell B. Reiss, eds., *The Perry Report, the Missile Quagmire, and the North Korean Question* (Seoul: Yonsei University Press, 2000).

31. Perry, *Review of U.S. Policy,* 8.

32. Stephen W. Bosworth, "After the Summit: American Policy towards Korea," Northeast Asia Peace and Security Network Special Report, *Nautilus Institute,* http://69.44.62.160/archives/pub/ftp/napsnet/special_reports/Bosworth_Speech.txt.

33. Bruce Cumings, *Parallax Visions: Making Sense of American–East Asian Relations at the End of the Century* (Durham, N.C.: Duke University Press, 2002), xiv.

34. "Der Sieg im Nuklearkonflikt wird unser sein" [We Will Be Victorious in the Nuclear Conflict], *Der Speigel*, February 17, 2003. For a similar representation see Tracy McVeigh, "UN official says U.S. and North Korea Sliding to War," *Guardian Weekly*, April 20, 2003, 8.

35. Murray Hiebert, John Larkin, and Susan Lawrence, "Consequences of Confession," *Far Eastern Economic Review*, October 31, 2002.

36. Nicholas D. Kristof, "Pentagon Targets in North Korea," *International Herald Tribune*, March 1, 2003.

37. Scott Ritter, "Arms Inspector Dares to Check the Doomsday Clock," *Sydney Morning Herald*, February 8, 2003.

38. Hugh White, "More Than One Catch-22 for West When It Comes to North Korea," *Sydney Morning Herald*, February 27, 2003.

39. Sigal, *Disarming Strangers*, 6.

40. See, most notably, Robert Jervis, *Perception and Misperception in International Politics* (Princeton, N.J.: Princeton University Press, 1976).

41. Oberdorfer, *The Two Koreas*, 252.

42. Article 2d obliged the parties to "cease the introduction into Korea of reinforcing combat aircraft, armored vehicles, weapons, and ammunition" (Armistice Agreement, July 27, 1953, as reprinted in Kim Chae-Han, *The Korean DMZ* [Seoul: Sowha Publishing, 2001], 246). North Korea did not, of course, abide by this agreement either.

43. Peter Hayes, "American Nuclear Hegemony in Korea," *Journal of Peace Research* 25, no. 4 (1988): 356.

44. Oberdorfer, *The Two Koreas*, 257.

45. Moon, *Arms Control on the Korean Peninsula*, 68, 260.

46. Hayes, "American Nuclear Hegemony in Korea," 355.

47. See Lee Chong-sik and Robert Scalapino, *Communism in Korea* (Berkeley: University of California Press, 1972), 1:558; William T. Tow, *Encountering the Dominant Player: U.S. Extended Deterrence Strategy in the Asia-Pacific* (New York : Columbia University Press, 1991), 256.

48. As reported in Oberdorfer, *The Two Koreas*, 258.

49. Bruce Cumings, *Korea's Place in the Sun: A Modern History* (New York: W. W. Norton, 1997), 481–82.

50. George W. Bush, "The President's State of the Union Address," January 29, 2002, http://www.whitehouse.gov/news/releases/2002/01/20020129-11.html.

51. Kristof, "Pentagon Targets in North Korea"; Urs Gehriger, "Washington erwägt Präventivschläge" [Washington Contemplates Preemptive Attacks], *Tages-Anzeiger*, June 12, 2002, 3.

52. See in particular chapter 5 of "The National Security Strategy of the United States of America," September 2002, http://www.whitehouse.gov/nsc/nss.html.

53. Kim Ji-ho, "Pyongyang's Threat Puzzles Analysts Concerned about Inter-Korean Relations," *Korea Herald,* March 15, 2002.

54. Tad Daley, "America's Nuclear Hypocrisy," *International Herald Tribune,* October 21, 2002.

55. Mark B.M. Suh, "North Korea Seen through the Confidential Documents of the Former East Germany," in Kang Myoung-kyu and Helmut Wagner, eds., *Germany and Korea: Lessons in Unification* (Seoul: Seoul National University Press, 1995), 394–98.

56. Kim Il Sung, quoted in Oberdorfer, *The Two Koreas,* 311. See also Michael J. Mazarr, "Going Just a Little Nuclear: Nonproliferation Lessons from North Korea," *International Security* 20, no. 2 (Fall 1995): 100–1.

57. Victor D. Cha, "North Korea's Weapons of Mass Destruction: Badges, Shields, or Swords?" *Political Science Quarterly* 117, no 2 (2002): 216–19.

58. Donald Gregg, speech to the Second Jeju Peace Forum, Jeju City, April 12, 2002.

59. See Peter Hartcher, "U.S. Gets Tough on North Korea," *Australian Financial Review,* March 22, 2002, 26; David I. Steinberg, "A Wrench in Korean Peace Machinery," *International Herald Tribune,* February 1, 2002, 6.

60. Joel S. Wit, "North Korea: The Leader of the Pack," *Washington Quarterly* 24, no. 11 (2000): 88.

61. Cumings, *Parallax Visions,* 142.

62. Leon V. Sigal, "U.S.–D.R.K. Relations and Military Issues on the Korean Peninsula," *KNDU Review: Journal of National Security Affairs* 6, no. 2 (December 2001): 96; "North Korea Understands Need for U.S. Troops," *New York Times,* June 24, 2000. See also William T. Tow, *Asia–Pacific Strategic Relations: Seeking Convergent Security* (Cambridge: Cambridge University Press, 2001), 87.

63. Kim Il Sung, *The U.S. Imperialist Army of Aggression Must Unconditionally Withdraw from South Korea* (Pyongyang: Foreign Language Publishing House, 1974), 8.

64. Markus Wehner, "Russland glaubt nicht an Pjöngjangs Bombe" [Russia Does Not Believe Reports about Pyongyang's Bomb], *Frankfurter Allgemeine Zeitung,* October 22, 2002, 12.

65. Kim Myong Chol, quoted in Nicholas D. Kristof, "Devil and Evil Axes," *New York Times,* February 26, 2002, A27.

66. Scott Snyder, *Negotiating on the Edge: North Korean Negotiating Behavior* (Washington, D.C.: U.S. Institute of Peace Press, 1999), 66; see also 43 and 70.

67. Nicholas Kristof, "A Sea of Fire, or Worse?" *New York Times,* May 2, 2003; "North Korea Warns of 'Sea of Fire' as U.S. Envoy Arrives," *Sydney Morning Herald,* January 3, 2003.

68. Kim, quoted in Kristof, "Devil and Evil Axes," A27.

69. "DPRK to React to Unreasonable 'Countermeasure' with Toughest Stance," *KCNA Bulletin,* January 19, 2003, http://www.kcna.co.jp/.

70. George W. Bush, "State of the Union Address," as reprinted in the *New York Times,* January 28, 2003.

71. Cumings, *Parallax Visions*; Hazel Smith, "Bad, Mad, Sad or Rational Actor? Why the 'Securitization' Paradigm Makes for Poor Policy Analysis of North Korea," *International Affairs* 76, no. 3 (July 2000): 594–96.

72. Powell, as quoted in *Newsweek,* April 22, 1991, and (later in) Cumings, *Parallax Visions,* 139.

73. See Jacques Derrida, *Voyous* [Rogues] (Paris: Galilée, 2003).

74. First aired on U.S. television between 1972 and 1983, *M*A*S*H* was set during the Korean War. Very few Koreans actually appeared on the show, and those who did were represented in rather paternalistic ways. The series was in no way intended to represent the war—it was generally interpreted as an indirect critique of the Vietnam War. And yet the mere popularity of *M*A*S*H* inevitably influenced American perceptions of Korea. This was particularly consequential since it was aired at a time when, as one commentator puts it, "the American news media was not making any great efforts to explain the background and reasons for events in Korea." Most correspondents, for instance, covered Korea from Tokyo, Beijing, or Hong Kong and drew much of their information from secondary sources. See Craig S. Coleman, *American Images of Korea: Korea and Koreans as Portrayed in Books, Magazines, Television, News Media, and Film* (Seoul: Hollym, 2000), 160.

75. Robert Dujarric, "North Korea: Risks and Rewards of Engagement," *Journal of International Affairs* 54, no. 2 (Spring 2001): 467.

76. Donald H. Rumsfeld, "Transforming the Military," *Foreign Affairs,* May–June 2002, 21.

77. Stephen M. Walt, "Beyond bin Laden: Reshaping U.S. Foreign Policy," *International Security* 26, no. 3 (Winter 2001–2002): 56.

78. CNN, November 6, 2001.

79. George W. Bush, "The President's State of the Union Address," January 29, 2002, http://www.whitehouse.gov/news/releases/2002/01/20020129-11.html. For analysis see Michael Cox, "American Power before and after 11 September: Dizzy with Success?" *International Affairs* 78, no. 2 (April 2002): 272–73.

80. Ira Katznelson, "Evil and Politics," *Daedalus,* Winter 2002, 7; Paul Valadir, "Le mal politique moderne" [Modern Political Evil], *Études,* February 2001, 394.

81. Allan Bloom, *The Closing of the American Mind* (New York: Simon and Schuster, 1987), 142.

82. Douglas Klusmeyer and Astri Suhrke, "Comprehending 'Evil': Challenges for Law and Policy," *Ethics and International Affairs* 16 (2002): 27, 29, 35–37; Roxanne L. Euben, "Killing (for) Politics: Jihad, Martyrdom, and Political Action," *Political Theory* 30, no. 1 (February 2002): 4; Manfred Henningsen, "Totalitarismus und politischer Realismus: Über die modernen Regime des Terrors" [Totalitarianism and Political Realism: About Modern Regimes of Terror], *Merkur* 56, no. 5 (May 2002): 383–92.

83. Thomas C. Hubbard (U.S. ambassador to South Korea), "The U.S. Approach to the Korean Peninsula," speech to the 2002 Jeju Peace Forum, Jeju City, April 13, 2002.

84. James Dao, "Bush Urges Chinese President to Press North Korea on Arms," *New York Times,* February 7, 2003.

85. William Safire, "The Asian Front," *New York Times,* March 10, 2003.

86. Victor D. Cha, "Korea's Place in the Axis," *Foreign Affairs,* May–June 2002, 79–92.

87. Quoted in Henrik Bork, "Annäherungen auf Umwegen" [Raprochement with Detours], *Süddeutsche Zeitung,* January 11, 2003, 2.

88. Lee Chung Min, "North Korean Missiles: Strategic Implications and Policy Responses," *Pacific Review* 14, no. 1 (2001): 98.

89. See Carol Cohn, "Sex and Death in the Rational World of Defense Intellectuals," in L. R. Forcey, ed., *Peace: Meanings, Politics, Strategies* (New York: Praeger, 1989), 334–37.

90. Jo Yung Hwan, "U.S. Policy towards the Two Koreas and Its Implications for Inter-Korea Relations," *Korea Observer,* Autumn 1986, 259.

91. Lho Kyong Soo, "The Military Balance in the Korean Peninsula," *Asian Affairs* 19, no. 1 (February 1988): 38.

92. As cited in John McBeth, "Safety in Numbers: Defense Paper Compares Quantity, Not Quality," *Far Eastern Economic Review,* January 26, 1989, 34.

93. *Defense White Paper* (Seoul: Ministry of National Defense, 1999), 59.

94. "Comparison of North–South Korean Military Capabilities," appendix 6 to *Defense White Paper,* Ministry of National Defense, Seoul, 2000, http://www.mnd.go.kr; *The Strategic Balance in Northeast Asia* (Seoul: Korean Research Institute of Strategy, 2001), 294–304.

95. McBeth, "Safety in Numbers," 34; Bruce Cumings, "The Conflict on the Korean Peninsula," in Y. Sakamoto, ed., *Asia, Militarization, and Regional Conflict* (Tokyo: United Nations University, 1988), 112–13.

96. Moon, *Arms Control on the Korean Peninsula,* 262; see also 56–66, 132–35.

97. Sigal, *Disarming Strangers,* 21.

98. Hazel Smith, "Threat or Opportunity?" *World Today,* January 2000.

99. "North Korea's Military Expenditures," appendix 5 to *Defense White Paper* (Seoul: Ministry of National Defense, 2000), Seoul, http://www.mnd.go.kr.

100. See Bjorn Moller, "Arms Control on the Korean Peninsula: Objectives and Prospects," *KNDU Review: Journal of National Security Affairs* 6, no. 2 (December 2001): 42–43; Kim Taehyun, "South Korean Perspectives on the North Korean Nuclear Question," *Mershon International Studies Review* 40 (1996): 259.

101. *The Strategic Balance in Northeast Asia,* 294.

4. TOWARD AN ETHICS OF DIALOGUE

1. Michel Wieviorka, "Le nouveau paradigm de la violence" [The New Paradigm of Violence], *Cultures et Conflits: Sociologie Politique de l'International,* no. 29–30 (Summer 1998): 15.

2. Roh Moo-hyun, "Presidential Inaugural Address," reprinted in *Korea Herald,* February 26, 2003.

3. Koh Byung Chul, "The Foreign and Unification Policies of the Republic of Korea," in Kil Soong Hoom and Moon Chung-in, eds., *Understanding Korean Politics* (Albany: State University of New York Press, 2001), 253.

4. According to South Korea's Ministry of Unification, the number of North–South talks for the past few years were 5 (1988), 8 (1999), 26 (2000), 8 (2001), and 33 (2002). See the ministry's website at http://www.unikorea.go.kr/.

5. Stephen Lunn, "South Korean Leader 'Bought' Peace Prize," *Australian,* June 26, 2003.

6. United Nations Development Programme, *Human Development Report* (New York: Oxford University Press, 1994), 22.

7. Lloyd Axworthy, "Human Security and Global Governance: Putting People First," *Global Governance* 7, no. 1 (January–March 2001): 19–23.

8. See, for instance, Edward Newman, "Human Security and Constructivism," *International Studies Perspectives* 2 (2001): 239–51; Roland Paris, "Human Security: Paradigm Shift or Hot Air?" *International Security* 26, no. 2 (Fall 2001): 87–102.

9. See Amitav Acharya, "Human Security: East Versus West," *International Journal* 56, no. 3 (Summer 2001): 442–60.

10. Paris, "Human Security," 89.

11. Yuen Foong Khong, "Human Security: A Shotgun Approach to Alleviating Human Misery?" *Global Governance* 7, no. 3 (July–September 2001): 232.

12. Hazel Smith, "Bad, Mad, Sad or Rational Actor? Why the 'Securitization' Paradigm Makes for Poor Policy Analysis of North Korea," *International Affairs* 76, no. 3 (2000): 596.

13. Stephen Noerper, "Regime Security and Military Tension in North Korea," in Moon Chung-in, ed., *Understanding Regime Dynamics in North Korea* (Seoul: Yonsei University Press, 1998), 167–74.

14. Paris, "Human Security," 93.

15. Quoted in Newman, "Human Security and Constructivism," 244.

16. Ibid., 240.

17. See Anthony Burke, "Caught between National and Human Security: Knowledge and Power in Post-Crisis Asia," *Pacifica Review* 13, no. 3 (October 2001): 215–39; Alex J. Bellamy and Matt McDonald, "The Utility of Human Security: Which Humans? What Security?" *Security Dialogue* 33, no. 3 (September 2002): 373–77.

18. Kent E. Calder, "The New Face of Northeast Asia," *Foreign Affairs,* January–February 2001, 16.

19. Ibid., 110.

20. Ibid., 107.

21. Cynthia Enloe, *Bananas, Beaches, and Bases: Making Feminist Sense of International Politics* (London: Pandora, 1989), xi. For an excellent application of this strategy of inquiry to Korea, see Katharine H. S. Moon, *Sex among Allies: Military Prostitution in U.S.–Korea Relations* (New York: Columbia University Press, 1997).

22. Moon Chung-in, "The Kim Dae Jung Government's Peace Policy towards North Korea," *Asian Perspective* 25, no. 2 (2001): 193.

23. Ahn Yinhay, "North Korea in 2001: At a Crossroads," *Asian Survey* 42, no. 1 (January–February 2002): 46–55; Moon Chung-in and Kim Tae-hwan, "Sustaining Inter-Korean Reconciliation: North–South Korea Cooperation," *Journal of East Asian Affairs,* Fall–Winter 2001, 240–41; Moon Chung-in and Kim Yonghoo, "The Future of the North Korean System," in Samuel S. Kim, ed., *The North Korean System in the Post–Cold War Era* (New York: Palgrave, 2001), 240–41.

24. John Gittings, "Reform Is Last Hope for Hungry North Korea," *Guardian Weekly,* August 15, 2002, 22; Bruce Pedroletti, "Pyongyang Gets Dose of Market Medicine," *Guardian Weekly,* August 22, 2002, 23.

25. Howard W. French, "North Korea Adding a Pinch of Capitalism to Its Economy," *New York Times,* August 9, 2002.

26. Marcus Noland, *Avoiding the Apocalypse: The Future of the Two Koreas* (Washington, D.C.: Institute for International Economics, 2000), 59–142; Oh Kongdan and Ralph C. Hassig, *North Korea through the Looking Glass* (Washington, D.C.: Brookings Institution Press, 2000), 41–80.

27. Hazel Smith, *Overcoming Humanitarian Dilemmas in the DPRK*

(Washington, D.C.: U.S. Institute of Peace, July 2002), 3; Ramsay Liem, "Silent Famine in North Korea," *Peace Review* 11, no. 2 (June 1999): 325–31.

28. Ahn, "North Korea in 2001," 2.

29. Shim Jae Hoon, "A Crack in the Wall," *Far Eastern Economic Review,* April 29, 1999. See also Oknim Chung, "The U.S.–ROK Private Sector Role in Peace and Security on the Korean Peninsula," *Korean Journal of Defense Analysis* 11, no. 1 (1999): 118–20; Elisabeth Rosenthal, "Famine in North Korea Creates Steady Human Flow into China," *New York Times,* June 10, 2000. For various statistical data on the number of North Koreans who crossed into China, see Noland, *Avoiding the Apocalypse,* 189.

30. See, for instance, Chung, "The U.S.–ROK Private Sector," 120–21; Timothy Savage and Nautilus Team, "NGO Engagement with North Korea: Dilemmas and Lessons Learned," *Asian Perspective* 26, no. 1 (2002): 151–67.

31. Omawale Omawale, "An Exercise in Ambivalence: Negotiating with North Korea," *Harvard Asia Pacific Review* 3, no. 2 (Summer 1999): 60–62; Hazel Smith, "Opening Up by Default: North Korea, the Humanitarian Community, and the Crisis," *Pacific Review* 12, no. 3 (1999): 467.

32. Smith, "Opening Up by Default," 454.

33. See, for instance, Hazel Smith, *Five-Year Review of the Caritas Programme in the DPRK* (Hong Kong: Caritas, 2001), and "Overcoming Humanitarian Dilemmas."

34. Chung, "The U.S.–ROK Private Sector Role," 122; Jim Williams et al., "The Wind Farm in the Cabbage Patch," *Bulletin of Atomic Scientists* 55, no. 3 (May–June 1999): 46, as cited in Smith, "Bad, Mad, Sad or Rational Actor?" 609. See also Savage and Nautilus Team, "NGO Engagement with North Korea," 151–67.

35. See Peter Hayes and Timothy Savage, "To Build Trust, Think Small," *Newsweek,* November 6, 2000, 48.

36. Nicholas Eberstadt, "South Korea's Economic Crisis and the Prospects for North–South Relations," *Korea and World Affairs* 22, no. 4 (Winter 1998): 539–40.

37. Moon Chung-in, "The Sunshine Policy and Ending the Cold War Structure," in Moon Chung-in, Odd Arne Westad, and Gyoo-hyoung Kahng, eds., *Ending the Cold War in Korea: Theoretical and Historical Perspectives* (Seoul: Yonsei University Press, 2001), 283. See also Moon, "The Kim Dae Jung Government's Peace Policy," 184, 186; and Kim Dae Jung, *The Korean Problem: Nuclear Crisis, Democracy, and Reunification* (Seoul: Kim Dae Jung Peace Foundation, 1994).

38. Moon and Kim, "Sustaining Inter-Korean Reconciliation," 213.

39. Lee Kap-soo, "Historic Cruiser Tour Full Steam Ahead," *Korea Herald,* November 18, 1998, 17; Peter M. Beck, "Beyond Balancing: Economic Cooperation on the Korean Peninsula," *International Journal of Korean Unification Studies* 8 (1999): 109; Moon and Kim, "Sustaining Inter-Korean Reconciliation," 223–24.

40. Kim Hyun-chul, "Two Koreas Break Ground in Gaesong," *Korea Herald,* June 30, 2003; James Brooke, "Koreas Open the DMZ," *New York Times,* February 15, 2003.

41. See Kim Kyung-ho, "Scandal-plagued Hyundai Chief Plunges to His Death," *Korea Herald,* August 5, 2003.

42. See Lee Tae Seop, "South Korean Business Investment Strategy in North Korea," *Korea Focus,* July–August 2000, 32–51; Richard Tait, "Playing by the Rules in Korea: Lessons Learned in the North–South Economic Engagement," *Asian Survey* 43, no. 2 (March–April 2003): 305–28; Bradley Babson, "Integrating North Korea with the World Economy," in Moon et al., *Ending the Cold War,* 445–68.

43. These data come from the South Korea Ministry of Unification, *White Paper,* 2002, http://www.unikorea.go.kr/.

44. See Noland, *Avoiding the Apocalypse,* 116–21; Bertil Lintner and Yoon Suh-kyung, "Coming in from the Cold?" *Far Eastern Economic Review,* October 25, 2001, 60–65.

45. James Brooke, "Tentatively, North Korea Solicits Foreign Investment and Tourism," *New York Times,* February 19, 2002, C1. See also Peter Smerdon, "The Road Less Traveled," *Far Eastern Economic Review,* December 27, 2001, 14–20.

46. Choi Won-Ki, "Dealing with North Korea 'as It Is,'" *Nautilus Institute Policy Forum Online,* 1999, http://www.nautilus.org/fora/security/9907K_Choi.html. See also *North Korea: Country Profile 2001* (London: Economist Intelligence Unit, 2001), 68.

47. Chung, "The U.S.–ROK Private Sector Role," 104.

48. See Moon, "The Kim Dae-jung Government's Peace Policy," 188–89.

49. Chung, "The U.S.–ROK Private Sector Role," 125.

50. Steven R. Weisman, "South Korea, Once a Solid Ally, Now Poses Problems for the U.S.," *New York Times,* January 2, 2003, 1.

51. For details see Chung, "The U.S.–ROK Private Sector Role," 104–6. Don Oberdorfer, *The Two Koreas: A Contemporary History* (London: Warner, 1998), 327; Leon V. Sigal, *Disarming Strangers: Nuclear Diplomacy with North Korea* (Princeton, N.J.: Princeton University Press, 1998).

52. On this issue see Selig S. Harrison, "The Kim Dae-jung Government, the Sunshine Policy, and the North–South Summit," in Moon Chung-in and David I. Steinberg, eds., *Korea in Transition: Three Years under the Kim Dae-jung Government* (Seoul: Yonsei University Press, 2002), 67–84.

53. See Han Sang-jin, "Four Critical Issues of the Korean Unification," in Han Sang-Jin, ed., *Habermas and the Korean Debate* (Seoul: Seoul National University Press, 1998), 138–59.

54. R. B. J. Walker, "The Subject of Security," in Keith Kraus and Michael C. Williams, eds., *Critical Security Studies* (Minneapolis: University of Minnesota Press, 1997), 62.

55. Seo Hyun-jin, "Tour Program Makes Inroads to Peace," *Korea Herald,* February 17, 2003; James Brooke, "South Koreans Visiting North, Despite Tensions," *New York Times,* February 15, 2003.

56. South Korea Ministry of Unification, *White Paper,* 2000, 2001, 2002. For these and other statistical indicators see http://www.unikorea.go.kr/.

57. Noland, *Avoiding the Apocalypse,* 115.

5. DILEMMAS OF ENGAGEMENT

1. Han Sang-jin, "Four Critical Issues of the Korean Unification," in Han Sang-Jin, ed., *Habermas and the Korean Debate* (Seoul: Seoul National University Press, 1998), 157. See also Jürgen Habermas, *Theorie des kommunikativen Handelns* (Frankfurt: Suhrkamp, 1988). For a translation by Thomas McCarthy, see *The Theory of Communicative Action* (Boston: Beacon Press, 1984).

2. Moon Chung-in, "The Sunshine Policy and Ending the Cold War Structure," in Moon Chung-in, Odd Arne Westad, and Gyoo-hyoung Kahng, eds., *Ending the Cold War in Korea: Theoretical and Historical Perspectives* (Seoul: Yonsei University Press, 2001), 304.

3. Lee Jung-Hoon and Moon Chung-in, "The North Korean Nuclear Crisis Revisited," *Security Dialogue* 34, no. 2 (June 2003): 148.

4. "Tête-a-Tête Talks Held between Kim Jong Il and Kim Dae Jung," *KCNA Bulletin,* June 15, 2000, http://www.kcna.co.jp/.

5. "Moves for Biochemical War by U.S. and South Korean Rulers Assailed," "U.S.–South Korean War Maneuver under Fire," and "U.S. and South Korean Warmongers' Preparations for War Blasted," all in *KCNA Bulletin,* April 20, 2000, http://www.kcna.co.jp/.

6. "Korean People's Absolute Worship of the Leader," *KCNA Bulletin,* July 17, 2000, http://www.kcna.co.jp/.

7. *Compendium of North Korea* (Seoul: Research Institute on Peace and Unification, 1986), 339.

8. Quoted in *Marshal Kim Il Sung Is Our Father* (Pyongyang: Youth Publishing House, 1985), 193.

9. Shim Jae Hoon, "Peace Breaks Out," *Far Eastern Economic Review,* December 26, 1991, 9.

10. Martin Heisler, "Cross-boundary Population Movements and Security in Korea," in Miranda A. Schreurs and Dennis Pirages, eds., *Ecological Security in Northeast Asia* (Seoul: Yonsei University Press, 1998), 181. For more details see Gert G. Wagner, "Migration before and after Unification," in Il SaKong and Kim Kwang Suk, eds., *Policy Priorities for the Unified Korean Economy* (Seoul: Institute for Global Economics, 1998), 91–121.

11. Quoted in Oh Kongdan and Ralph C Hassig, *North Korea through the Looking Glass* (Washington, D.C.: Brookings Institution Press, 2000), 108.

12. Pyongyang Institute for the Reunification of the Fatherland, "Die Berechtigung der DVRK zum Besitz militärischer Abschreckungskraft" [The DPRK's Right to Possess Military Weapons for Purposes of Deterrence], trans. Shin Yho-Eun and Yi Hee-Young, paper presented at the symposium "Wohin steuert Nordkorea?" [What Future for North Korea?], June 25, 2003, Berlin, 11.

13. See Ministry of Unification, "Overview of Intra-Korean Interchange and Cooperation," http://152.99.76.131/en/.

14. Or so argues Marcus Noland in "Turmoil on the Peninsula: The Need for Economic Reform in North Korea," *Harvard Asia Pacific Review* 3, no. 2 (Summer 1999): 49.

15. Park Syung Je, "The Promised Land: Reopening Borders with the Kumkangsan Tours," *Harvard Asia Pacific Review* 3, no. 2 (Summer 1999): 58.

16. See James Cotton, "A Radical Experiment: The Evidence Is in from North Korea's Rajin-Seonbong Area," *Harvard Asia Pacific Review* 2, no. 1 (1997–1998): 57–60.

17. Christoph Hein, "Nordkorea errichtet eine kapitalistische Sonderzone hinter Mauern" [North Korea Is Erecting a Capitalist Special Zone behind Walls], *Frankfurter Allgemeine Zeitung,* September 25, 2002, 15; Lee Young-jong, "North Names Sinuiju Special Economic Zone," *Joong-Ang Ilbo,* September 20, 2002.

18. Omawale Omawale, "An Exercise in Ambivalence: Negotiating with North Korea," *Harvard Asia Pacific Review* 3, no. 2 (Summer 1999): 60–62.

19. See, for instance, Hazel Smith, *Five-Year Review of the Caritas Programme in the DPRK* (Hong Kong: Caritas, 2001).

20. Marcus Noland, *Avoiding the Apocalypse: The Future of the Two Koreas* (Washington, D.C.: Institute for International Economics, 2000), 8. See also Douglas Paal, "Achieving Korean Reunification," in Nicholas Eberstadt and Richard Ellings, eds., *Korea's Future and the Great Powers* (Seattle: University of Washington Press, 2001), 305.

21. Nicholas Eberstadt, "Hastening Korean Unification," *Foreign Affairs,* March–April 1997, 82.

22. Noland, *Avoiding the Apocalypse,* 183.

23. Fiona Terry, "Food Aid to North Korea Is Propping Up a Stalinist Regime," *Guardian Weekly,* September 6, 2001.

24. See, for instance, Selig S. Harrison, "Promoting a Soft Landing in Korea," in *Foreign Policy,* no. 106 (Spring 1997): 57–75; Scott Snyder, "Managing Integration on the Korean Peninsula: The Positive and Normative Case for Gradualism with or without Integration," in Marcus Noland, ed., *Economic Integration of the Korean Peninsula* (Washington, D.C.: Institute for International Economics, 1998), 39–50; Moon Chung-in and David I. Steinberg, eds., *Kim Dae-jung Government and Sunshine Policy* (Seoul: Yonsei University Press, 1999).

25. See Hazel Smith, *Overcoming Humanitarian Dilemmas in the DPRK* (Washington, D.C.: U.S. Institute of Peace, July 2002), especially 14–15.

26. Timothy Savage and Nautilus Team, "NGO Engagement with North Korea: Dilemmas and Lessons Learned," *Asian Perspective* 26, no. 1 (2002): 155.

27. See, for instance, Christopher W. Hughes, "Japanese Policy and the North Korean 'Soft Landing,'" *Pacific Review* 11, no. 3 (1998): 389–415; Kwak Tae-Hwan, ed., *The Four Powers and Korean Unification Strategies* (Seoul: Kyungnam University, 1997); Kwak Tae-Hwan and Edward A. Olsen, eds., *The Major Powers of Northeast Asia: Seeking Peace and Security* (Boulder, Colo.: Lynne Rienner, 1996).

28. See Smith, "Overcoming Humanitarian Dilemmas," 4.

29. George W. Bush, in a conversation with Bob Woodward, quoted in Martin Woolacott, "Korea United in Anger at U.S.," *Guardian Weekly,* February 2, 2003.

30. See Koh Byung Chul, "The Foreign and Unification Policies of the Republic of Korea," in Kil Soong Hoom and Moon Chung-in, eds., *Understanding Korean Politics* (Albany: State University of New York Press, 2001), 249; *A Comparison of Unification Policies of South and North Korea* (Seoul: National Unification Board, 1990), 66; Moon Chung-in, *Arms Control on the Korean Peninsula* (Seoul: Yonsei University Press, 1996), 32.

31. Shin Gi-Wook, "Nation, History, and Politics: South Korea," in Hyung Il Pai and Timothy R. Tangherlini, eds., *Nationalism and the Construction of Korean Identity* (Berkeley, Calif.: Institute of East Asian Studies, 1998), 152.

32. Dennis Hart, "Creating the National Other: Opposing Images of Nationalism in South and North Korean Education," *Korean Studies* 23 (1999): 79.

33. Cited in Kihl Young Whan, "Seoul's Engagement Policy and U.S.–DPRK Relations," *Korean Journal of Defense Analysis* 10, no. 1 (1998): 23.

34. See, for instance, Kim Dae-jung, "The South–North Summit: A Year in Review," in Woo Keun-Min, ed., *Building Common Peace and Prosperity in Northeast Asia* (Seoul: Yonsei University Press, 2002), 28. See also *Defense White Paper* (Seoul: Ministry of National Defense, 2000), 64.

35. Quoted in Kim Young-sae, "U.S. Says It Recognizes the North as 'Sovereign,'" *Yoong Ang Ilbo,* November 19, 2002.

36. *A Comparison of Unification Policies,* 65.

37. Don Oberdorfer, *The Two Koreas: A Contemporary History* (London: Warner, 1998), 364.

38. *Korea Herald,* September 15, 1999.

39. Ibid.

40. "Kukkun Kimu saryeongbu-e osin geoseul hwanyeong imnida" [Welcome to Army Headquarters], *Ganjeop singo* [Reporting Spies], undated, http://www.dsc.or.kr/singo/singo.html.

41. Helmut Schmidt (chair), "The Lessons of the German Unification Process for Korea," *InterAction Council,* February 1993, http:/www.asiaawide .or.jp/iac/meetings. See also previous discussion in chapter 2; Koh Il-dong, ed., *Economic Assessment of German Unification and Policy Implications for the Korean Peninsula* (Seoul: Korea Development Institute, 1995); and Moon, *Arms Control on the Korean Peninsula,* 79.

42. Bernhard Seliger, "Ten Years after German Economic Unification: Are There Any Lessons for Korean Unification?" *International Journal of Korean Unification Studies* 10 (2001): 122.

43. For an excellent discussion see Hans J. Giessmann, "German Ostpolitik and Korean Unification," *Pacific Focus* 16, no. 2 (Fall 2001): 25–41.

44. Werner Pfennig, "From Division through Normalization to Unification: A Comparative View on Developments in Germany and Korea," *Korea Observer,* Spring 2001, 26.

45. See Günter Grass, "Das war im Mai, als Willy zurücktrat" [It was May when Willie resigned], *Frankfurter Allgemeine Zeitung,* October 8, 2002, 37.

46. Kim Dae-jung, interview in *Time,* March 2, 1998, 23.

47. Lim Dong-won, "Inter-Korean Summit Meeting and Future Talks," *Korea Focus,* September–October 2002, 63.

48. Koh Byung Chul, "The Foreign and Unification Policies of the Republic of Korea," 249.

49. *Defense White Paper* (Seoul: Ministry of National Defense, 1998), 73.

50. Ibid., 94.

51. Scott Snyder, "U.S. Policy toward North Korea in the Aftermath of

the Perry Report," testimony before the U.S. House Committee on International Relations, March 16, 2000, http://www.globalsecurity.org/wmd/library/congress/2000_h/000316-snyder.htm.

52. Moon Chung-in, "The Kim Dae Jung Government's Peace Policy towards North Korea," *Asian Perspective* 25, no. 2 (2001): 188.

53. Heiner Meulemann, "Values and Social Integration in Korea and Germany," paper presented at "Pursuing Peace beyond the Korean War," conference held in Seoul, April 27–28, 2000.

54. Min Kyung-Hwan, "Psychological Preparations for the Korean Unification," in Kang Myoung-kyu and Helmut Wagner, eds., *Germany and Korea: Lessons in Unification* (Seoul: Seoul National University Press, 1995), 305.

55. Kim Myongsob, "Reexamining Cold War History and the Korean Question," *Korea Journal* 41, no. 2 (Summer 2001): 21.

56. Victor D. Cha, "Korea's Place in the Axis," *Foreign Affairs,* May–June 2002, 83.

57. For an excellent discussion see Roy Richard Grinker, *Korea and Its Futures: Unification and the Unfinished War* (London: Macmillan, 1998).

58. See Werner Pfennig, "Steps towards Normalization: A Comparative Look at Divided Nations," in Kang and Wagner, *Germany and Korea,* 51; Peter Polomka, *The Two Koreas: Catalyst for Conflict in East Asia?* (Letchworth, U.K: International Institute for Strategic Studies, 1986), 13.

59. Baek Yong-cheol, a Southern delegate, representing the position of Northerners, is quoted in "Nam-Buk-haewoe dongpo hakja tongil hoeui: Nam-Buk daepyodanjang daehan interview" [Unification conference for North–South–Overseas Korean scholars: Interviews with Southern and Northern Delegates], *Donga Ilbo,* October 28, 1999, 23.

6. TOWARD AN ETHICS OF DIFFERENCE

1. Moon Chung-in, introduction to Moon Chung-in, ed., *Understanding Regime Dynamics in North Korea* (Seoul: Yonsei University Press, 1998), 12.

2. Martin Heisler, "Cross-boundary Population Movements and Security in Korea," in Miranda A. Schreurs and Dennis Pirages, eds., *Ecological Security in Northeast Asia* (Seoul: Yonsei University Press, 1998), 172; Aidan Foster-Carter, "North Korea: All Roads Lead to Collapse—All the More Reason to Engage Pyongyang," in Marcus Noland, ed., *Economic Integration of the Korean Peninsula* (Washington, D.C.: Institute for International Economics, 1998), 27–38.

3. Oh Kongdan and Ralph C. Hassig, *North Korea through the Looking Glass* (Washington, D.C.: Brookings Institution Press, 2000), 191.

4. Nicholas Eberstadt, "Hastening Korean Unification," *Foreign Affairs,* March–April 1997, 79, 81.

5. Paik Nak-Chung, "Habermas on National Unification in Germany and Korea," in Han Sang-Jin, ed., *Habermas and the Korean Debate* (Seoul: Seoul National University Press, 1998), 162.

6. Martin Hart-Landsberg, "Korean Unification: Learning from the German Experience," *Journal of Contemporary Asia* 26, no. 1 (1996): 72.

7. Jürgen Habermas, *Die nachholende Revolution* (Frankfurt: Suhrkamp, 1991). Parts of this book have been translated as "What Does Socialism Mean Today? The Rectifying Revolution and the Need for New Thinking on the Left," *New Left Review,* September–October 1990, 3–21. See also Habermas, "National Unification and Popular Sovereignty," in Han, *Habermas and the Korean Debate,* 116–17.

8. Marcus Noland, Sherman Robinson, and Li-gang Liu, "The Costs and Benefits of Korean Unification," *Asian Survey* 38, no. 8 (August 1998): 814.

9. See, for instance, Emmanuel Levinas, *Time and the Other,* trans. R. Cohen (Pittsburgh, Pa.: Duquesne University Press, 1987); Levinas, *Totality and Infinity,* trans. Alphonso Lingis (Pittsburgh: Duquesne University Press, 1969). For applications to the international realm see Michael J. Shapiro, *Violent Cartographies: Mapping Cultures of War* (Minneapolis: University of Minnesota Press, 1997), and David Campbell, "The Deterritorialisation of Responsibility: Levinas, Derrida, and Ethics after the End of Philosophy," *Alternatives* 19, no. 4 (December 1994): 455–85; and Campbell, *National Deconstruction: Violence, Identity, and Justice in Bosnia* (Minneapolis: University of Minnesota Press, 1998).

10. Roxanne L. Euben, *Enemy in the Mirror: Islamic Fundamentalism and the Limits of Modern Rationalism* (Princeton, N.J.: Princeton University Press, 1999), 16.

11. Kwon Hyeok-beom, "Symposium—Jeongsang Hoedam hu Hanbando-e Tongil Gwajeong" [Symposium—The Process of Unification on the Korean Peninsula after the Summit], proceedings, June 2001, http://dragon.taejon.ac.kr/kwonhb/papers/buddalec.htm; and "Tongil gyoyuk-eseo talbundan simin gyoyuk-euro—pyeonghwa, inkwon geurigo chai-ui kongjon" [From Unification Education to Postdivision Popular Education: The Coexistence of Peace, Human Rights, and Difference], June 2001, http://dragon.taejon.ac.kr/kwonhb/papers/postuni.htm.

12. Roy Richard Grinker, *Korea and Its Futures: Unification and the Unfinished War* (London: Macmillan, 1998), xvi; see also x–xvi.

13. See Park Jae Kyu, "North Korea's Democratic Confederal Republic of Koryo," in Kwak Tae-Hwan, Kim Chonghan, and Kim Hong Nack, eds., *Korean Reunification* (Seoul: Institute for Far Eastern Studies, Kyungnam University, 1984), 69; Volker Grabowsky, *Zwei-Nationen-Lehre oder*

Wiedervereinigung? [Two-Nation Theory or Unification?] (Bochum: Studien-verlag Brockmeyer, 1987), 319.

14. Dennis Hart, "Creating the National Other: Opposing Images of Nationalism in South and North Korean Education," *Korean Studies* 23 (1999): 68–93.

15. Guksa Pyeonchan Wiwonhoe and Il Jong Doseo Yeoungu Gaebal Wiwonhoe [National Institute of Korean History and the Commission for Developing Textbooks], *Guksa* [Korean History] (Seoul: Taehan Gyogwaseo, 1996/2001), 199.

16. *Wuidaehan Suryeong Kim Il Sung Wonsunim Hyeokmeongsa* [The Great Leader General Kim Il Sung's Revolutionary History] (Pyong-yang: Gyoruk Doseo Chulpansa, 1995/1999), 120.

17. Oh and Hassig, *North Korea through the Looking Glass*, 30.

18. Chung Tae-hon, "Godeunghakkyo guksa gyogwaseo-ui keunhyeun-daesa naeyong bunseok" [A Contextual Analysis of Modern History Taught in Korean High School History Books], *Sachong* 45 (1996): 201–29.

19. Bruce Cumings, *Korea's Place in the Sun: A Modern History* (New York: W. W. Norton, 1997), 265.

20. See Henry H. Em, "Overcoming Korea's Division: Narrative Strate-gies in Recent South Korean Historiography," *Positions* 1, no. 2 (1993): 450–85.

21. Friedrich Nietzsche, "Vom Nutzen und Nachteil der Historie für das Leben," in *Unzeitgemässe Betrachtungen* (Frankfurt: Insel Taschen-buch, 1981), 118. For a translation by Ian C. Johnson, available on-line, see *On the Use and Abuse of History for Life*, September 1998, http://www .mala.bc.ca/johnstoi/Nietzsche/history.htm.

22. Nietzsche, "Vom Nutzen und Nachteil der Historie für das Leben," 106–7, 111.

23. Quoted in Choi Hae Won, "Seoul's Textbook Détente: Revised History Reader Reflects South's Waning Fear of the North," *Wall Street Journal*, January 14, 2003.

24. Ku Nan Hee, quoted in Choi, "Seoul's Textbook Détente."

25. Park Sung Soo, quoted in Choi, "Seoul's Textbook Détente." See also Chong Hyunmuk, "Battle of Bocheonbo in Our Textbook?" *JoongAng Ilbo*, August 7, 2002.

26. Grinker, *Korea and Its Futures*, 128, 130–32.

27. Ibid., 132–34.

28. Kim Ki-Jung and Park Jae-min, "Paradox of Dismantling the Cold War Structure," in Chung-in Moon, Odd Arne Westad, and Kahng Gyoo-hyoung, eds., *Ending the Cold War in Korea: Theoretical and Historical Perspectives* (Seoul: Yonsei University Press, 2001), 320.

29. Duncan S. A. Bell, "Mythscapes: Memory, Mythology, and Na-tional Identity," *British Journal of Sociology* 54 (2003): 63–81.

30. Paul Ricoeur, "Imagination, Testimony, and Trust," a dialogue with Paul Ricoeur, in Richard Kearney and Mark Dooley, eds., *Questioning Ethics: Contemporary Debates in Philosophy* (London: Routledge, 1999), 13.

31. Richard Kearney, "Narrative and the Ethics of Remembrance," in Kearney and Dooley, *Questioning Ethics,* 26–27.

32. Dipesh Chakrabarty, *Provincializing Europe: Postcolonial Thought and Historical Difference* (Princeton, N.J.: Princeton University Press, 2000), 97. See also Gilles Deleuze and Félix Guattari, *Kafka: pour une littérature mineure* (Paris: Éditions de Minuit, 1975). For a good translation of Deleuze and Guattari, see Dana Polan's, *Kafka: Toward a Minor Literature* (Minneapolis: University of Minnesota Press, 1986).

33. Em, "Overcoming Korea's Division," 452, 479–80.

34. See the festival's website at http://piff.org.

35. See James Brooke, "The Power of Film: A Bond That United Koreans," *New York Times,* February 2, 2003, A4.

36. Jeon Woo-Taek, "Promoting National Harmony in a Unified Korea," paper presented at Yonsei University, Seoul, December 21, 2001, 3.

37. William A. Callahan, "Laughter, Critical Theory, and Korea," in Han, *Habermas and the Korean Debate,* 445–71.

38. Choi Chungmoo, "The Discourse of Decolonization and Popular Memory: South Korea," *Positions* 1, no. 1 (1993): 92–95.

39. Mikhail Bakhtin, *Rabelais and His World,* trans. Helene Iswolsky (Cambridge, Mass.: MIT Press, 1968), 10; François Rabelais, *The Histories of Gargantua and Pantagruel,* trans. J. M. Cohen (Harmondsworth, U.K.: Penguin, 1966).

40. Bakhtin, *Rabelais and His World,* 123.

41. Administrator, Busan Metropolitan City Office of Education, interview by Hoang Young-ju, August 30, 2002. All interviews referred to in this chapter were conducted as part of my joint research project with Hoang Young-ju.

42. History teachers at Haeundae Girls' High School, interviews by Hoang Young-ju, September 4, 2002, and at Keumjeon High School, September 13, 2002.

43. History teacher at Haeundae Girls' High School, interview by Hoang Young-ju, September 4, 2002.

44. Ch'oe Yong-ho et al., eds., *Sources of Korean Tradition: From the Sixteenth to the Twentieth Centuries* (New York: Columbia University Press, 2000), 2:38.

45. History teacher at Namsan High School, interview by Hoang Young-ju, September 13, 2002.

46. Two administrators at the Busan Metropolitan City Office of Education, interviews by Hoang Young-ju, August 30, 2002. Interviews with

about sixty students at Haeundae Girls' High School and Namsan High School largely confirmed this pattern although not unanimously.

47. Susan Dwyer, "Reconciliation for Realists," *Ethics and International Affairs* 13 (1999): 89.

48. Ibid.

49. Kwon, "Tongil gyoyuk-eseo talbundan simin gyoyuk-euro," and *Symposium*. See also Sheila Miyoshi Jager, "Women, Resistance, and the Divided Nation: The Romantic Rhetoric of Korean Reunification," *Journal of Asian Studies* 55, no. 1 (February 1996): 3–21.

50. Øyvind Østerud, "Antinomies of Postmodernism in International Studies," *Journal of Peace Research* 33, no. 4 (1996): 386.

51. Ricoeur, "Imagination, Testimony, and Trust," 15.

52. Gerrit W. Gong, "A Clash of Histories," in Gerrit W. Gong, ed., *Memory and History in East and Southeast Asia: Issues of Identity in International Relations* (Washington, D.C.: Center for Strategic and International Studies, 2001), 30.

53. Claus Offe, *Der Tunnel am Ende des Lichts: Erkundungen der politischen Transformation im Neuen Osten* [The Tunnel at the End of the Light: Inquiries into the Political Transformation of the New East] (Frankfurt: Campus Verlag, 1994), 188.

54. Paul Ricoeur, "Memory and Forgetting," in Kearney and Dooley, *Questioning Ethics*, 11.

55. Kearney, "Narrative and the Ethics of Remembrance," 27.

56. Ricoeur, "Imagination, Testimony, and Trust," 12.

57. See F. R. Ankersmit, *Aesthetic Politics: Political Philosophy beyond Fact and Value* (Stanford, Calif.: Stanford University Press, 1996).

58. Ricoeur, "Imagination, Testimony, and Trust," 15.

59. Hayden White, *The Content of the Form: Narrative Discourse and Historical Representation* (Baltimore: Johns Hopkins University Press, 1987), 4, 14.

60. Chakrabarty, *Provincializing Europe*, 98.

61. U.S. Department of Defense, "Statement of Mutual Understanding between the United States and the Republic of Korea on the No Gun Ri Investigations," January 2001, http//www.defenselink.mil/news/Jan2001/smu20010111.html. See also Choe Sang-hun, Charles J. Hanley, and Martha Mendoza, "American Veterans Speak Out on Massacre during Korean War," *Korea Herald,* October 1, 1999; Elizabeth Becker, "Army Admits G.I.'s in Korea Killed Civilians at No Gun Ri," *New York Times,* January 12, 2001; Bruce Cumings, "Occurrence at Nogun-ri Bridge: An Inquiry into the History and Memory of a Civil War," *Critical Asian Studies* 33, no. 4 (2001): 509–26.

62. William E. Connolly, *The Ethos of Pluralization* (Minneapolis: University of Minnesota Press, 1995), xxi–xxii.

CONCLUSION

1. Zaki Laïdi, *A World without Meaning: The Crisis of Meaning in International Politics* (London: Routledge, 1998), 52.

2. See Elict Cohen, "A Revolution in Warfare," *Foreign Affairs,* March–April 1996, 37–54; Paul F. Hermann, "Revolution in Military Affairs," *Strategic Review,* September 1996.

3. Park Chung Hee, "North Korean Communists' Deceptive Double Tactics," in *Towards Peaceful Unification: Selected Speeches and Interviews by Park Chung Hee* (Seoul: Kwongmyong, 1976), 120.

4. Park Tong Whan, "Nation Versus State: The Dilemma of Seoul's Foreign Policy-Making towards Pyongyang," *Pacific Focus* 14, no. 2 (Fall 1999): 60–65. See also Paik Nak-Chung, "South Korea: Unification and the Democratic Challenge," *New Left Review,* January–February 1993, 67–84.

5. Ken Conca, "Environmental Confidence Building and Regional Security in Northeast Asia," in Miranda A. Schreurs and Dennis Pirages, eds., *Ecological Security in Northeast Asia* (Seoul: Yonsei University Press, 1998), 41–65.

6. Jürgen Habermas, *Die postnationale Konstellation: Politische Essays* (Frankfurt: Suhrkamp, 1998), 120. A fine translation is Max Pensky's, *The Postnational Constellation: Political Essays* (Cambridge: Polity Press, 2001).

7. Gearóid Ó Tuathail, *Critical Geopolitics: The Politics of Writing Global Space* (London: Routledge, 1996), 228–30; Arjun Appadurai, *Modernity at Large: Cultural Dimensions of Globalization* (Minneapolis: University of Minnesota Press, 1996), 37–38.

8. Stephen D. Krasner, *Sovereignty: Organized Hypocrisy* (Princeton, N.J.: Princeton University Press, 1999).

9. Thomas Bernauer, *Staaten im Weltmarkt: Zur Handlunsfähigkeit von Staaten trotz wirtschaftlicher Globalisierung* [States in the World Market: The Ability of States to Act Despite Economic Globalization] (Opladen: Leske und Budrich, 2000).

10. Kang Chol-Hwan and Pierre Rigoulot, *Aquariums of Pyongyang: Ten Years in the North Korean Gulag,* trans. Yair Reiner (New York: Basic Books, 2001), 186.

11. See Moon Chung-in and Mo Jongryn, eds., *Democratization and Globalization in Korea: Assessments and Prospects* (Seoul: Yonsei University Press, 1999).

12. See, for instance, Peter Van Ness, "Globalization and Security in East Asia," *Asian Perspective* 23, no. 4 (1999): 315–42; Kihl Young Hwan, "Globalization and Korean Diplomacy," in Yim Yong Soon and Kim Ki-Jung, eds., *Korea in the Age of Globalization and Information* (Seoul: Korean Association for International Studies, 1997), 243–62.

13. See Moon Chung-in and Lee Yongwhan, "The State, Market, and Institutions: A Comparative Analysis of Internet Diffusion in Japan and South Korea," paper presented at the Convention of the International Studies Association, Hong Kong, July 26–28, 2001, 7.

14. Kim Deok-hyun, "Telecom Industry Sets Eye on North Korean Mart," *Korea Times*, April 20, 2001, 7; Moon Chung-in and Kim Yonghoo, "The Future of the North Korean System," in Samuel S. Kim, ed., *The North Korean System in the Post–Cold War Era* (New York: Palgrave, 2001), 221.

15. Kwon Hyeok-ryeol, "Bukhan-seodo Internet sayong ganeunghalka" [Will It Be Possible to Use the Internet in North Korea Too?], *Sinangge: The Monthly Magazine of the Youido Full Gospel Church*, April 2001, http://www.sinangge.com/200104/200104_068.htm; Tim Beal, "Digital Divide on the Korean Peninsula: Constructive Engagement Offers Solutions," *Institute for Corean-American Studies*, ICAS Special Contribution No. 2002-0218-TxB, June 10, 2002, http://www.icasinc.org.

16. Lee Kyeong-woo, "Bukhan Internet hwangkyeong-kwa kwallyeon site" [Sites Related with North Korea's Internet Environment], *Soccer World*, http://www.soccer4u.co.kr/ninternet.htm.

17. Song Yeong-hui, "Techno gune-uro ganeun gil" Internet-euro Bukhan jireyong song-su sin [On the Way to Techno-Soldiers: Sending and Receiving North Korean Orders over the Internet], *Hankuk Ilbo*, September 23, 1999, http://www.hankooki.com/whan/last/990923/w615221.htm.

18. "Bukhan network and Internet" [North Korea's Networks and the Internet], *Chungcheon Center Evangelical Holiness Church*, 2000, http://www.cccehc.com/noh/north/northkorea3.html.

19. Eric Harwit and Duncan Clark, "Shaping the Internet in China: Evolution of Political Control over Network Infrastructure and Content," *Asian Survey* 41, no. 3 (May–June 2001): 377. See also report from the Rand Corporation, "You've Got Dissent!" www.rand.org/publications/mr/mr1543/; and Jonathan Watts, "China Tightens Net around Online Dissenters," *Guardian Weekly*, February 12, 2004, 3.

20. Brian McWilliams, "North Korea's School for Hackers," *Wired News*, June 2, 2003.

21. "Bukhan Internet ajik chobo dangye" [North Korean Internet Still at Beginners' Level], *Ministry of National Defense*, September 5, 1999, http://www.dapis.go.kr/mndweb/daily/1999/09/0905-16.htm.

22. Kwon, "Bukhan-seodo Internet sayong ganeunghalka."

23. Emmanuel Levinas, "Peace and Proximity," in Adriaan T. Peperzak, Simon Critchley, and Robert Bernasconi, eds., *Basic Philosophical Writings* (Bloomington: Indiana University Press, 1996), 166; David Campbell, *National Deconstruction: Violence, Identity, and Justice in Bosnia* (Minneapolis: University of Minnesota Press, 1998), ix.

24. John Paul Lederach, *Building Peace: Sustainable Reconciliation in Divided Societies* (Washington, D.C.: U.S. Institute of Peace Press, 1997), 27.

25. William E. Connolly, *The Ethos of Pluralization* (Minneapolis: University of Minnesota Press, 1995), 27.

26. R. B. J. Walker, *Inside/Outside: International Relations as Political Theory* (Cambridge: Cambridge University Press, 1993), 51. See also Chris Brown, "Theories of International Justice," *British Journal of Political Science* 27 (1977): 273–97.

27. J. G. Ballard, *Cocaine Nights* (London: Flamingo, 1997), 293.

28. Costas Constantinou, "Poetics of Security," *Alternatives* 25, no. 3 (July–September 2000): 290, 303; Anthony Burke, "Poetry Outside Security," *Alternatives* 25, no. 3 (July–September 2000): 308.

Index

absorption: fear of North Korea, 29, 83, 93; in other divided countries, 101; South Korean policy toward, 81, 87, 88, 90–92, 98. *See also* collapse of North Korea

academic disciplines: lack of communication between, xlix, 111; role in obstructing new solutions to conflict, xvi–xviii, 67; role in upholding attitudes to conflict, xvi–xviii, xlviii–xlix, 67. *See also* interdisciplinary research

Agreed Framework of 1994: breakdown of, xxix, 49; nature of, xxix; role in diffusing nuclear tension, xxix

Ahn Pyong-Seong: on inter-Korean relations, xxx

aid: role in development of South Korea, 39, 40, 41; from Soviet Union and China to North Korea, 38–39, 70. *See also* humanitarian assistance

alterity. *See* difference

amnesty: role in Korea, 111–12

antagonistic perceptions of the other: constructed nature of, xiv, 76, 100; historical roots of, 5, 8, 99; in Korea, xiv, 90, 98, 99, 100, 109–10, 115, 117, 122; link to security issues, xxxi, 18, 46, 61, 64, 110, 117, 118. *See also* identities

antagonistic rhetoric: persistence of, 23, 110–11, 122; role in fueling conflict, xxvii, xxx, 115–16

anti-Americanism: in North Korea, 14; in South Korea, 22, 75

anti-Communism: and construction of identity, 8, 91; and education, 12, 88; in South Korea, 12–13, 22, 23, 25, 91

Armistice Agreement: nature of, xii, xxvii, 9, 118; provisions of, 144; violations of, xv, 47

arms control: in Korea, 47

ROLAND BLEIKER is reader in peace studies and political theory at the University of Queensland, Australia. From 1986 to 1988 he was chief of the office of the Swiss delegation to the Neutral Nations Supervisory Commission in Panmunjom. He has since frequently returned to Korea and served as visiting fellow at Yonsei University and as visiting professor at Pusan National University. The research for this book was generously supported by the United States Institute of Peace and the Alexander von Humboldt Stiftung.

BORDERLINES